Autism Spectrum Disorder in Children and Adolescents

SCHOOL PSYCHOLOGY BOOK SERIES

Autism Spectrum Disorder in Children and Adolescents

Evidence-Based Assessment and Intervention in Schools

Edited by **Lee A. Wilkinson**

American Psychological Association • Washington, DC

Published by
American Psychological Association
750 First Street, NE
Washington, DC 20002
www.apa.org

To order
APA Order Department
P.O. Box 92984
Washington, DC 20090-2984
Tel: (800) 374-2721; Direct: (202) 336-5510
Fax: (202) 336-5502; TDD/TTY: (202) 336-6123
Online: www.apa.org/pubs/books
E-mail: order@apa.org

In the U.K., Europe, Africa, and the Middle East, copies may be ordered from
American Psychological Association
3 Henrietta Street
Covent Garden, London
WC2E 8LU England

Typeset in Goudy by Circle Graphics, Inc., Columbia, MD

Printer: United Book Press, Baltimore, MD
Cover Designer: Mercury Publishing Services, Inc., Rockville, MD

The opinions and statements published are the responsibility of the authors, and such opinions and statements do not necessarily represent the policies of the American Psychological Association.

Library of Congress Cataloging-in-Publication Data
Autism spectrum disorder in children and adolescents : evidence-based assessment and intervention in schools / edited by Lee A. Wilkinson. — First edition
    pages cm
Includes bibliographical references and index.
ISBN 978-1-4338-1615-4 — ISBN 1-4338-1615-6
1. Autistic children—Education—United States. 2. School psychology—United States.
3. Educational counseling—United States. I. Wilkinson, Lee A. (Lee Anthony)
LC4718.A88 2014
371.94—dc23
                    2013034269

British Library Cataloguing-in-Publication Data
A CIP record is available from the British Library.

Printed in the United States of America
First Edition

http://dx.doi.org/10.1037/14338-000

CONTENTS

CONTRIBUTORS

Alyssa A. Altomare, MS, Faculty of Education, University of Calgary, Calgary, Alberta, Canada

Brea M. Banks, BS, Department of Psychology, Illinois State University, Normal

Gena P. Barnhill, PhD, BCBA-D, NCSP, School of Education and Human Development, Lynchburg College, Lynchburg, VA

Jonathan M. Campbell, PhD, Department of Educational, School, and Counseling Psychology, University of Kentucky, Lexington

Linda C. Caterino, PhD, ABPP, School Psychology Program, Mary Lou Fulton Teachers College, Arizona State University, Tempe

Karla J. Doepke, PhD, Department of Psychology, Illinois State University, Normal

Laura J. Hall, PhD, Department of Special Education, San Diego State University, San Diego, CA

Rachel K. Hammond, PhD, Department of Educational, School, and Counseling Psychology, University of Kentucky, Lexington

Katia Jitlina, MSc, Department of Educational and Counseling Psychology, and Special Education, University of British Columbia, Vancouver, British Columbia, Canada

Susan Kabot, EdD, CCC-SLP, Mailman Segal Center for Human Development, Nova Southeastern University, Fort Lauderdale, FL

Steven Landau, PhD, Department of Psychology, Illinois State University, Normal

Ryan L. Matchullis, MS, Faculty of Education, University of Calgary, Calgary, Alberta, Canada

Jennifer F. Mays, BS, Department of Psychology, Illinois State University, Normal

Adam W. McCrimmon, PhD, Faculty of Education, University of Calgary, Calgary, Alberta, Canada

Sarah R. Reed, PhD, Rady Children's Hospital, University of California, San Diego

Christine Reeve, PhD, BCBA-D, Reeve Autism Consulting, Plantation, FL

Lisa A. Ruble, PhD, Department of Educational, School, and Counseling Psychology, University of Kentucky, Lexington

Donald H. Sakofske, PhD, Department of Psychology, University of Western Ontario, London, Ontario, Canada

Laura Schreibman, PhD, Autism Research Program, University of California, San Diego

Amanda D. Smith, BA, Faculty of Education, University of Calgary, Calgary, Alberta, Canada

Aubyn C. Stahmer, PhD, Rady Children's Hospital, University of California, San Diego

Jessica Suhrheinrich, PhD, Rady Children's Hospital, University of California, San Diego

Lauryn M. Toby, MS, Department of Psychology, Illinois State University, Normal

Jennifer Twachtman-Bassett, MS, CCC-SLP, Addcon Center, LLC, Higganum, CT

Diane Twachtman-Cullen, PhD, CCC-SLP, Addcon Center, LLC, Higganum, CT

Sheila J. Wagner, MEd, Emory Autism Center, Emory University, Atlanta, GA

Lee A. Wilkinson, PhD, NCSP, Center for Psychological Studies, Nova Southeastern University, Ft. Lauderdale, FL

Perry A. Zirkel, PhD, JD, LLM, College of Education, Lehigh University, Bethlehem, PA

SERIES FOREWORD

Outside of their homes, children spend more time in schools than in any other settings. From tragedies such as Sandy Hook and Columbine to more hopeful developments such as the movement toward improved mental health, physical health, and academic achievement, there is an ongoing need for high-quality writing that explains how children, families, and communities associated with schools worldwide can be supported through the application of sound psychological research, theory, and practice.

Thus, for the past several years the American Psychological Association (APA) Books and APA Division 16 (School Psychology) have partnered to produce the School Psychology Book Series. The mission of this series is to increase the visibility of psychological science, practice, and policy for those who work with children and adolescents in schools and communities. The result has been a strong collection of scholarly work that appeals not only to psychologists but also to individuals from all fields who have reason to seek and use what psychology has to offer in schools.

Many individuals have made significant contributions to the School Psychology Book series. First, we would like to acknowledge the dedication of past series editors: Sandra L. Christensen, Jan Hughes, R. Steve McCallum, LeAdelle Phelps, Susan Sheridan, and Christopher H. Skinner. Second, we would like to acknowledge the outstanding editorial vision of the scholars who have edited or authored books for the series. The work of these scholars has significantly advanced psychological science and practice for children and adolescents worldwide.

We welcome your comments about this volume and other topics you would like to see explored in this series. To share your thoughts, please visit the Division 16 website at www.apadivisions.org/division-16.

Linda A. Reddy, PhD
Series Editor

ACKNOWLEDGMENTS

This book would not have been possible without the efforts of many people. I am extremely grateful to all of the contributing authors. It was truly an honor to work with such an outstanding group of scholars. For your dedication, patience, and time commitment, I gratefully acknowledge your exceptional work. I would like to express my appreciation to Linda Reddy, the editor of the Division 16 book series, for her support and encouragement in bringing the project forward. Special thanks to Linda McCarter, senior acquisitions editor for APA Books, for her guidance and timely attention to my questions regarding the editorial process. I also extend my appreciation to Susan Herman, development editor for APA Books, for her valuable review and skillful editing of the manuscript. Last, I am grateful to my family who supported my efforts. As always, I happily express my sincere gratitude to my wife, Amy, for her love, patience, and understanding.

Autism Spectrum Disorder in Children and Adolescents

INTRODUCTION: EVIDENCE-BASED PRACTICE FOR AUTISM SPECTRUM DISORDER

LEE A. WILKINSON

Learning about autism is an unfolding process. We get to know the child through the particular filter of autism. But in doing so, we start to see him clearly and wholly. And that perspective is the beginning of our peace and progress.
—Susan Senator, *The Autism Mom's Survival Guide*.

More children and youth are being diagnosed with autism spectrum disorder (ASD) than ever before. Epidemiological research has indicated a progressively rising prevalence trend for ASD over the past decade (Wing & Potter, 2009). Autism is much more prevalent than previously thought, especially when it is viewed as a spectrum condition with varying levels of symptom severity. Surveys focusing on this broader definition of autism have indicated that ASD is one of the fastest growing disability categories in the world. Recent findings of the Centers for Disease Control and Prevention (CDC) Autism and Developmental Disabilities Monitoring Network (2012) indicated that one in every 88 school-age children in the United States has an ASD. This represents an estimated increase of 78% in the prevalence of ASD when compared with the data for earlier surveillance years. Autism is now considered the second most serious developmental disability after

http://dx.doi.org/10.1037/14338-001
Autism Spectrum Disorder in Children and Adolescents: Evidence-Based Assessment and Intervention in Schools, L. A. Wilkinson (Editor)

intellectual disability and more prevalent among children than cancer, diabetes, and Down syndrome (Filipek et al., 1999, Wilkinson, 2010).

A number of explanations for this dramatic increase in the incidence and prevalence of ASD have been proposed. They include changes in diagnostic criteria, improved identification, growing awareness among parents and professionals, conception of autism as a spectrum disorder, and greater availability of services (Fombonne, 2005; Wilkinson, 2010; Wing & Potter, 2009). Whatever the reasons, the current prevalence figures carry clear-cut implications for school professionals who share the challenge of identifying and providing interventions for an increasing number of children with ASD who comprise approximately 1% of the school-age population (Wilkinson, 2010).

AUTISM SPECTRUM DISORDER IN THE SCHOOLS

The increase in the occurrence of autism is also evident in the number of students with ASD receiving special educational services. According to the U.S. Department of Education, Office of Special Education Programs, Data Analysis System (2010), more than 5 million children ages 6 to 21 years received services through 13 disability categories in public special education programs in 2010. Although the overall population of special education students, after decades of increases, peaked in the 2004–2005 school year and has declined since that time, the data indicate a divergence in the trajectories of the individual disability categories. Although the number of students identified with specific learning disabilities, emotional disturbance, and intellectual disability decreased relative to other disability categories, the number of students with autism quadrupled between 2000–2001 and 2009–2010, rising from 93,000 to 378,000 students and increasing from 1.5% to 5.8% of all identified disabilities. Clearly, school professionals are now expected to participate in the identification and treatment of children with ASD more than at any other time in the recent past. They must be prepared to recognize the presence of risk factors and/or early warning signs of ASD, engage in case finding, and be familiar with assessment tools and interventions to ensure that students are being identified and provided with the appropriate programs and services.

The Challenge to School Professionals

From the age of 6 to 12, the child with ASD faces many challenges with transitions to new learning environments and contact with unfamiliar peers and adults. The social-communication domains of development become more divergent from typical expectations as the student with ASD progresses through school. These children frequently experience problems related to their social-communication deficits, such as poor regulation of attention, emotional distress, academic difficulties, and high rates of externalizing problem behavior (Mazzone, Ruta, & Reale, 2012; Sikora, Vora, Coury, & Rosenberg, 2012; Wilkinson, 2010). As a result, they are at risk of academic underachievement, school dropout, peer rejection, and co-occurring (comorbid) internalizing disorders such as anxiety and depression (Mazzone et al., 2012; Ozsivadjian, Knott, & Magiati 2012).

The unique needs and multifaceted nature of autism, including co-occurring disabilities, have significant implications for planning and intervention in the school context. Most students with ASD receive their education in general education classrooms with teachers who often have limited experience and training in working with children with special needs (Wilkinson, 2010). In fact, more than half of all students ages 6 through 21 served under the Individuals With Disabilities Education Improvement Act (2004) are educated for most of their school day in the general education classroom; that is, they participate in the regular class 80% or more of the day (U.S. Department of Education, Office of Special Education Programs, Data Analysis System, 2010). Because autistic traits exist along a spectrum of severity with respect to the core symptomatology, mild deficits in social and communicative competence can be associated with teacher-reported problems in socialization and a wide range of behavioral and academic difficulties (Skuse et al., 2009). As a result, social skills deficits that fall below the threshold for a clinical diagnosis of ASD can still result in functional impairment (Russell, Ford, Steer, & Golding, 2010; Wilkinson, 2010). Providing effective behavioral supports and interventions to the ever-increasing numbers of children with ASD presents a major challenge to the educational communities that serve them.

Adopting Evidence-Based Practice for Autism Spectrum Disorder

The challenge to improve the services to children with ASD in our schools centers on the adoption of evidence-based practices in diagnosis and identification, assessment, and intervention. The term *evidence-based practice* first appeared in the professional literature in the early 1990s. Since that time the interest in evidence-based practice has increased dramatically. This includes policy statements by the Task Force on Evidence-Based Interventions in School Psychology (Kratochwill & Stoiber, 2002) and the American Psychological Association (APA) Presidential Task Force on Evidence-Based Practice (2006; Kratochwill & Hoagwood, 2006; Kratochwill & Shernoff, 2004). The following statement was approved as policy of the APA by the APA Council of Representatives: "Evidence-based practice in psychology (EBPP) is the integration of the best available research with clinical expertise in the context of client characteristics, culture, and preferences"

(APA Presidential Task Force on Evidence-Based Practice, 2006, p. 5). According to the APA Presidential Task Force on Evidence-Based Practice (2006), "The purpose of EBPP is to promote effective psychological practice and enhance public health by applying empirically supported principles of psychological assessment, case formulation, therapeutic relationship, and intervention" (p. 5). More recently, the APA Task Force on Evidence-Based Practice With Children and Adolescents (2008) recommended that evidence-based practice be given priority and that children and adolescents receive the best available evidence-based mental health services through the integration of science and practice.

The use of evidence-based practice has also been emphasized in education policy and legislation. For example, the federal government has recognized the importance of evidence-based practice with the passage of two laws: the No Child Left Behind Act (NCLB; 2001) and the Individuals With Disabilities Education Act (IDEA; 2004). Both were designed to ensure that students receive services that are based on scientific evidence. According to IDEA and federal and state regulations, scientifically based research involves the application of rigorous, systematic, and objective procedures to obtain reliable and valid knowledge relevant to educational activities, programs, and strategies. A salient element of NCLB also relates to using effective education practices developed from scientifically based research. These practices are defined as those that have met rigorous peer review and other standards and that, when consistently and reliably applied with fidelity, have a history of yielding positive results (NCLB, 2001).

The call for effective and scientifically supported methods of practice extends beyond legislative and policy statements to special populations of children. This appeal has been particularly evident within the field of autism (National Research Council, 2001). For example, the National Autism Center (NAC) and the National Professional Development Center (NPDC) on Autism Spectrum Disorders promote the use of evidence-based practice for children and youth with ASD and have established standards for effective, research-validated educational and behavioral interventions for children on the spectrum (NAC, 2009; NPDC, 2010).

ELEMENTS OF EVIDENCE-BASED PRACTICE

The scientific literature identifies two primary elements of evidence-based practice: (a) *intervention* that includes, but is not limited to, those treatment programs for which randomized controlled trials have shown empirical support for the target population and (b) *assessment* that guides diagnosis, intervention planning, and outcome evaluation (APA Task Force on Evidence-Based

Practice With Children and Adolescents, 2008). Both include practices and procedures that have a knowledge base confirming their efficacy and effectiveness. Treatment *efficacy* generally refers to whether a particular intervention or treatment has been found to work by means of experimental procedures (e.g., random assignment, control groups), whereas *effectiveness* involves determining whether a particular intervention has been found to produce a positive outcome in settings and conditions in which the intervention is implemented (e.g., classroom, clinic). Evidence-based intervention includes, but is not limited to, treatment programs and strategies with documented efficacy. In fact, differences between the dimensions of research (efficacy) and typical practice (effectiveness) mean that interventions developed through efficacy trials may need to be adapted to real-world practice contexts. Although a certain intervention or treatment may have a strong evidence base, it must also have "utility" and be effective in applied settings (Mash & Hunsley, 2005; Rogers & Vismara, 2008; Silverman & Hinshaw, 2008).

The dimensions of efficacy and effectiveness can also be applied to assessment. Evidence-based assessment requires using instruments with strong reliability and validity for the accurate identification of children's problems and disorders, for ongoing monitoring of children's response to interventions, and for evaluation of the outcomes of intervention (Mash & Hunsley, 2005; Ozonoff, Goodlin-Jones, & Solomon, 2005). These procedures must also have demonstrated effectiveness in diagnosis, clinical formulation, intervention planning, and outcome assessment (Wilkinson, 2010).

To adequately meet the needs of students with ASD, it is essential that professionals understand the characteristics of this neurodevelopmental disorder, use appropriate assessment tools, provide evidence-based recommendations for intervention across the continuum of services, and offer consultation to educational staff and families (APA Task Force on Evidence-Based Practice With Children and Adolescents, 2008; Wilkinson, 2010; Williams, Johnson, & Sukhodolsky, 2005). In this volume, empirically supported principles of assessment and intervention are integrated with the key practice issues facing school psychologists and other professionals who are increasingly called on to work with children on the autism spectrum.

PURPOSE OF THIS BOOK

There is an extensive body of educational, medical, and psychological literature outlining comprehensive information regarding educational practices, supports, and processes that are reportedly effective for students with ASD. Likewise, statutes, case laws, regulations, and policies provide a framework for educational planning and development of individualized educational programs for students on the spectrum. Nevertheless, the extant literature can be confusing and even conflicting at times, and although there are myriad books describing the clinical diagnosis and treatment of ASD, there is a need for an up-to-date text that provides school psychologists and allied professionals with a best-practice guide to screening, assessment, and intervention in the school context. Moreover, recent national and statewide surveys of school psychologists' knowledge, training, and practice in autism assessment and intervention in their respective school systems suggest that they are in need of additional resources and training in meeting the unique needs of students identified with ASD (Aiello & Ruble, 2011; Rasmussen, 2009; Williams et al., 2005).

The overarching goal in preparing this book was to assemble a set of chapters that provide comprehensive summaries of the evidence base for assessing and intervening with children and youth with ASD. It brings the areas of assessment and intervention together in a single volume consistent with recent advances in evidence-based practice. Each chapter features a consolidated and integrative description of best-practice assessment and intervention and treatment approaches for children and youth with ASD. Although no single text can provide a complete examination of the emerging research in ASD, this volume provides an up-to-date view of the status of the field that will guide practitioners in the selection, use, and interpretation of evidence-based assessment tools and intervention strategies for students with ASD. This includes best-practice procedures to help identify children on the basis of symptom criteria for the new *Diagnostic and Statistical Manual of Mental Disorders* (5th edition; *DSM–5*; American Psychiatric Association, 2013) single diagnostic category of autism spectrum disorder, which now encompasses the previous *DSM–IV–TR* (4th edition, text revision; American Psychiatric Association, 2000) categorical subgroups of autistic disorder (autism), Asperger's disorder, and pervasive developmental disorder not otherwise specified.

AUDIENCE

This book was written for practitioners in educational and school psychology, child and adolescent clinical psychology, general and special education, counseling, educational administration, and social work, as well as for graduate and preservice students. It can be used in school psychology and in clinical child, developmental, pediatric, and child and adolescent psychiatry courses. This text will also find interdisciplinary use as a guide to help a variety of school-based support professionals (counselors, speech and language therapists, occupational therapists, case managers, and many others) make informed decisions regarding the assessment, identification, and treatment of ASD. Because the dramatic increase in the number of school-age children being identified with ASD extends well beyond the United States to Europe and other countries, this book will also find an audience among the international educational community that shares the challenges of screening, evaluating, and intervention planning to meet the unique needs of children with ASD.

ORGANIZATION OF THE TEXT

The term *autism spectrum disorder* is used throughout the volume to reflect the scientific consensus that symptoms of the various autism subgroups represent a single continuum of impairment that varies in level of severity and need for support (*DSM–5*; American Psychiatric Association, 2013). This shift from a multicategorical model to a single diagnostic entity of ASD is consistent with the extant research and better describes our current understanding of the features and course of the neurodevelopmental disorders. Each chapter is based on the principles of evidence-based practice and provides detailed procedural guidelines for the screening and assessment of ASD, current description of assessment instruments used in the screening and assessment process, and application of evidence-based interventions to the school setting.

The volume is divided into two parts. Part I focuses on evidence-based assessment. Chapters 1 through 6 present critical information and guidance on evidence-based screening and assessment, including the selection, use, and interpretation of specific tools for ASD. The first chapter begins with an overview and historical view of ASD, providing the reader with an important foundation and current perspective of the field. Chapter 2 presents an overview of the basic psychometric principles that practitioners need to know when selecting and interpreting screening tools and provides a multitier approach to screening for children who may require a more comprehensive assessment. Chapter 3 introduces the practitioner to the comprehensive development approach to assessment and describes the components of an evidence-based assessment battery. Chapter 4 provides a comprehensive review of tools to assess the domains of cognitive, academic, neuropsychological, and adaptive functioning. In Chapter 5, the pragmatic, social-communicative functions of language are considered together with assessments to identify pragmatic language deficits. Chapter 6 focuses on the assessment of co-occurring emotional and behavior problems of children with ASD that can affect daily functioning and complicate intervention.

In Part II, the focus shifts from assessment to intervention. Chapters 7 through 11 present information on evidence-based interventions in the classroom, curriculum and class structure, special education continuum and placement, working with families and teachers, and legal issues. Chapter 7 describes current "established" treatments for ASD and provides an example of how a scientifically based intervention can be adapted to the classroom. Chapters 8 and 9 focus on the continuum of special education services and placement options, individual education planning, curriculum and classroom structure, and instructional and support strategies. Both chapters use case vignettes to illustrate best practice in the school setting. Chapter 10 presents techniques and strategies to enhance the home–school partnership and provides guidance on how to involve parents as active partners in the decision-making process. Chapter 11 concludes the volume with a primer on ASD-related litigation issues and discusses relationships between special education law, provision of services, and placement decisions.

Because of the dimensional nature of ASD, impact on multiple domains of functioning, and specific evidence-based practice parameters, an overlap in content among the various chapters was necessary. To foster the overall integration of the subject matter, the volume includes numerous cross-references to direct the reader's attention to related topics across chapters. It should also be noted that to effectively cover the breadth of assessment and intervention for ASD, it was necessary for each chapter to maintain a level of brevity.

CONCLUSION

Evidence-based practice in ASD relies on the presence of a sound body of scientific knowledge relevant to a broad range of programs, products, practices, and policies that optimizes the effectiveness of assessment and intervention or treatment (APA Task Force on Evidence-Based Practice with Children and Adolescents, 2008; Kratochwill, 2007). Because the knowledge base in ASD is changing so rapidly, school professionals are challenged to stay current with the latest research and methods of evaluation and treatment, to acquire and become skilled with the most up-to-date screening and assessment tools, and to maintain an awareness of community resources. As our scientific knowledge and thinking about ASD continues to develop, school psychologists will play an increasingly important role in the educational programming of children with ASD by providing support, information, and recommendations to teachers, other school personnel and administrators, and families (Wilkinson, 2010; Williams et al., 2005). Being knowledgeable about assessment and intervention strategies, including their strengths and limitations, will help form cohesive educational support networks for children with ASD (Bryson, Rogers, & Fombonne, 2003; Wilkinson, 2010). The sine qua non for assessment and intervention is the utility in helping to bring about a positive outcome and meaningful difference in the lives of children and families with whom we work and to whom we provide services (Mash & Hunsley, 2005). The chapters that follow provide the foundation for meeting this important goal.

REFERENCES

Aiello, R., & Ruble, L. A. (2011, February). *Survey of school psychologists' autism knowledge, training, and experiences*. Poster session presented at the meeting of the National Association of School Psychologists, San Francisco, CA.

American Psychiatric Association. (2000). *Diagnostic and statistical manual of mental disorders* (4th ed., text rev.). Washington, DC: Author.

American Psychiatric Association. (2013). *Diagnostic and statistical manual of mental disorders* (5th ed.). Washington, DC: Author.

American Psychological Association Presidential Task Force on Evidence-Based Practice. (2006). Evidence-based practice in psychology. *American Psychologist, 61*, 271–285. doi:10.1037/0003-066X.61.4.271

American Psychological Association Task Force on Evidence-Based Practice With Children and Adolescents. (2008). *Disseminating evidence-based practice for children and adolescents: A systems approach to enhancing care.* Washington, DC: Author.

Bryson, S. E., Rogers, S. J., & Fombonne, E. (2003). Autism spectrum disorders: Early detection, intervention, education, and psychopharmacological management. *Canadian Journal of Psychiatry/La Revue de Canadienne de Psychiatrie, 48*, 506–516.

Centers for Disease Control and Prevention. (2012). *Prevalence of autism spectrum disorders—Autism and Developmental Disabilities Monitoring Network, United States, 2008.* Retrieved from http://www.cdc.gov/mmwr/preview/mmwrhtml/ss6103a1.htm

Filipek, P. A., Accardo, P. J., Baranek, G. T., Cook, E. H., Dawson, G., Gordon, B., . . . Volkmar, F. R. (1999). The screening and diagnosis of autistic spectrum disorders. *Journal of Autism and Developmental Disorders, 29*, 439–484. doi:10.1023/A:1021943802493

Fombonne, E. (2005). The changing epidemiology of autism. *Journal of Applied Research in Intellectual Disabilities, 18*, 281–294. doi:10.1111/j.1468-3148.2005.00266.x

Individuals With Disabilities Education Improvement Act of 2004, Pub. L. No. 108-446, § 602, 118 Stat. 2647 (2004).

Kratochwill, T. R. (2007). Preparing psychologists for evidence-based school practice: Lessons learned and challenges ahead. *American Psychologist, 62*, 829–843. doi:10.1037/0003-066X.62.8.829

Kratochwill, T. R., & Hoagwood, K. E. (2006). Evidence-based interventions and system change: Concepts, methods and challenges in implementing evidence-based practices in children's mental health. *Child and Family Policy and Practice Review, 2*, 12–17.

Kratochwill, T. R., & Shernoff, E. S. (2004). Evidence-based practice: Promoting evidence-based interventions in school psychology. *School Psychology Review, 33*, 34–48.

Kratochwill, T. R., & Stoiber, K. C. (2002). Evidence-based interventions in school psychology: Conceptual foundations of the Procedural and Coding Manual of Division 16 and the Society for the Study of School Psychology Task Force. *School Psychology Quarterly, 17*, 341–389. doi:10.1521/scpq.17.4.341.20872

Mash, E. J., & Hunsley, J. (2005). Evidence-based assessment of child and adolescent disorders: Issues and challenges. *Journal of Clinical Child and Adolescent Psychology, 34*, 362–379. doi:10.1207/s15374424jccp3403_1

Mazzone, L., Ruta, L., & Reale, L. (2012). Psychiatric comorbidities in Asperger syndrome and high functioning autism: Diagnostic challenges. *Annals of General Psychiatry, 11*, 16. doi:10.1186/1744-859X-11-16

National Autism Center. (2009). *The National Standards Project—Addressing the need for evidence-based practice guidelines for autism spectrum disorders*. Randolph, MA: Author.

National Professional Development Center on Autism Spectrum Disorders. (2010). *Evidence-based practices*. Retrieved from http://autismpdc.fpg.unc.edu/content/briefs

National Research Council. (2001). *Educating children with autism*. Washington, DC: National Academy Press.

No Child Left Behind Act of 2001. 20 U.S.C. 70 § 6301 *et seq.* (2002).

Ozonoff, S., Goodlin-Jones, B. L., & Solomon, M. (2005). Evidence-based assessment of autism spectrum disorders in children and adolescents. *Journal of Clinical Child and Adolescent Psychology, 34*, 523–540. doi:10.1207/s15374424jccp3403_8

Ozsivadjian, A., Knott, F., & Magiati, I. (2012). Parent and child perspectives on the nature of anxiety in children and young people with autism spectrum disorders: A focus group study. *Autism, 16*, 107–121. doi:10.1177/1362361311431703

Rasmussen, J. E. (2009). *Autism: Assessment and intervention practices of school psychologists and the implications for training in the United States* (Doctoral dissertation). Available from ProQuest Dissertations and Theses database. (UMI Number: 3379197)

Rogers, S. J., & Vismara, L. A. (2008). Evidence-based comprehensive treatments for early autism. *Journal of Clinical Child and Adolescent Psychology, 37*, 8–38. doi:10.1080/15374410701817808

Russell, G., Ford, T., Steer, C., & Golding, J. (2010). Identification of children with the same level of impairment as children on the autism spectrum, and analysis of their service use. *Journal of Child Psychology and Psychiatry, 51*, 643–651. doi:10.1111/j.1469-7610.2010.02233.x

Senator, S. (2010). *The autism mom's survival guide*. Boston, MA: Trumpeter Books.

Sikora, D. M., Vora, P., Coury, D. L., & Rosenberg, D. (2012). Attention-deficit/hyperactivity disorder symptoms, adaptive functioning, and quality of life in

children with autism spectrum disorder. *Pediatrics, 130,* S91–S97. doi:10.1542/
peds.2012-0900G

Silverman, W. K., & Hinshaw, S. P. (2008). The second special issue on evidence-
based psychosocial treatments for children and adolescents: A 10-year update.
Journal of Clinical Child and Adolescent Psychology, 37, 1–7. doi:10.1080/
15374410701817725

Skuse, D. H., Mandy, W., Steer, C., Miller, L. L., Goodman, R., Lawrence,
K., . . . Golding, J. (2009). Social communication competence and functional
adaptation in a general population of children: Preliminary evidence for sex-by-
verbal IQ differential risk. *Journal of the American Academy of Child & Adolescent
Psychiatry, 48,* 128–137. doi:10.1097/CHI.0b013e31819176b8

U.S. Department of Education, Office of Special Education Programs, Data Analysis
System. (2010). *Children with disabilities receiving special education under Part B
of the Individuals With Disabilities Education Act, 2010* (OMB 1820–0043).
Washington, DC: Author.

Wilkinson, L. A. (2010). *A best practice guide to assessment and intervention for autism
and Asperger syndrome in schools.* London, England: Kingsley.

Williams, S. K., Johnson, C., & Sukhodolsky, D. G. (2005). The role of the school
psychologist in the inclusive education of school-age children with autism
spectrum disorders. *Journal of School Psychology, 43,* 117–136. doi:10.1016/
j.jsp.2005.01.002

Wing, L., & Potter, D. (2009). The epidemiology of autism spectrum disorders: Is the
prevalence rising? In S. Goldstein, J. A. Naglieri, & S. Ozonoff (Eds.), *Assessment of autism spectrum disorders* (pp. 18–54). New York, NY: Guilford Press.

I

EVIDENCE-BASED ASSESSMENT OF AUTISM SPECTRUM DISORDER

1

OVERVIEW OF AUTISM SPECTRUM DISORDER

ADAM W. McCRIMMON, ALYSSA A. ALTOMARE,
AMANDA D. SMITH, KATIA JITLINA, RYAN L. MATCHULLIS,
AND DONALD H. SAKOFSKE

The clinical origin of autism spectrum disorder (ASD) can be traced to the early 1900s when the term *autism* was coined by Bleuler in 1911 (Bleuler, 1950). Leo Kanner (1943) first introduced the term as a clinical syndrome to the scientific literature by describing 11 children with "early infantile autism." These children were characterized as relating better to objects than people and showing severe social and communication abnormalities as well as narrow and restricted interests. One year later, Hans Asperger separately published a work characterizing children with "autistic psychopathology" (Asperger, 1944/1991). These children were described as being verbally fluent but with peculiar language use and abnormal prosody. They were also socially isolated and demonstrated repetitive behaviors, a desire for sameness, interest in unusual topics, motor clumsiness, and a propensity toward rote memorization of facts.

http://dx.doi.org/10.1037/14338-002
Autism Spectrum Disorder in Children and Adolescents: Evidence-Based Assessment and Intervention in Schools, L. A. Wilkinson (Editor)

Clinical descriptions of ASD have changed considerably since 1943. Initial clinical accounts were defined in the *Diagnostic and Statistical Manual of Mental Disorders* (*DSM*; American Psychiatric Association, 1952) as schizophrenic reaction, childhood type, and later modified to schizophrenia, childhood type, in the *DSM–II* (American Psychiatric Association, 1968). These early descriptions related the symptomatology to schizophrenia, a classification that differed from initial accounts and that received little empirical support (Bregman, 2005).

Reconceptualization of autism into a distinct class of neurobehaviorally based disorders occurred with the publication of the *DSM–III* (American Psychiatric Association, 1980). Autistic disorder was introduced in the *DSM–III–R* (American Psychiatric Association, 1987) with new diagnostic criteria that required behavioral evidence in addition to guidance for clinicians when conducting an assessment.

ASD was most recently an umbrella term referring to five disorders described under the category of pervasive developmental disorders (PDDs) in the *DSM–IV–TR* (American Psychiatric Association, 2000). According to the *DSM–IV–TR*, autistic disorder (autism), Rett's disorder, childhood disintegrative disorder, Asperger's disorder (syndrome), and pervasive developmental disorder not otherwise specified are characterized by a varying degree of qualitative impairment in three key areas of development that result in a distinct abnormality in comparison with expected developmental or mental age. This includes impairment in reciprocal social interaction, communication, and restrictive and repetitive patterns of interests, activities, and behaviors, which together are often referred to as the *autistic triad of impairments*. Differential diagnosis in *DSM–IV–TR* is based on cognitive and language development, physical and motor characteristics, age of onset of symptoms, and developmental trajectory.

Autistic disorder is commonly diagnosed at a young age, with individuals showing a lack of or delay in normal verbal and nonverbal language development in conjunction with impairment in social interaction and restrictive and repetitive behaviors and interests (American Psychiatric Association, 2000). Autistic disorder is also more prevalent in males, with affected females displaying greater severity of symptoms. *Rett's disorder*, which occurs only in females, is characterized by apparently normal development up to 5 months of age, followed by an observable decrease in head growth, fine and gross motor skills, social engagement, and language development. *Childhood disintegrative disorder* (CDD) is more common in males and involves a loss of previously acquired communicative, play, and adaptive abilities between the ages of 2 and 10 years after apparently normal development. Individuals with *Asperger's syndrome* demonstrate impairment in social interaction and restrictive, repetitive interests and behaviors in conjunction with typical language and cognitive development. Finally, *pervasive developmental disorder not otherwise specified* (PDDNOS) refers to individuals with clear impairments in reciprocal social interaction associated with impairment in either verbal or nonverbal communication skills or with the presence of restricted patterns of behavior, but who did not qualify for the specific criteria outlined for another specific PDD.

Research since the publication of the *DSM–IV–TR* has again prompted changes to the definition and diagnostic framework of ASD. Changes in the *DSM–5* (American Psychiatric Association, 2013) include elimination of the separate disorders and the introduction of a unitary ASD diagnosis. Clinically, this modification also reflects a change in diagnostic criteria, with the previous three core impairments becoming two: social-communication deficits and fixated interests and repetitive behaviors. Individuals meeting criteria for ASD also receive a rating of 1, 2, or 3 (*requiring support, requiring substantial support,* or *requiring very substantial support,* respectively), with each level indicating an increase in symptom severity.

PREVALENCE

Historically, epidemiological studies have indicated substantially lower prevalence rates for autism than those reported in the current literature (Rutter, 2005). The first survey completed in 1966 indicated an estimated prevalence rate of four to five per 10,000 young children (Lotter, 1966). Recent studies have estimated the prevalence of the broad ASD category to be 50 to 100 per 10,000 (Baird et al., 2000; Centers for Disease Control and Prevention [CDC], 2012; Chakrabarti & Fombonne, 2005; Newschaffer et al., 2007).

There have been few epidemiological studies of Asperger's syndrome, PDDNOS, or CDD (Fombonne, 2009; Newschaffer et al., 2007); however, Fombonne (2009) estimated a prevalence of six per 10, 000 for Asperger's syndrome, 37.1 per 10, 000 for PDDNOS, and less than two per 10, 000 for CDD. Overall, there is also a ratio ranging from 4.3 to 4.6:1 for males to females presenting with ASD (CDC, 2012; Newschaffer et al., 2007). The U.S. Department of Education (2005) estimated that ASD is increasing at a rate of 10% to 17% per year, and the CDC (2012) recently reported a 78% estimated increase in prevalence from 2002 to 2008. It is unknown whether these increasing prevalence rates are directly related to an increase in the occurrence of this disorder; however, the concepts of better ascertainment and broadening of the ASD concept do not rule out an actual rise in incidence (CDC, 2012; Rutter, 2005). As the *DSM–5* conceptualization of ASD is new, prevalence studies based on that description have yet to be conducted.

CORE DIFFICULTIES

Individuals with ASD experience pervasive primary social challenges resulting from impairment in understanding and responding to social information (Dawson, Meltzoff, Osterling, Rinaldi, & Brown, 1998; Travis & Sigman, 1998). As children, they do not show typical developmental levels of imitation, sharing of attention and focus with social partners, orienting to socially important stimuli, and the perception and expression of emotions, all of which interfere with the development of social reciprocity (Dawson et al., 1998; Osterling & Dawson, 1994). Communication symptoms involve atypical language development, including delayed acquisition of single words and/or phrase speech, delayed or atypical expansion of abilities, loss of previously developed skills, and difficulties with conversational and socially appropriate usage (Stephanatos & Baron, 2011). Research has indicated that as much as 50% of individuals with ASD remain nonverbal (Rutter, 1978); however, more recent research found this estimate high and reported that a more conservative estimate would be that up to 40% of children develop some speech by 9 years of age, with only 15% remaining nonverbal (Lord et al., 2006). Spoken language impairments include echolalia, pronoun reversal, and difficulties with pragmatic language use (Tager-Flusberg, 1999, 2000). Communicative behaviors involved in play with others, such as imitation and role playing, is often an additional area of deficit (Haq & Le Couteur, 2004).

Restricted and repetitive patterns of behavior manifest as lower and/or higher level behaviors. *Lower level behaviors* include repetitive motor movements such as hand flapping, rocking, and spinning, whereas *higher level behaviors* include circumscribed interests, fixations on established behavioral routines, preoccupations, and interests with certain topics (e.g., street signs or birth dates) or attachment to unusual objects, such as toilet brushes or spoons (Campbell et al., 1990; Turner, 1999). Some individuals with ASD may also manifest adverse reactions to sensory sensations (Steyn & Le Couteur, 2003).

Continuum of Symptom Severity

One of the most important developments in our understanding of ASD is the heterogeneity in phenotypic expression that exists beyond the classical presentation of autism (Szatmari et al., 2002). The number of symptoms displayed, as well as their severity, varies across individuals and, in some domains, over time (Richler, Huerta, Bishop, & Lord, 2010; Szatmari et al., 2002).

A continuum, or spectrum, of severity exists in the symptom domains of ASD (National Research Council, 2001). The *DSM–IV–TR* subtypes of

Asperger's syndrome and PDDNOS are generally considered to be on the milder end of the spectrum (Volkmar, Lord, Bailey, Schultz, & Klin, 2004), whereas autistic disorder is found across the entire spectrum of severity (Rutter, 2003). Individuals with Rett's disorder and CDD commonly fall more on the severe end of the spectrum (*DSM–IV–TR*; American Psychiatric Association, 2000). Moreover, some family members of children with ASD may exhibit milder autism-like symptoms that are not severe enough to be considered clinically impairing, a phenomenon that has been termed the *broader autism phenotype* (Gerdts & Bernier, 2011). The new *DSM–5* diagnostic category of ASD conceptualizes the symptoms of the previous *DSM–IV–TR* subtypes as falling on a single dimension from mild to severe impairment.

Although many individuals diagnosed with ASD evidence high cognitive potential, as reflected by intelligence test scores, the ability to translate this potential to real-life activities required for personal and social self-sufficiency may still be impaired (Klin et al., 2007). The typical profile of adaptive functioning in ASD consists of severe impairments in social functioning, moderate impairments in communication, and relative strengths in activities of daily living (Klin et al., 2007). However, the degree of impairment in each of these domains varies across individuals. For example, individuals with higher verbal abilities may display substantial communication impairments similar to individuals with poor verbal skills.

The language abilities of individuals with ASD also vary significantly (Bishop, 2003), with some acquiring language within normal developmental timelines and even developing a high level of language. Others develop language late and may only acquire simplistic speech. Moreover, a substantial number of individuals with ASD are nonverbal and have minimal comprehension (Volkmar et al., 2004).

Although individuals with average or above average verbal abilities may evidence some understanding of various aspects of communication, incorporating this understanding into their daily interactions poses difficulty (McPartland & Klin, 2006). Subtleties of social interaction such as gesturing, eye contact, and other nonverbal communication may be explicitly identified and explained through social skills training, but the application of this knowledge to dynamic, real-life situations remains a challenge for these individuals. Individuals with ASD are challenged by skills that are integral to conversation, such as initiating new topics, conveying a specific message, organizing speech, and concluding and shifting topics. Similarly, the ability to perceive and react to the social cues expressed by others involved in social interaction may also be lacking and contribute to failed social interactions. The range of facial expression in individuals with ASD also varies, with some individuals unable to communicate their affect through their facial expressions. Despite these impairments, individuals vary from having a deep desire for friendships to a dampened or complete lack of interest in social relationships (McPartland & Klin, 2006; Spiker, Lotspeich, Dimiceli, Myers, & Risch, 2002).

Severity in the broad category of repetitive behaviors (RBs) also varies, with higher frequencies of RB typically observed in children with autistic disorder compared with children with PDDNOS (Richler et al., 2010; Walker et al., 2004). Severity of sensorimotor RBs, such as repetitive motor patterns or sensory interests, appears more consistent over time, whereas RBs characterized by insistence on sameness tend to worsen throughout childhood (Richler et al., 2010). Moreover, there is significant variation in developmental trajectories of RBs across individuals, with very young children typically not exhibiting a significant level of any type of RB (Richler et al., 2010). Thus, lower order behaviors may decrease or remain stable throughout childhood (Kim & Lord, 2010; Murphy et al., 2005; Richler et al., 2010), whereas higher order RBs become more intense with age (Richler et al., 2010).

Cognitive Functioning

Cognitive functioning is strongly indicative of the type and severity of presenting symptomatology. Measured general intelligence varies substantially in individuals with ASD, ranging from significantly impaired to superior. Indeed, the severity of presenting ASD symptomology has often, though not always, shown a strong negative correlation with cognitive intelligence (IQ; Spiker et al., 2002). Individuals with CDD and Rett's disorder typically present with comorbid intellectual impairment, often in the moderate to severe range (DSM–IV–TR; American Psychiatric Association, 2000). Conversely, individuals with Asperger's syndrome present with average and often well-developed cognitive abilities, whereas those with autistic disorder or PDDNOS present with varying degrees of intellectual capacity, from highly developed skills to severe impairment (American Psychiatric Association, 2000).

Theory of Mind

Theory of mind (ToM) is defined as the ability to conceive of the mental states of another individual, specifically, their knowledge, wants, feelings, and beliefs. As first discussed by Premack and Woodruff (1978), deficits in ToM ability have been proposed to underlie the social communication impairments observed in individuals with ASD (Baron-Cohen, Leslie, & Frith, 1985). Research evidence has linked difficulties on ToM tasks to failures with understanding complex social situations, recognizing self-conscious emotions such as embarrassment and shame, attributing false beliefs to others, and understanding personal mental states (e.g., Mitchell & O'Keefe, 2008). ToM and social communication are discussed in Chapter 5 of this volume.

Weak Central Coherence

Frith (1989) proposed that a central deficit in ASD is the inability to integrate information at different levels. The term *central coherence* refers to the capacity to form a higher level meaning in context by combining diverse information. This theory has been hypothesized to underlie the tendency of individuals with ASD to focus on parts of objects, display sensitivities to small changes in one's environment, and have circumscribed interests and perseverative behaviors (Hoy, Hatton, & Hare, 2004). This focus may account for the average to superior performance of individuals with ASD on noncontextual perceptual tasks, such as the Embedded Figures Test or block-design test (Jolliffe & Baron-Cohen, 1997; Shah & Frith, 1993), and may account for their difficulties with integrating contextual information such as complex facial features and expressions for accurate face processing (López, Donnelly, Hadwin, & Leekam, 2004).

Executive Functions

Associated with the prefrontal cortex, *executive functions* (EFs) are higher order cognitive processes that are required to respond to novel or complex situations (Calhoun, 2006). EF deficits in ASD have been reported in planning, mental flexibility, inhibition, and self-monitoring abilities (E. L. Hill, 2004). Deficits in planning and in the ability to predetermine, monitor, and change one's actions as necessary to accomplish a goal have been observed on neuropsychological tasks (Ozonoff & Jensen, 1999), but results are inconsistent (Mari, Castiello, Marks, Marraffa, & Prior, 2003). This population may also exhibit difficulty in mental flexibility, shifting thoughts and actions to suit a particular situation (Ozonoff, Pennington, & Rogers, 1991), underlying their characteristic perseverative behavior especially observed on cognitive flexibility tasks. Although some inhibition abilities appear intact (Ozonoff & Jensen, 1999), individuals with ASD appear to have difficulty inhibiting a prepotent response, especially those with lower IQ scores, who may have problems following more complex rules and directions to determine an alternate, more appropriate response (Bíró & Russell, 2001). Finally, individuals with ASD may have deficits in monitoring their actions and thoughts and correcting them as necessary to guide behavior, which is possibly related to their perseverative behavior (Russell, 2002). Neuropsychological assessment and measurement of executive functioning are described in Chapter 3.

COMORBID CONDITIONS

Estimates of comorbid conditions in individuals with ASD vary significantly from 4% to 81% (e.g., Davis et al., 2011; Leyfer et al., 2006). The most common comorbid condition is intellectual disability, with an estimated comorbidity rate between 40% (Baird et al., 2000) and 69% (Chakrabarti & Fombonne, 2001). In addition, a recent meta-analysis found that the prevalence of epilepsy among individuals with ASD and comorbid intellectual disability was 22%, compared with 8% among individuals with ASD but without intellectual disability (Amiet et al., 2008). Furthermore, the prevalence of epilepsy was reported to be higher among individuals with ASD than the general population, with the highest rates occurring in adolescence and young adulthood (Tuchman & Rapin, 2002).

Tic disorders are also highly prevalent (Klinger, Dawson, & Renner, 2003), with research suggesting a strong genetic predisposition to tic disorders among this population (Baron-Cohen, Scahill, Izaguirre, Hornsey, & Robertson, 1999).

Mood disorders are also common in the ASD population. Leyfer and colleagues (2006) examined a sample of 109 mid- to high-functioning children and adolescents with ASD ranging from 5 to 17 years old and reported that 44% met criteria for specific phobia, 37% for obsessive–compulsive disorder, 31% for attention-deficit/hyperactivity disorder, 13% for depression, 12% for separation anxiety disorder, 7% for oppositional defiant disorder, and 2% for generalized anxiety disorder. It should be noted that the rate of major depression increased to nearly 24% when subsyndromal cases were included (i.e., children who fell just short of meeting criteria for this disorder). Comorbid conditions that have been less frequently reported in the literature include bipolar disorder (Frazier, Doyle, Chiu, & Coyle, 2002), schizophrenia (Chang et al., 2003), and isolated psychotic symptoms, such as delusions (Bryson & Smith, 1998) and hallucinations (Howlin, 2005).

It is evident that comorbid conditions are common in the ASD population. Most alarming is the young age at which comorbid conditions first manifest in this population, especially given the additional negative impact such conditions can have on the lives of these individuals (Bellini, 2004). Chapter 6 focuses on the assessment of co-occurring (comorbid) emotional and behavior problems.

EDUCATIONAL CONSIDERATIONS

Educational systems strive to foster independence and social responsibility in all students, including those with ASD (National Research Council, 2001). The introduction of the Individuals With Disabilities Education Act

(IDEA; 1990) into U.S. federal legislation brought about a new approach to identification and support for children with ASD. Autism is one of the 13 categories of disability recognized in IDEA, which guarantees children free appropriate public education in the least restrictive environment and an individualized education plan that addresses the student's specific learning needs.

Several issues have arisen in the years since this legislation was first implemented. For example, the recent alarming increase in the prevalence of diagnosed ASD has posed challenges in the educational realm, and as a result, school-based professionals are being required to address the educational needs of greater numbers of these students (Zirkel, 2011). And because the educational identification of students with ASD has lagged behind the increase in prevalence (Safran, 2008), many affected students with ASD, particularly those with mild presentation of symptoms, are not receiving appropriate educational services (Wilkinson, 2010). Moreover, a discrepancy exists between clinical identification of ASD (e.g., diagnosis) and educational identification in that the latter requires evidence of negative impact on educational performance, thus precluding some diagnosed individuals from receiving educational support (Safran, 2008).

Additional difficulties have arisen in regard to the *least restrictive environment* (LRE), which is defined in IDEA as the educational setting (from full inclusion in a general education classroom to residential placement, with many options in between) that ensures that the student with a disability is educated alongside students without disabilities to the maximum extent possible (IDEA, 1990, 2004). The selection of environment has been a passionately contested topic for parents and educators as they struggle to meet the educational needs of students with ASD (D. A. Hill & Hill, 2012). At the same time, there has been an increase in litigation focusing on the educational placement and needs of students with ASD (D. A. Hill & Hill, 2012; Zirkel, 2011). In many instances, the specific needs of students with ASD remain underserved because financial limitations increasingly restrict the capability of educational systems to meet these needs. The continuum of special education services and legal issues related to LRE are examined in Chapters 8 and 11, respectively.

INTERVENTIONS

Although ASD was once considered to be untreatable, there is now general agreement that early identification and appropriate intervention can improve the outcomes for many individuals with ASD (National Research Council, 2001). Since the disorder's initial recognition in the 1940s, treatment approaches for ASD have ranged from psychoanalytic therapies and electroconvulsive treatments to the present-day focus on behavioral inter-ventions and enhancement of developmental abilities (Howlin, 2003). Moreover, identification of specific intervention approaches has been the focus of targeted efforts, with specific intervention approaches now recog-nized as having established empirical support (e.g., behavioral approaches, pivotal response training), emerging support (e.g., augmentative communi-cation, language training), or no support (e.g., auditory integration training; National Autism Center, 2009).

Although there is no known cure for ASD, treatments have attempted to target both the core symptoms and associated comorbid features (Ospina et al., 2008). The most widely used approach is *applied behavior analysis* (ABA), which involves early, intensive, individualized behavioral interven-tion. This approach aims to enhance, reduce, or maintain targeted behaviors through manipulation of environmental variables (Virués-Ortega, 2010). When used intensively in early life (20–40 hours a week), ABA has been shown to have medium to large positive effects, particularly on language acquisition and communication, adaptive skills, intellectual and social functioning, and academic performance. Indeed, it is one of the interven-tion approaches empirically supported by the National Standards Project (National Autism Center, 2009), an effort by the National Autism Center in the United States to publish standards for evidence-based intervention methods for ASD.

Although the degree of structure and the level of intensity required to produce positive effects remain hotly debated topics among researchers, some important guidelines have been identified: (a) treatment should be individualized to the presenting behavioral pattern of each child; (b) prompt-ing, shaping, and reinforcement techniques should be used to develop skills; (c) functional analysis should be used to understand problematic behav-iors; (d) verbal and nonverbal communication skills should be developed to minimize problematic behaviors; (e) the environment should be modified to promote communication, understanding, and interaction; (f) opportunities for teaching and reinforcement should be used even outside the therapeutic setting; and (g) new skills should be taught in the framework of predictable schedules and consistency (Howlin, 2003).

In addition to an increase in research on ABA therapy, recent years have seen an explosion in interventions delivered both in the home and at school that involve and educate parents or use inclusive methods such as peer involvement (Schreiber, 2011). Advances in technology are being harnessed to develop personalized computer software that is specifically adapted for augmenting communication abilities, particularly for nonverbal and mini-mally verbal individuals with ASD; however, research in this area is still in its infancy (Wainer & Ingersoll, 2011).

Lower order RBs, including stereotyped movements, repetitive self-injurious behaviors, and manipulations of objects, have been treated through antecedent- and consequence-based interventions, with some positive results (Boyd, McDonough, & Bodfish, 2012). Higher order RBs have largely also been treated with behavioral interventions, with the exception of obsessive–compulsive behaviors (Boyd et al., 2012). The compulsive and ritualistic behaviors that manifest in ASD, as well as the insistence on sameness, have been approached from a cognitive–behavioral therapy perspective, but research on such interventions is limited (Boyd et al., 2012).

In individuals with higher functioning ASD, social skills deficits have been addressed with social skills training in a variety of formats and settings (Schreiber, 2011). Many children on the higher functioning end of the spectrum have a desire for social relationships but do not develop the necessary skills when immersed in a classroom with typically developing peers where they are exposed to a variety of social situations (Klin & Volkmar, 2000). As such, social skills have been explicitly taught through a variety of approaches.

The *social stories* approach uses simple stories to describe social situations and offers the child different perspectives and strategies to use in situations that may pose difficulty for them (Gray & Garand, 1993). Social skills training groups focus on breaking down social behaviors and conventions into small, understandable steps appropriate for the group's developmental level. These sessions attempt to make the rules of conversation, topic selection, topic shifting, social expectations across different settings, and understanding of audience interest explicit (Cappadocia & Weiss, 2011; Klin & Volkmar, 2000). A comprehensive review of the research literature on social skills training in school settings has found that this format of delivery has been minimally effective in producing treatment effects or generalizing across settings (Bellini, Peters, Benner, & Hopf, 2007). However, few studies have examined the effects of such intervention at session durations longer than a few hours a week over several months (Bellini et al., 2007). For practitioners, this means that in addition to formal social skills training, any opportunity to reinforce social skills techniques should be taken advantage of throughout the child's day. These reviewers also concluded that the weak outcomes may be attributed to the intervention's "decontextualized" settings of delivery, such as pullout groups, rather than the child's typical classroom. Thus, school personnel should select interventions that can be implemented across multiple settings.

Although some researchers have rigorously collected data to examine the effectiveness of various approaches, many claims about interventions have been made with little or no empirical support. Indeed, some treatment approaches have captured the attention of the popular media despite a complete lack of evidence to support the claims made by their proponents

(Howlin, 2003). Treatments such as facilitated communication, auditory integration therapy, and several medical and dietary interventions such as secretin, immunoglobulin injections, and anti-yeast treatments have not been shown to be effective through empirical research (Howlin, 2003).

Significant gains have been made in the area of intervention research, but there are still gaps in our understanding of how to best improve outcomes for individuals with ASD. Controversy remains regarding the required intensity of treatment for positive effect, and there is a limited understanding of which interventions are most effective for such a diverse population (Ospina et al., 2008). In addition, the longer term effects of various treatments are currently unknown (Howlin, 2003). Some long-term follow-up studies of individuals as they progress through adolescence into young and later adulthood have indicated that a lack of supports through these transitions may negatively affect outcomes (Howlin, Goode, Hutton, & Rutter, 2004). Chapter 7 provides an overview of evidence-based treatments for ASD and describes how a scientifically based intervention can be adapted to the classroom.

OUTCOMES

The two best predictors of positive outcomes in individuals with ASD are higher cognitive abilities (e.g., IQ greater than 70) and the development of at least some speech prior to age 5 (Howlin, Mawhood, & Rutter, 2000). Nevertheless, even with an IQ above 70, the outcomes for individuals with ASD are mixed (Howlin et al., 2004). Howlin and colleagues (2004) found that of the 45 participants with an initial childhood IQ of 70 or higher, only 16% were considered to have "very good" outcomes, which consisted of living independently, keeping a job, and having friends. However, 44% of the participants were considered to be significantly impaired, with the majority living with their families or in some form of residential provision. Interestingly, the participants with an initial childhood IQ between 70 and 99 were found to have made more progress in terms of academic achievement, employment, and general level of functioning than those with an IQ above 100 (Howlin et al., 2004). These results indicate that higher IQ levels do not necessarily equate to better outcomes. In fact, the fundamental deficits associated with ASD (e.g., social difficulties) may at times negate the impact of a high IQ (Mawhood & Howlin, 1999). Consistent with these findings, Green, Gilchrist, Burton, and Cox (2000) reported that individuals with high functioning ASD often struggle in adolescence and adulthood because they lack independent daily living skills and have significant difficulties forming social relationships.

Dawson and Osterling (1997) contended that early intervention improves positive outcomes in individuals with ASD because there is a greater likelihood that such individuals will develop language, have higher cognitive abilities, and be a part of a regular classroom. However, Howlin et al. (2004) commented that over the past 30 years the vast increase in educational opportunities for children with ASD has not necessarily resulted in significant improvements in adult outcomes. It has been suggested that the availability of continued services for adults with ASD (e.g., supportive living, employment) may be crucial in promoting more positive outcomes in this population (Howlin et al., 2004; Mawhood & Howlin, 1999). Overall, it can be concluded that future studies are needed to discover factors that are predictive of positive outcomes in individuals with ASD.

CONCLUSION

Following the clinical descriptions of ASD by Kanner (1943) and Asperger (1944/1991), progress in understanding and conceptualizing ASD was relatively slow until more recent years. Although much more is now known about the prevalence, symptoms, and comorbid conditions of ASD, intervention efforts have yet to effectively treat individuals in this population, and we are still unaware of the causes of ASD. Thus, it is of primary importance that future research efforts be devoted to identifying the causal factors of ASD. Many active research and clinical programs also hold great potential for identifying interventions that will improve the quality of life for those children and adults with varying degrees and clinical expressions of ASD.

The role of school psychologists is integral to positive outcomes for students with ASD. Given the recent change in *DSM* diagnostic criteria, new knowledge from research, and the ongoing commitment to providing students with appropriate and effective education, school psychologists will continue to be challenged by the need to support an increasing population of students with ASD in schools as well as in other educational and postsecondary settings. Presently, school psychological services are mainly directed at the more traditional roles of formal (e.g., diagnosis) and informal (e.g., identification of specific learning needs and communication skills) assessment, in addition to providing direct and recommended intervention services (e.g., academic, behavioral, socioemotional). However, expanding this current function to include greater ongoing consultation and collaboration that would provide teachers with "best-practice approaches" to educating and supporting students with ASD may be another effective approach. School psychologists are also in a key position to provide a liaison between the school, home, community, and other health, social, and educational agencies that are committed to the well-being of children and adolescents with ASD. Such wraparound services are integral to meeting the full range of needs of these children in various contexts. Moreover, school psychologists can enhance the capacity of teachers and schools in meeting the educational needs of students with ASD by continually contributing to, being informed by, and applying evidence-based research knowledge. As our understanding of ASD grows, so too will our ability to support positive outcomes, and this is a goal for which all school psychologists strive.

REFERENCES

American Psychiatric Association. (1952). *Diagnostic and statistical manual of mental disorders*. Washington, DC: Author.

American Psychiatric Association. (1968). *Diagnostic and statistical manual of mental disorder* (2nd ed.). Washington, DC: Author.

American Psychiatric Association. (1980). *Diagnostic and statistical manual of mental disorders* (3rd ed.). Washington, DC: Author.

American Psychiatric Association. (1987). *Diagnostic and statistical manual of mental disorders* (3rd ed., rev.). Washington, DC: Author.

American Psychiatric Association. (2000). *Diagnostic and statistical manual of mental disorders* (4th ed., text rev.). Washington, DC: Author.

American Psychiatric Association. (2013). *Diagnostic and statistical manual of mental disorders* (5th ed.). Washington, DC: Author.

Amiet, C., Gourfinkel-An, I., Bouzamondo, A., Tordjman, S., Baulac, M., Lechat, P., . . . Cohen, D. (2008). Epilepsy in autism is associated with intellectual disability and gender: Evidence from a meta-analysis. *Biological Psychiatry, 64*, 577–582. doi:10.1016/j.biopsych.2008.04.030

Asperger, H. (1991). Autistic psychopathy in childhood. In U. Frith (Ed. & Trans.), *Autism and Asperger's syndrome* (pp. 37–92). New York, NY: Cambridge University Press. (Original work published 1944)

Baird, G., Charman, T., Baron-Cohen, S., Cox, A., Swettenham, J., Wheelwright, S., . . . Kemal, L. (2000). A screening instrument for autism at 18 months of age: A six-year follow-up study. *Journal of the American Academy of Child & Adolescent Psychiatry, 39*, 694–702. doi:10.1097/00004583-200006000-00007

Baron-Cohen, S., Leslie, A. M., & Frith, U. (1985). Does the autistic child have a "theory of mind"? *Cognition, 21*, 37–46. doi:10.1016/0010-0277(85)90022-8

Baron-Cohen, S., Scahill, V. L., Izaguirre, J., Hornsey, H., & Robertson, M. M. (1999). The prevalence of Gilles de la Tourette syndrome in children and adolescents with autism: A large scale study. *Psychological Medicine, 29*, 1151–1159. doi:10.1017/S003329179900896X

Bellini, S. (2004). Social skill deficits and anxiety in high-functioning adolescents with autism spectrum disorders. *Focus on Autism and Other Developmental Disabilities, 19*, 78–86. doi:10.1177/10883576040190020201

Bellini, S., Peters, J. K., Benner, L., & Hopf, A. (2007). A meta-analysis of school-based social skills interventions for children with autism spectrum disorders. *Remedial and Special Education, 28*, 153–162. doi:10.1177/07419325070280030401

Bíró, S., & Russell, J. (2001). The execution of arbitrary procedures by children with autism. *Development and Psychopathology, 13*, 97–110. doi:10.1017/S0954579401001079

Bishop, D. V. M. (2003). Autism and specific language impairment: Categorical distinction or continuum? In G. Bock & J. Goode (Eds.), *Autism: Neural basis and treatment possibilities* (pp. 213–226). Chichester, England: Wiley.

Bleuler, E. (1950). *Dementia praecox.* New York, NY: International Universities Press.

Boyd, B. A., McDonough, S. G., & Bodfish, J. W. (2012). Evidence-based behavioral interventions for repetitive behaviors in autism. *Journal of Autism and Developmental Disorders, 42*, 1236–1248. doi:10.1007/s10803-011-1284-z

Bregman, J. (2005). Definitions and characteristics of the spectrum. In D. Zager (Ed.), *Autism spectrum disorders: Identification, education, and treatment* (pp. 3–46). Mahwah, NJ: Erlbaum.

Bryson, S. E., & Smith, I. M. (1998). Epidemiology of autism: Prevalence, associated characteristics, and implications for research and service delivery. *Mental Retardation and Developmental Disabilities Research Reviews, 4*, 97–103. doi: 10.1002/(SICI)1098-2779(1998)4:2<97::AID-MRDD6>3.0.CO;2-U

Calhoun, J. (2006). Executive functions: A discussion of the issues facing children with autism spectrum disorders and related disorders. *Seminars in Speech and Language, 27*, 60–71. doi:10.1055/s-2006-932439

Campbell, M., Locascio, J., Choroco, M., Spencer, E. K., Malone, R. P., Kafantaris, V., & Overall, J. E. (1990). Stereotypies and tardive dyskinesia: Abnormal movements in autistic children. *Psychopharmacology Bulletin, 26*, 260–266.

Cappadocia, C. M., & Weiss, J. A. (2011). Review of social skills training groups for youth with Asperger syndrome and high functioning autism. *Research in Autism Spectrum Disorders, 5*, 70–78. doi:10.1016/j.rasd.2010.04.001

Centers for Disease Control and Prevention. (2012). *Prevalence of autism spectrum disorders—Autism and Developmental Disabilities Monitoring Network, United States, 2008.* Retrieved from http://www.cdc.gov/mmwr/preview/mmwrhtml/ss6103a1.htm

Chakrabarti, S., & Fombonne, E. (2001). Pervasive developmental disorders in preschool children. *JAMA, 285*, 3093–3099. doi:10.1001/jama.285.24.3093

Chakrabarti, S., & Fombonne, E. (2005). Pervasive developmental disorders in preschool children: Confirmation of high prevalence. *The American Journal of Psychiatry, 162*, 1133–1141. doi:10.1176/appi.ajp.162.6.1133

Chang, H. L., Juang, Y., Wang, W., Huang, C., Chen, C., & Hwang, Y. (2003). Screening for autism spectrum disorder in adult psychiatric outpatients in a clinic in Taiwan. *General Hospital Psychiatry, 25*, 284–288. doi:10.1016/S0163-8343(03)00053-7

Davis, T. E., Hess, J. A., Moree, B. N., Fodstad, J. C., Dempsey, T., Jenkins, W. S., & Matson, J. L. (2011). Anxiety symptoms across the lifespan in people diagnosed with autistic disorder. *Research in Autism Spectrum Disorders, 5*, 112–118. doi:10.1016/j.rasd.2010.02.006

Dawson, G., Meltzoff, A. N., Osterling, J., Rinaldi, J., & Brown, E. (1998). Children with autism fail to orient to naturally occurring social stimuli. *Journal of Autism and Developmental Disorders, 28*, 479–485. doi:10.1023/A:1026043926488

Dawson, G., & Osterling, J. (1997). Early intervention in autism. In M. J. Guralnick (Ed.), *The effectiveness of early intervention* (pp. 307–326). Baltimore, MD: Brookes.

Fombonne, E. (2009). Epidemiology of pervasive developmental disorders. *Pediatric Research, 65*, 591–598. doi: 0031-3998/09/6506-0591.

Frazier, J. A., Doyle, R., Chiu, S., & Coyle, J. T. (2002). Treating a child with Asperger's disorder and comorbid bipolar disorder. *The American Journal of Psychiatry, 159*, 13–21. doi:10.1176/appi.ajp.159.1.13

Frith, U. (1989). *Autism: Explaining the enigma*. Oxford, England: Blackwell.

Gerdts, J., & Bernier, R. (2011). The broader autism phenotype and its implications on the etiology and treatment of autism spectrum disorders. *Autism Research and Treatment*. doi:10.1155/2011/545901

Gray, C. A., & Garand, J. D. (1993). Social stories: Improving responses of students with autism with accurate social information. *Focus on Autism and Other Developmental Disabilities, 8*, 1–10. doi:10.1177/108835769300800101

Green, J., Gilchrist, A., Burton, D., & Cox, A. (2000). Social and psychiatric functioning in adolescents with Asperger syndrome compared with conduct disorder. *Journal of Autism and Developmental Disorders, 30*, 279–293. doi:10.1023/A:1005523232106

Haq, I., & Le Couteur, A. (2004). Autism spectrum disorder. *Medicine, 32*(8), 61–63. doi:10.1383/medc.32.8.61.43165

Hill, D. A., & Hill, S. J. (2012). Autism spectrum disorder, individuals with disabilities education act, and case law: Who really wins? *Preventing School Failure: Alternative Education for Children and Youth, 56*, 157–164. doi:10.1080/1045988X.2011.633282

Hill, E. L. (2004). Evaluating the theory of executive dysfunction in autism. *Developmental Review, 24*, 189–233. doi:10.1016/j.dr.2004.01.001

Howlin, P. (2003). Can early interventions alter the course of autism? In G Bock & J. Goode (Eds.), *Autism: Neural basis and treatment possibilities* (pp. 213–226). Chichester, England: Wiley

Howlin, P. (2005). Outcomes in autism spectrum disorders. In F. R. Volkmar, R. Paul, A. Klin, & D. Cohen (Eds.), *Handbook of autism and pervasive developmental disorders: Vol. 1. Diagnosis, development, neurobiology* (3rd ed., pp. 201–220). Hoboken, NJ: Wiley.

Howlin, P., Goode, S., Hutton, J., & Rutter, M. (2004). Adult outcome for children with autism. *Journal of Child Psychology and Psychiatry, 45,* 212–229. doi:10.1111/j.1469-7610.2004.00215.x

Howlin, P., Mawhood, L., & Rutter, M. (2000). Autism and developmental receptive language disorder: A follow-up comparison in early adult life: II. Social, behavioral, and psychiatric outcomes. *Journal of Child Psychology and Psychiatry, 41,* 561–578. doi:10.1111/1469-7610.00643

Hoy, J. A., Hatton, C., & Hare, D. (2004). Weak central coherence: A cross-domain phenomenon specific to autism? *Autism, 8,* 267–281. doi:10.1177/136236130 4045218

Individuals With Disabilities Education Act of 1990, Pub. L. No. 101-476, 20 U.S.C. (1990).

Individuals With Disabilities Education Improvement Act of 2004, Pub. L. No. 108-446, § 602, 118 Stat. 2647 (2004).

Jolliffe, T., & Baron-Cohen, S. (1997). Are people with autism and Asperger syndrome faster than normal on the Embedded Figures Test? *Journal of Child Psychology and Psychiatry, 38,* 527–534. doi:10.1111/j.1469-7610.1997.tb01539.x

Kanner, L. (1943). Autistic disturbances of affective contact. *Nervous Child, 2,* 217–250.

Kim, S. H., & Lord, C. (2010). Restrictive and repetitive behaviors in toddlers and preschoolers with autism spectrum disorders based on the Autism Diagnostic Observation Schedule (ADOS). *Autism Research, 3,* 162–173. doi:10.1002/aur.142

Klin, A., Saulnier, C. A., Sparrow, S. S., Cicchetti, D. V., Volkmar, F. R., & Lord, C. (2007). Social and communication abilities and disabilities in higher functioning individuals with autism spectrum disorders: The Vineland and the ADOS. *Journal of Autism and Developmental Disorders, 37,* 748–759. doi:10.1007/s10803-006-0229-4

Klin, A., & Volkmar, F. (2000). Treatment and intervention guidelines for individuals with Asperger syndrome. In A. Klin, F. Volkmar, & S. Sparrow. (Eds.), *Asperger syndrome* (pp. 340–366). New York, NY: Guilford Press.

Klinger, L. G., Dawson, G., & Renner, P. (2003). Autistic disorder. In E. J. Mash & R. A. Barkley (Eds.), *Child psychopathology* (2nd ed., pp. 409–454). New York, NY: Guilford Press.

Leyfer, O. T., Folstein, S. E., Bacalman, S., Davis, N. O., Dinh, E., Morgan, J., . . . Lainhart, J. E. (2006). Comorbid psychiatric disorders in children with autism: Interview development and rates of disorders. *Journal of Autism and Developmental Disorders, 36,* 849–861. doi:10.1007/s10803-006-0123-0

López, B., Donnelly, N., Hadwin, J. A., & Leekam, S. R. (2004). Face-processing in high-functioning adolescents with autism: Evidence for weak central coherence. *Visual Cognition, 11,* 673–688. doi:10.1080/13506280344000437

Lord, C., Risi, S., DiLavore, P., Shulman, C., Thurm, A., & Pickles, A. (2006). Autism from 2 to 9 years of age. *Archives of General Psychiatry, 63*, 694–701. doi:10.1001/archpsyc.63.6.694

Lotter, V. (1966). Epidemiology of autistic conditions in young children: 1. Prevalence. *Social Psychiatry and Psychiatric Epidemiology, 1*, 124–135. doi:10.1007/BF00584048

Mari, M., Castiello, U., Marks, D., Marraffa, C., & Prior, M. (2003). The reach-to-grasp movement in children with autism spectrum disorder. *Philosophical Transactions of the Royal Society of London: B. Biological Sciences, 358*, 393–403. doi:10.1098/rstb.2002.1205

Mawhood, L., & Howlin, P. (1999). The outcome of a supported employment scheme for high-functioning adults with autism or Asperger syndrome. *Autism, 3*, 229–254. doi:10.1177/1362361399003003003

McPartland, J. & Klin, A. (2006). Asperger's syndrome. *Adolescent Medicine Clinics, 17*, 771–788. doi: 0.1016/j.admecli.2006.06.010

Mitchell, P., & O'Keefe, K. (2008). Brief report: Do individuals with autism spectrum disorder think they know their own minds? *Journal of Autism and Developmental Disorders, 38*, 1591–1597. doi:10.1007/s10803-007-0530-x

Murphy, G. H., Beadle-Brown, J., Wing, L., Gould, J., Shah, A., & Holmes, N. (2005). Chronicity of challenging behaviors in people with severe intellectual disabilities and/or autism: A total population sample. *Journal of Autism and Developmental Disorders, 35*, 405–418. doi:10.1007/s10803-005-5030-2

National Autism Center. (2009). *National standards report*. Randolph, MA: Author.

National Research Council. (2001). Educating children with autism. In C. Lord & J. P. McGee (Eds.), *Committee on Educational Interventions for Children with Autism* (pp. 211–229). Washington, DC: National Academy Press.

Newschaffer, C. J., Croen, L. A., Daniels, J., Giarelli, E., Grether, J. K., Levy, S. F., & Windham, G. C. (2007). The epidemiology of autism spectrum disorders. *Annual Review of Public Health, 28*, 235–258. doi:10.1146/annurev.publhealth.28.021406.144007

Ospina, M. B., Krebs Seida, J., Clark, B., Karkhaneh, M., Hartling, L., Tjosvold, L., . . . Smith, V. (2008). Behavioral and developmental interventions for autism spectrum disorder: A clinical systematic review. *PLoS ONE, 3*(11), e3755. doi:10.1371/journal.pone.0003755

Osterling, J., & Dawson, G. (1994). Early recognition of children with autism: A study of first birthday home video-tapes. *Journal of Autism and Developmental Disorders, 24*, 247–257. doi:10.1007/BF02172225

Ozonoff, S., & Jensen, J. (1999). Brief report: Specific executive function profiles in three neurodevelopmental disorders. *Journal of Autism and Developmental Disorders, 29*, 171–177. doi:10.1023/A:1023052913110

Ozonoff, S., Pennington, B. F., & Rogers, S. J. (1991). Executive function deficits in high-functioning autistic individuals: Relationship to theory of mind. *Journal of*

Child Psychology and Psychiatry, 32, 1081–1105. doi:10.1111/j.1469-7610.1991.tb00351.x

Premack, D., & Woodruff, G. (1978). Does the chimpanzee have a theory of mind? *Behavioral and Brain Sciences, 1*, 515–526. doi:10.1017/S0140525X00076512

Richler, J., Huerta, M., Bishop, S., & Lord, C. (2010). Developmental trajectories of restricted and repetitive behaviors and interests in children with autism spectrum disorders. *Development and Psychopathology, 22*, 55–69. doi:10.1017/S0954579409990265

Russell, J. (2002). Cognitive theories of autism. In J. E. Harrison & A. A. M. Owen (Eds.), *Cognitive deficits in brain disorders* (pp. 295–323). London, England: Martin Dunitz.

Rutter, M. (1978). Diagnosis and definition of childhood autism. *Journal of Autism & Childhood Schizophrenia, 8*, 139–161. doi:10.1007/BF01537863

Rutter, M. (2003). Introduction: Autism—The challenges ahead. In G. Bock & J. Goode (Eds.), *Autism: Neural basis and treatment possibilities* (pp. 213–226). Chichester, England: Wiley.

Rutter, M. (2005). Incidence of autism spectrum disorders: Changes over time and their meaning. *Acta Paediatrica, 94*, 2–15. doi:10.1080/08035250410023124

Safran, S. P. (2008). Why youngsters with autistic spectrum disorders remain under-represented in special education. *Remedial and Special Education, 29*, 90–95. doi:10.1177/0741932507311637

Schreiber, C. (2011). Social skills interventions for children with high-functioning autism spectrum disorders. *Journal of Positive Behavior Interventions, 13*, 49–62. doi:10.1177/1098300709359027

Shah, A., & Frith, U. (1993). Why do autistic individuals show superior performance on the block design task? *Journal of Child Psychology and Psychiatry 34*, 1351–1364. doi:10.1111/j.1469-7610.1993.tb02095.x

Spiker, D., Lotspeich, L. J., Dimiceli, S., Myers, R. M., & Risch, N. (2002). Behavioral phenotypic variation in autism multiplex families: Evidence for a continuous severity gradient. *American Journal of Medical Genetics, 114*, 129–136. doi:10.1002/ajmg.10188

Stephanatos, G. A., & Baron, I. S. (2011). The ontogenesis on language impairment in autism: A neuropsychological perspective. *Neuropsychology Review, 21*, 252–270. doi:10.1007/s11065-011-9178-6

Steyn, B., & Le Couteur, A. (2003). Understanding autism spectrum disorders. *Current Paediatrics, 13*, 274–278. doi:10.1016/S0957-5839(03)00049-6

Szatmari, P., Merette, C., Bryson, S. E., Thivierge, J., Roy, M., Cayer, M., & Maziade, M. (2002). Quantifying dimensions in autism: A factor-analytic study. *Journal of the American Academy of Child & Adolescent Psychiatry, 41*, 467–474. doi:10.1097/00004583-200204000-00020

Tager-Flusberg, H. (1999). A psychological approach to understanding the social and language impairments in autism. *International Review of Psychiatry, 11*, 325–334. doi:10.1080/09540269974203

Tager-Flusberg, H. (2000). Understanding the language and communicative impairments in autism. *International Review of Research in Mental Retardation, 23*, 185–205. doi:10.1016/S0074-7750(00)80011-7

Travis, L. L., & Sigman, M. (1998). Social deficits and interpersonal relationships in autism. *Mental Retardation and Developmental Disabilities Research Reviews, 4*, 65–72. doi:10.1002/(SICI)1098-2779(1998)4:2<65::AID-MRDD2>3.0.CO;2-W

Tuchman, R., & Rapin, I. (2002, October). Epilepsy in autism. *The Lancet Neurology, 1*(6), 352–358. doi:10.1016/S1474-4422(02)00160-6

Turner, M. (1999). Annotation: Repetitive behavior in autism: A review of psychological research. *Journal of Child Psychology and Psychiatry, 40*, 839–849. doi:10.1111/1469-7610.00502

U.S. Department of Education. (2005). *Twenty-seventh annual report to congress on the implementation of the individuals with disabilities education act.* Retrieved from http://www2.ed.gov/about/reports/annual/osep/2005/parts-b-c/index.html

Virués-Ortega, J. (2010). Applied behavior and analytic intervention for autism and early childhood: Meta-analysis, meta-regression and dose-response meta-analysis of multiple outcomes. *Clinical Psychology Review, 30*, 387–399. doi: 10.1016/j.cpr.2010.01.008

Volkmar, F. R., Lord, C., Bailey, A., Schultz, R. T., & Klin, A. (2004). Autism and pervasive developmental disorders. *Journal of Child Psychology and Psychiatry, 45*, 135–170. doi:10.1046/j.0021-9630.2003.00317.x

Wainer, A. L., & Ingersoll, B. R. (2011). The use of innovative computer technology for teaching social communication to individuals with autism spectrum disorders. *Research in Autism Spectrum Disorders, 5*, 96–107. doi:10.1016/j.rasd.2010.08.002

Walker, D. R., Thompson, A., Zwaigenbaum, L., Goldberg, J., Bryson, S. E., Mahoney, W. J., . . . Szatmari, P. (2004). Specifying PDD-NOS: A comparison of PDD-NOS, Asperger syndrome, and autism. *Journal of the American Academy of Child & Adolescent Psychiatry, 43*, 172–180. doi:10.1097/00004583-200402000-00012

Wilkinson, L. A. (2010). Facilitating the identification of autism spectrum disorders in school-age children. *Remedial and Special Education, 31*, 350–357. doi:10.1177/0741932509338372

Zirkel, P. A. (2011). Autism litigation under the IDEA: A new meaning of "disproportionality"? *Journal of Special Education Leadership, 24*, 92–103.

2

MULTITIER SCREENING AND IDENTIFICATION

LEE A. WILKINSON

Although autism spectrum disorder (ASD) affects approximately 1% of the school-age population, it is not unusual for children with mild levels of impairment (e.g., without intellectual disability or noticeable language delay) to remain unidentified until well after entering school (Brock, Jimerson, & Hansen, 2006; Wilkinson, 2010). For example, a recent study examining the timing of identification among children with autism using a population-based sample from an ongoing surveillance effort across 13 sites in the United States found the gap between potential and actual age of identification (for those identified) to be in the range of 2.7 to 3.7 years. Combined with the fact that more than one quarter of cases were never identified as having ASD through age 8, these results illustrate the need for a more effective system of screening and identification for ASD in our schools (Shattuck et al., 2009).

As described in the Introduction and Chapter 1 of this volume, a defining feature of ASD is impairment in interpersonal relating and social

http://dx.doi.org/10.1037/14338-003
Autism Spectrum Disorder in Children and Adolescents: Evidence-Based Assessment and Intervention in Schools, L. A. Wilkinson (Editor)

communication. This includes difficulties in communicating with others, processing and integrating information from the environment, establishing and maintaining reciprocal social relationships, taking another person's perspective, inferring the interests of others, and transitioning to new learning environments (Carter, Davis, Klin, & Volkmar, 2005; Wilkinson, 2010). Although all children with ASD experience core social-communication deficits, we now recognize that autism-related traits are quantitatively distributed in the general population and that autism is best conceptualized as a spectrum disorder rather than a categorical diagnosis (Constantino & Gruber, 2012; Skuse et al., 2009). Even mild degrees of what might be called autistic social impairment can significantly interfere with classroom performance and adaptation. Likewise, a combination of mild autistic symptomatology and other psychological liabilities (e.g., attention problems, mood problems, aggression) can have an adverse effect on children's learning and behavior (Constantino & Gruber, 2012; Skuse et al., 2009). It is also important to recognize that socialization deficits are a major cause of impairment in ASD regardless of the individual's level of cognitive or language ability (Carter et al., 2005).

The core features of ASD may not diminish with development. Typically, children do not "outgrow" their limitations. Distress may actually increase as they approach adolescence and the social milieu becomes more complex and challenging. These difficulties may then persist into adulthood, where they would continue to negatively affect adaptive functioning. Because children with mild or even moderate deficits in social and communicative competence are often overlooked, are misdiagnosed with another psychiatric condition, or experience co-occurring disorders, it is critical that support professionals, particularly school psychologists, give greater priority to case finding and screening to ensure that children with symptoms of ASD are identified and have access to the appropriate intervention services (Brock et al., 2006; Wilkinson, 2010). The objective of this chapter is to provide school psychologists and allied professionals with a review of five ASD-specific screening instruments with promising psychometric properties and to present a multitier model for identifying children who are most likely to have ASD and thus require a comprehensive assessment.

DIAGNOSTIC VALIDITY AND ACCURACY IN SCREENING FOR AUTISM SPECTRUM DISORDER

Screening is an important first step for securing the appropriate educational services for children with ASD. Developing screening tools to identify students with less severe symptoms of ASD tends to be especially difficult because the autism spectrum consists of a wide range of impairment without clear-cut boundaries (Wing & Potter, 2009). Until recently, there were few validated screening measures available to assist school psychologists in the identification of students with the core symptoms of ASD (Campbell, 2005; Lord & Corsello, 2005). Because autism has traditionally been viewed as a "categorical" diagnosis, most rating scales were developed to categorically determine the presence or absence of ASD rather than dimensionally assess the severity of ASD symptoms. Yet research indicates that children with the same diagnostic classification are likely to be heterogeneous and that many childhood disorders, including ASD, fall along a continuum in the general population (Constantino & Gruber, 2012). Categorical classification fails to account for these quantitative differences between children with the same core symptoms. However, there are now several reliable and valid screening tools and rating scales to quantify the severity of symptoms across the autism spectrum and/or as a function of response to intervention.

Diagnostic validity is an especially important psychometric characteristic to consider when evaluating the quality and usefulness of a test or screening instrument. It refers to a test's accuracy in predicting group membership (e.g., ASD vs. non-ASD). Diagnostic validity can be expressed through metrics such as sensitivity and specificity and positive predictive value and negative predictive value. Sensitivity and specificity are measures of a test's ability to correctly identify someone as having a given disorder or not having the disorder. *Sensitivity* refers to the percentage of cases with a disorder that screen positive. A highly sensitive test means that there are few false negative results (i.e., individuals with a disorder who screen negative), and thus fewer cases of the disorder are missed. *Specificity* is the percentage of cases without a disorder that screen negative. A highly specific test means that there are few false positive results (i.e., individuals without a disorder who screen positive). False negatives decrease sensitivity, whereas false positives decrease specificity. An efficient screening tool should minimize false negatives because these are individuals with a likely disorder who remain unidentified (National Research Council, 2001; Norris & Lecavalier, 2010; Wilkinson, 2010). Sensitivity and specificity levels of .80 or higher are generally recommended (Norris & Lecavalier, 2010).

Positive predictive value and negative predictive value are also important validity statistics that describe how well a screening tool or test performs. The probability of having a given disorder, given the results of a test, is called the *predictive value*. *Positive predictive value* (PPV) is interpreted as the percentage of all positive cases that truly have the disorder. PPV is a critical measure of the performance of a diagnostic or screening measure because it reflects the probability that a positive test or screen identifies the disorder for which the individual is being evaluated or screened. *Negative predictive value* (NPV) is the percentage of all cases screened negative that are truly without the disorder. The higher the PPV and NPV, the more efficient the instrument at correctly identifying cases. It is important to recognize that PPV is influenced by the sensitivity and specificity of the test as well as the prevalence of the disorder in the sample under study. For example, an ASD-specific screening measure may be expected to have a higher PPV when used with a known group of high-risk children who exhibit signs or symptoms of developmental delay, social skills deficits, or language impairment. In fact, for any diagnostic test, when the prevalence of the disorder is low, the PPV will also be low, even using a test with high sensitivity and specificity.

SCREENING MEASURES

Third-party screening questionnaires have been shown to discriminate well between children with and without ASD. Parent and teacher screening tools are especially ideal instruments for identifying children who are in need of a more comprehensive evaluation. They yield important information from individuals who know the child the best, and they are relatively easy to administer and score (Wilkinson, 2010). The following measures have demonstrated utility in screening for ASD in educational settings and can be used to determine which children are likely to require further assessment and/or who might benefit from additional support. They also afford the ability to measure autistic characteristics on a quantitative scale across a wide range of severity. All measures have strong psychometric qualities, are appropriate for school-age children, and are time efficient (5–20 minutes to complete). Although training needs are minimal and require little or no professional instruction to complete, interpretation of the results requires familiarity with ASD and experience in administering, scoring, and interpreting psychological tests. Table 2.1 shows the ASD screening measures, together with information regarding format, administration time, diagnostic validity, and applicable age ranges.

Autism Spectrum Rating Scales

The Autism Spectrum Rating Scales (ASRS; Goldstein & Naglieri, 2010) is a norm-referenced instrument designed to effectively identify symptoms and behaviors associated with autistic disorder, Asperger's disorder (syndrome), and pervasive developmental disorder not otherwise specified, in children and adolescents from 2 to 18 years of age. The ASRS was standardized on 2,560 cases from across the United States and provides strong evidence that the measure can accurately distinguish ASD from general population groups as rated by teachers and parents (Goldstein & Naglieri, 2010). The

TABLE 2.1
Screening Measures for Autism Spectrum Disorder

Measure	Age range	Format (no. of items)	Sensitivity	Specificity	Time to complete
ASRS	6–18 years	Questionnaire—Parent/Teacher (15/71)	.94	.92	5–15 min
ASSQ	6–17 years	Questionnaire—Parent/Teacher (27)	.91	.86	10 min
CCC–2	4–16 years, 11 months	Questionnaire—Parent/Professional (70)	.89	.97	10–15 min
SCQ	4 years–Adult	Questionnaire—Parent (40)	.96	.80	10 min
SRS–2	4–18 years	Questionnaire—Parent/Teacher (65)	.92	.92	10–20 min

Note. ASRS = Autism Spectrum Rating Scales (Short and Long Forms); ASSQ = Autism Spectrum Screening Questionnaire; CCC–2 = Children's Communication Checklist—Second Edition; SCQ = Social Communication Questionnaire; SRS–2 = Social Responsiveness Scale, Second Edition (School-Age Form).

ASRS has full-length and short forms for young children ages 2 to 5 years and for older children and adolescents ages 6 to 18 years. The full-length ASRS (2–5 Years) consists of 70 items, and the full-length ASRS (6–18 Years) contains 71 items. The short form was developed for screening purposes and contains 15 items from the full-length form that have been shown to differentiate children diagnosed with ASD from children in the general population.

Each item is scored on a Likert scale from 0 (*never*) to 4 (*very frequently*). All scales are set to the *T* score metric, with a normative mean of 50 and a standard deviation of 10. *T* scores and percentiles are categorized as *low, average* (typical), *slightly elevated, elevated,* and *very elevated.* The full-length form provides the most comprehensive assessment information, including the various scales (Total score, ASRS scales, and Treatment scales). It also includes a *DSM–IV–TR* Scale related to the symptom criteria from the *Diagnostic and Statistical Manual of Mental Disorders* (4th ed., text rev.; American Psychiatric Association, 2000). The short form provides a single total score and can be used as a screening measure to determine which children and youth are likely to require a more comprehensive assessment for an ASD. It is also suitable for monitoring response to treatment and intervention. Reliability data indicate high levels of internal consistency, good interrater agreement, and excellent test–retest reliability. The discriminative validity (classification accuracy) of both the ASRS full-length and ASRS short forms indicates that the scales were able to accurately predict group membership with a mean overall correct classification rate of 90.4% on the ASRS (2–5 Years) and 90.1% on the ASRS (6–18 Years). The full-length form can be completed in approximately 15 minutes, whereas the short form can be completed in approximately 5 minutes.

Autism Spectrum Screening Questionnaire

The Autism Spectrum Screening Questionnaire (ASSQ; Ehlers, Gillberg, & Wing, 1999) is a parent and teacher questionnaire that consists of 27 items designed to discriminate between more capable children with ASD and typically developing peers. The ASSQ has been widely used in clinical practice and is well validated in research, both with general population and clinical samples (Ehlers et al., 1999; Mattila et al., 2009; Posserud, Lundervold, & Gillberg, 2009). The ASSQ content addresses social interaction (11 items), verbal and nonverbal communication (six items), restricted and repetitive behaviors (five items), and motor clumsiness and associated symptoms (five items). Social items include questions related to difficulties with friendship, prosocial behavior, and social communication. The respondent rates behavioral descriptions on a 3-point scale, 0 (*not true*), 1 (*sometimes true*), and 2 (*certainly true*). Positively endorsed items are summed for a total score (range of 0–54). Various cutoffs and their corresponding sensitivity and specificity are reported to allow more flexible interpretation. For a nonclinical sample, the authors suggest a score of ≥ 13 when parents served as raters (sensitivity = .91, specificity = .77) and ≥ 11 for teachers (sensitivity = .90, specificity = .58). This threshold is recommended for use when it is essential to minimize the risk of missing mild autism cases (false negatives; Ehlers et al., 1999; Posserud et al., 2009). For a clinical setting, the authors suggest a cutoff of ≥ 19 for parent raters (sensitivity = .62, specificity = .90) and ≥ 22 for teacher raters (sensitivity = .70, specificity = .91).

A recent validation study found the ASSQ to be an effective screening tool for identifying ASD and the broader autism phenotype in a general population sample (e.g., public schools) of 7- to 9-year-old children. Analyses indicated an optimal cutoff score of ≥ 17 on either parent or teacher questionnaire for discriminating between ASD and non-ASD cases. Combining the results for both informants and using this cutoff score provided the most efficient screening results, with a sensitivity value of .91 and a specificity value of .86 (Posserud et al., 2009). Research has indicated that the ASSQ possesses strong test–retest reliability, acceptable interrater reliability, and good internal consistency and that it significantly differentiates high-functioning ASD from other childhood disorders (Ehlers et al., 1999; Posserud et al., 2009).

Children's Communication Checklist—Second Edition

The Children's Communication Checklist—Second Edition (CCC–2; Bishop, 2006) is a measure intended to assess communication skills in the areas of pragmatics, syntax, morphology, semantics, and speech of children ages 4 to 16 years, 11 months. Initially developed in the United Kingdom, the CCC–2 has been adapted for use in the United States and has shown utility in identifying children who may require further assessment for an ASD (Bishop, 2006). A caregiver response form is completed by an adult who has regular contact with the child, usually a parent, teacher, therapist, or other professional. The CCC–2 consists of 70 items that are divided into 10 scales, each with seven items. The first four scales address specific aspects of language and communication skills (content and form). The next four scales assess the pragmatic aspects of communication. The last two scales assess behaviors that are usually impaired in children with ASD. The respondent rates the frequency of the communication behavior described in each item from 0 (*less than once a week or never*) to 3 (*several times a day or always*).

Interpretation is based on a General Communication Composite and Social Interaction Difference Index (SIDI), a metric specifically designed for use in identifying a communication profile that might be characteristic of ASD. Disproportionately depressed communicative competence, coupled with a score of −11 or less on the SIDI, suggests a profile of ASD and the need for further evaluation. The CCC–2 reports a sensitivity value of .89 and specificity value of .97 for identifying children with autistic symptomatology and social impairment (Bishop, 2006). Previous versions of the CCC–2 have been strongly associated with the Autism Diagnostic Interview—Revised (ADI–R; Rutter, Le Couteur, & Lord, 2003) total score and International Classification of Diseases (10th Rev.; World Health Organization, 2010) diagnostic criteria (Charman et al., 2007; Verté et al., 2006). In a recent study (Volden & Phillips, 2010), the CCC–2 was found to be a more sensitive tool than the Test of Pragmatic Language (Phelps-Terasaki & Phelps-Gunn, 2007) for identifying pragmatic language impairment in high-functioning individuals with ASD who have structural language and nonverbal cognitive scores within typical limits. The CCC–2 also has the advantage of sampling pragmatic skills in the child's natural environment.

Social Communication Questionnaire

The Social Communication Questionnaire (SCQ; Rutter, Bailey, & Lord, 2003), previously known as the Autism Screening Questionnaire (ASQ), was initially designed as a companion screening measure for the ADI–R. The SCQ is a parent and caregiver dimensional measure of ASD symptomatology, appropriate for children of any chronological age older than 4 years. It can be completed by the informant in less than 10 minutes. The SCQ is available in two forms, Lifetime and Current, each with 40 questions presented in a yes-or-no format. Scores on the questionnaire provide an index of symptom severity and indicate the likelihood that a child has ASD. Questions include items in the reciprocal social interaction domain, the communication domain, and the restricted, repetitive, and stereotyped patterns of behavior domain. The authors recommend using different cutoff scores for different purposes and populations (e.g., a cutoff of ≥ 22 when differentiating autism from other ASD and a cutoff of ≥ 15 when differentiating ASD from non-ASD). A threshold raw score of >15 is recommended to minimize the risk of false negatives and indicate the need for a comprehensive evaluation. This threshold score resulted in a sensitivity value of .96, a specificity value of .80, and a PPV of .93 in a large population of children with autism and other developmental disorders. Compared with other screening measures, the SCQ has received significant scrutiny and has consistently demonstrated its effectiveness in predicting ASD versus non-ASD status in multiple studies (Chandler et al., 2007; Norris & Lecavalier, 2010).

Social Responsiveness Scale (Second Edition)

The second edition of the Social Responsiveness Scale (SRS–2; Constantino & Gruber, 2012) identifies the various dimensions of interpersonal behavior, communication, and repetitive and stereotypic behavior characteristic of ASD and quantifies symptom severity. The SRS–2 maintains continuity with the original instrument and extends the age range from 2.5 years through adulthood. There are four forms, each consisting of 65 items: Preschool Form (2.5–4.5 years), School-Age Form (4–18 years), Adult Form (ages 19 and up), and Adult Self-Report Form (ages 19 and up). Nationally representative standardization samples were collected to support each form.

The School-Age Form is unchanged in its item content from the first edition of the SRS and can be completed in 15 to 20 minutes by informants (e.g., parents, teachers, day care providers) who have observed the child's social interactions in naturalistic contexts. Each item is scored on a 4-point scale: 1 (not true), 2 (sometimes true), 3 (often true), and 4 (almost always true). Scores are obtained for five treatment subscales: Social Awareness, Social Cognition, Social Communication, Social Motivation, and Restricted Interests and Repetitive Behavior. There are also two Diagnostic and Statistical Manual of Mental Disorders (5th ed.; DSM–5; American Psychiatric Association, 2013) compatible subscales (Social Communication and Interaction and Restricted Interests and Repetitive Behavior) that allow comparison of symptoms with the new DSM–5 diagnostic criteria for ASD.

Interpretation is based on a single score reflecting the sum of responses to all 65 SRS questions. Raw scores are converted to T scores for gender and respondent. A total T score of 76 or higher is considered severe and strongly associated with a clinical diagnosis of ASD. T scores of 66 through 75 are interpreted as indicating moderate deficiencies in reciprocal social behavior that are clinically significant and lead to substantial interference in everyday social interactions, whereas T scores of 60 to 65 are in the mild range and indicate deficiencies in reciprocal social behavior that are clinically significant and may lead to mild to moderate problems in social interaction. T scores of 59 and below fall within typical limits and are not generally associated with clinically significant ASD.

Findings across studies and groups consistently report sensitivity ranging from .78 to .91, with values clustering around .80. Specificity values range from .85 to .90 when contrasts involve a typically developing group. In a large-scale clinical sample (School-Age Form), analyses indicated sensitivity and specificity values of .92 at a raw score of 62. This suggests that the SRS–2 is a robust instrument for discriminating between individuals with ASD and those unaffected by the condition. Large samples also provide evidence of good interrater reliability, high internal consistency, and convergent validity with the ADI–R, Autism Diagnostic Observation Schedule (Lord, Rutter, DiLavore, & Risi, 1999), and SCQ.

A MULTITIER SCREENING MODEL

The following three-tier (or three-step) model is recommended for screening students who demonstrate risk factors and/or warning signs of atypical development or where caregiver and parent concerns strongly suggest the presence of ASD symptoms.

Tier One

The initial step is *case finding*. This involves recognizing the risk factors and/or warning signs of ASD. All school professionals should be aware of those students who display atypical social and/or communication behaviors that might be associated with ASD. Although no two children are alike, at-risk students may demonstrate difficulties in the areas of social interaction, attention, impulse control, and behavioral regulation. They may have difficulty interacting with peers and may display a narrow range of interests or intense preoccupation with specific objects. Delays in language milestones or pragmatic skills (social language), repetitive behaviors, inflexibility, and difficulty transitioning have been associated with ASD.

Pedantic or overly mature speech, stereotypic mannerisms, poor eye contact, and sensory sensitivity may also be observed in at-risk children. The failure to make friends, understand social rules and conventions, or display social reciprocity in interpersonal relationships is considered a warning sign at all age and grade levels. Case finding also requires that attention be given not only to teacher concerns about children's development but also to parental worry as well. Parent and/or teacher reports of social impairment combined with communication and behavioral concerns constitute a red flag and indicate the need for screening. Children who are identified with risk factors during this case-finding phase should be referred for formal screening.

Tier Two

Once screened, individual scores can be used as an indication of the approximate severity of ASD symptomatology for students who present with elevated developmental risk factors and/or warning signs of ASD identified through case finding. Screening results are shared with parents and school-based teams, with a focus on intervention planning and ongoing observation. Scores can also be used for progress monitoring and to measure change over time. Students with a positive screen who continue to show minimal progress at this level are then considered for a more comprehensive assessment and intensive interventions as part of Tier Three. However, as with all screening tools, there will be some false negatives (children with ASD who are not identified). Thus, children who screen negative but who have a high level of risk and/or parent and/or teacher concerns indicating developmental variations and behaviors consistent with an autism-related disorder should continue to be monitored, regardless of screening results.

Tier Three

Students who meet the threshold criteria in Tier Two may then be referred for an in-depth assessment and intensive intervention. When used in combination with other assessment information, the results from these screening measures can be integrated into a comprehensive developmental assessment to assist in determining eligibility for special education services and guide intervention planning. A multidisciplinary team of school professionals (e.g., school psychologist, general and special educator, speech or language pathologist, and occupational therapist) should collaborate to determine an appropriate classification and intervention plan. Qualitative measures should include parent or caregiver interviews, developmental history, direct observation, and interaction with the student, together with a quantitative assessment of social behavior, cognitive functioning, academic achievement, language and communication, adaptive behavior, and when indicated, motor skills, sensory processing, and atypical behavior (National Research Council, 2001; Wilkinson, 2010). The essential elements of a comprehensive developmental assessment are described in the next chapter.

LIMITATIONS

Although the screening measures discussed in this chapter can be recommended as reliable and valid tools for identifying children across the broad autism spectrum, they are not without limitations. Some students who screen positive will not be identified with ASD (false positive). However, some children who were not initially identified will go on to meet the diagnostic and/or classification criteria (false negative). Therefore, it is especially important to carefully monitor those students who screen negative so as to ensure access to intervention services (Bryson, Rogers, & Fombonne, 2003). Gathering information from family and school resources during screening will also facilitate identification of possible cases.

Gender differences should also be taken into consideration when screening. Research has suggested that there may be sex differences in the expression of the broader autism phenotype (Wilkinson, 2010). Although few studies have examined effects of gender-specific differences on various screening measures, the ASRS, ASSQ, and SRS–2 have generally reported higher mean scores for boys than girls. Both the SRS–2 and ASSQ found higher scores for boys than girls in both the parent and teacher questionnaires, with the greatest difference in reports from teachers (Constantino & Gruber, 2012; Posserud et al., 2009). These lower symptom scores for girls may reflect gender differences in autistic traits and expression of the phenotype. Recent research has also suggested that certain single items may be more typical of girls than of boys with ASD, and examining symptom gender differences at the individual item level might lead to a better understanding of gender differences in ASD (Kopp & Gillberg, 2011). Although this phenomenon continues to be studied, a higher cutoff threshold for boys might be considered when screening for autism traits in the general population.

Finally, a screening tool's efficiency will be influenced by the practice setting in which it is used. ASD-specific tools are not currently recommended for the universal screening of typical school-age children. Focusing on case finding and children with identified risk-factors and/or developmental delays increases predictive values and results in more efficient screening (Wilkinson, 2010).

CONCLUSION

Epidemiological studies have indicated a progressively rising prevalence trend for ASD over the past decade (Wing & Potter, 2009). Research has indicated that outcomes for children on the autism spectrum can be significantly enhanced with the delivery of intensive intervention services (National Research Council, 2001). However, intervention services can only be implemented if students are identified. Screening is the initial step in this process. School psychologists should be prepared to recognize the presence of risk factors and/or early warning signs of ASD and be familiar with screening tools to ensure children with ASD are being identified and provided with the appropriate programs and services (Wilkinson, 2010).

REFERENCES

American Psychiatric Association. (2000). *Diagnostic and statistical manual of mental disorders* (4th ed., text rev.). Washington, DC: Author.

American Psychiatric Association. (2013). *Diagnostic and statistical manual of mental disorders* (5th ed.). Washington, DC: Author.

Bishop, D. V. M. (2006). *Children's Communication Checklist* (2nd ed.). San Antonio, TX: Psychological Corporation.

Brock, S. E., Jimerson, S. R., & Hansen, R. L. (2006). *Identifying, assessing, and treating autism at school*. New York, NY: Springer.

Bryson, S. E., Rogers, S. J., & Fombonne, E. (2003). Autism spectrum disorders: Early detection, intervention, education, and psychopharmacological management. *Canadian Journal of Psychiatry/La Revue de Canadienne de Psychiatrie, 48,* 506–516.

Campbell, J. M. (2005). Diagnostic assessment of Asperger's disorder: A review of five third-party rating scales. *Journal of Autism and Developmental Disorders, 35,* 25–35. doi:10.1007/s10803-004-1028-4

Carter, A. S., Davis, N. O., Klin, A., & Volkmar, F. R. (2005). Social development in autism. In F. R. Volkmar, R. Paul, A. Klin, & D. Cohen (Eds.), *Handbook of autism and pervasive developmental disorders: Vol. 1. Diagnosis, development, neurobiology, and behavior* (pp. 312–334). Hoboken, NJ: Wiley.

Chandler, S., Charman, T., Baird, G., Simonoff, E., Loucas, T., Meldrum, D., . . . Pickles, A. (2007). Validation of the Social Communication Questionnaire in a population cohort of children with autism spectrum disorders. *Journal of the American Academy of Child & Adolescent Psychiatry, 46,* 1324–1332. doi:10.1097/chi.0b013e31812f7d8d

Charman, T., Baird, G., Simonoff, E., Loucas, T., Chandler, S., Meldrum, D., & Pickles, A. (2007). Efficacy of three screening instruments in the identification of autistic-spectrum disorders. *The British Journal of Psychiatry, 191*, 554–559. doi:10.1192/bjp.bp.107.040196

Constantino, J. N., & Gruber, C. P. (2012). *Social Responsiveness Scale* (2nd ed.). Los Angeles, CA: Western Psychological Services.

Ehlers, S., Gillberg, C., & Wing, L. (1999). A screening questionnaire for Asperger syndrome and other high-functioning autism spectrum disorders in school-age children. *Journal of Autism and Developmental Disorders, 29*, 129–141. doi:10.1023/A:1023040610384

Goldstein, S., & Naglieri, J. A. (2010). *Autism Spectrum Rating Scales*. North Tonawanda, NY: Multi-Health Systems, Inc.

Kopp, S., & Gillberg, C. (2011). The Autism Spectrum Screening Questionnaire (ASSQ)—Revised Extended Version (ASSQ-REV): An instrument for better capturing the autism phenotype in girls? A preliminary study involving clinical cases and community controls. *Research in Developmental Disabilities, 32*, 2875–2888. doi:10.1016/j.ridd.2011.05.017

Lord, C., & Corsello, C. (2005). Diagnostic instruments in autistic spectrum disorders. In F. R. Volkmar, R. Paul, A. Klin, & D. Cohen (Eds.), *Handbook of autism and pervasive developmental disorders: Vol. 2. Assessment, interventions, and policy* (3rd ed., pp. 730–771). Hoboken, NJ: Wiley.

Lord, C., Rutter, M., DiLavore, P. C., & Risi, S. (1999). *Autism Diagnostic Observation Schedule (ADOS): Manual*. Los Angeles, CA: Western Psychological Services.

Mattila, M. L., Jussila, K., Kuusikko, S., Kielinen, M., Linna, S. L., Ebeling, H., . . . Moilanen, I. (2009). When does the Autism Spectrum Screening Questionnaire (ASSQ) predict autism spectrum disorders in primary school-aged children? *European Child & Adolescent Psychiatry, 18*, 499–509. doi:10.1007/s00787-009-0044-5

National Research Council. (2001). *Educating children with autism*. Washington, DC: National Academy Press.

Norris, M., & Lecavalier, L. (2010). Screening accuracy of Level 2 autism spectrum disorder rating scales: A review of selected instruments. *Autism, 14*, 263–284. doi:10.1177/1362361309348071

Phelps-Terasaki, D., & Phelps-Gunn, T. (2007). *Test of Pragmatic Language: Examiner's manual* (2nd ed.). Austin, TX: Pro-Ed.

Posserud, M., Lundervold, A. J., & Gillberg, C. (2009). Validation of the Autism Spectrum Screening Questionnaire in a total population sample. *Journal of Autism and Developmental Disorders, 39*, 126–134. doi:10.1007/s10803-008-0609-z

Rutter, M., Bailey, A., & Lord, C. (2003). *Social Communication Questionnaire*. Los Angeles, CA: Western Psychological Services.

Rutter, M., Le Couteur, A., & Lord, C. (2003). *Autism Diagnostic Interview—Revised*. Los Angeles, CA: Western Psychological Services.

Shattuck, P. T., Durkin, M., Maenner, M., Newschaffer, C., Mandell, D. S., Wiggins, L., . . . Cuniff, C. (2009). Timing of identification among children with an autism spectrum disorder: Findings from a population-based surveillance study. *Journal of the American Academy of Child & Adolescent Psychiatry, 48,* 474–483. doi:10.1097/CHI.0b013e31819b3848

Skuse, D. H., Mandy, W., Steer, C., Miller, L. L., Goodman, R., Lawrence, K., . . . Golding, J. (2009). Social communication competence and functional adaptation in a general population of children: Preliminary evidence for sex-by-verbal IQ differential risk. *Journal of the American Academy of Child & Adolescent Psychiatry, 48,* 128–137. doi:10.1097/CHI.0b013e31819176b8

Verté, S., Geurts, H. M., Roeyers, H., Rosseel, Y., Oosterlaan, J., & Sergeant, J. A. (2006). Can the Children's Communication Checklist differentiate autism spectrum subtypes? *Autism, 10,* 266–287. doi:10.1177/1362361306063299

Volden, J., & Phillips, L. (2010). Measuring pragmatic language in speakers with autism spectrum disorders: Comparing the Children's Communication Checklist—2 and the Test of Pragmatic Language. *American Journal of Speech-Language Pathology, 19,* 204–212. doi:10.1044/1058-0360(2010/09-0011)

Wilkinson, L. A. (2010). *A best practice guide to assessment and intervention for autism and Asperger syndrome in schools.* London, England: Kingsley.

Wing, L., & Potter, D. (2009). The epidemiology of autism spectrum disorders: Is the prevalence rising? In S. Goldstein, J. A. Naglieri, & S. Ozonoff (Eds.), *Assessment of autism spectrum disorders* (pp. 18–54). New York, NY: Guilford Press.

World Health Organization. (2010). *ICD–10: International statistical classification of diseases and related health problems* (10th rev.). Geneva, Switzerland: Author.

3

COMPREHENSIVE DEVELOPMENTAL APPROACH ASSESSMENT MODEL

JONATHAN M. CAMPBELL, LISA A. RUBLE,
AND RACHEL K. HAMMOND

In this chapter, we describe the importance of conducting a comprehensive and evidence-based psychological assessment when working with a student where concerns about autism are relevant. We highlight two classification systems frequently used to identify and diagnose autism spectrum disorder (ASD), and we provide an overview of ASD focused on what school psychologists need to know. We then provide an introduction to the comprehensive developmental approach and the evidence-based assessment movement in the field of autism assessment. The chapter continues with the identification and description of various psychological assessments with sound evidence base for use in professional practice. We conclude with general comments about the use and value of psychological assessment in the context of school practice.

http://dx.doi.org/10.1037/14338-004
Autism Spectrum Disorder in Children and Adolescents: Evidence-Based Assessment and Intervention in Schools, L. A. Wilkinson (Editor)

TWO CLASSIFICATION SYSTEMS FOR AUTISM SPECTRUM DISORDER

The defining characteristics of ASD are the pervasive impairments in social and communication skills relative to other areas of development (American Psychiatric Association, 2000). Although symptoms of autism are often evident in the first 3 years of life and children can be identified reliably during this period, children often remain undiagnosed until 4 years of age or older. The delay in diagnosis is especially true for children who are non-White or Hispanic (Fountain, King, & Bearman, 2011). Further, research suggests that, in addition to minority status, children who are poor or have mothers with less education are most likely to be identified by schools rather than by medical professionals (Yeargin-Allsopp et al., 2003). These circumstances suggest that school psychologists play a critical role in the diagnosis of children with autism, especially children from minority or low-income families.

Psychiatric Classification

The *Diagnostic and Statistical Manual of Mental Disorders* (5th ed.; *DSM–5*; American Psychiatric Association, 2013) specifies the current diagnostic features and criteria for ASD. In this section, we highlight several important points regarding the potential impact of the new *DSM–5* category of ASD. In contrast to the *DSM–IV–TR* (American Psychiatric Association, 2000), which included several subtypes of ASD (e.g., autistic disorder, Asperger's disorder, and pervasive developmental disorder not otherwise specified), the current definition consists of a single diagnosis of ASD. The three *DSM–IV–TR* symptom domains (social impairment; communication impairment; and restrictive, repetitive behaviors and interests) have been reduced to two (social communication impairments and restricted, repetitive patterns of behavior). The American Psychiatric Association has acknowledged that individuals with currently defined pervasive developmental disorder diagnoses will retain a diagnosis of ASD. In the *DSM–5*, a new diagnostic category of social communication disorder is also included that is designed to capture social-communication impairments not accompanied by restrictive and repetitive interests (American Psychiatric Association, 2013). It is important for school psychologists to understand that the changes have resulted in concern among parents, advocates, and some researchers. For example, there is concern that the new category of ASD may not identify higher functioning individuals with autism as suggested in independent field trials. The general consensus, however, is that higher functioning individuals will meet the new *DSM–5* criteria.

Educational Classification

A challenge for school psychologists is that many states have adopted the educational classification system outlined in the Individuals With Disabilities Education Improvement Act (IDEA; 2004), rather than the psychiatric system just described. The federal definition of autism is as follows:

> A developmental disability significantly affecting verbal and nonverbal communication and social interaction, usually evident before age 3 that adversely affects a child's educational performance. Other characteristics often associated with ASD are engagement in repetitive activities and stereotyped movements, resistance to environmental change or change in daily routines, and unusual responses to sensory experiences. The term does not apply if a child's educational performance is adversely affected because the child has an emotional disturbance. (34 C.F.R. 300.8(c)(1) (2004))

Therefore, school psychologists must be prepared to assist teachers, administrators, and parents in understanding the similarities and differences between the two diagnostic frameworks.

Where the Two Systems Differ: Educational Impact

Because of differences between the psychiatric and educational classification systems, issues may arise. For example, it is not unusual for parents to obtain a diagnosis of ASD from a medical professional outside the educational system; however, unlike the IDEA (2004) criteria, the psychiatric criteria do not require presence of an educational impact. The differences between the two systems are particularly salient for students with ASD who have average or above average intelligence and are able to complete academic work at the expected grade level. Despite cognitive and academic strengths, these students experience significant social challenges in and outside the classroom, which can lead to deleterious effects if not addressed through appropriate interventions that should be provided by the educational system and specified in the child's individualized education program (IEP) or 504 plan. The continuum of special education services, IEP process, and educational programming for effective intervention are discussed in Chapters 8 and 9.

WHAT SCHOOL PSYCHOLOGISTS NEED TO KNOW ABOUT AUTISM SPECTRUM DISORDER

It is imperative that school psychologists keep up-to-date with new information about ASD, particularly as current findings apply to initial diagnosis and psychological assessment. In the next section, we provide a brief introduction to current findings regarding etiology, epidemiology, and comorbidities.

Etiology and Cure

School psychologists will likely be asked about the cause of autism, particularly in instances where an initial diagnosis is delivered to parents and an educational team. Although it is helpful that most people have heard of autism today, the unfortunate consequence of public media attention is the perpetuation of incorrect and sometimes harmful information. The role of vaccines vis-à-vis etiology is a good example of a controversial issue that could result in divisiveness between parents and professionals. Autism is also a target of untested and possibly harmful interventions that promise a cure and can be costly for families, emotionally and financially. Front-line practitioners need to stay informed about the latest findings in autism and have a response to questions about the cause and possibility of a cure.

Unfortunately, we are unable to provide clear answers to parents about the cause of autism. The etiology remains unknown, and there are no known cures; however, there are significant advances in research that provide direction. Neuroimaging and autopsy studies suggest an alteration of normal brain processes early in development, such as increased cerebrum and cerebellar growth during the preschool years, followed by decreased growth later (Amaral, Schumann, & Nordahl, 2008). More recent functional imaging studies have identified deficient connectivity within and between brain regions important for social information processing (e.g., Courchesne & Pierce, 2005).

Evidence for the role of genetics in autism is based on increased sibling occurrence rates, monozygotic (MZ) twin concordance rates, and dizygotic twin concordance rates. Also observed is an increased risk of associated genetic and chromosomal abnormalities such as fragile X syndrome and tuberous sclerosis. As a result of the etiological heterogeneity in ASD, there is growing support for autism as a behavioral manifestation of tens or even hundreds of related genetic or genomic disorders (Betancur, 2011). Genetic research on cellular and molecular pathways that regulate the development of neural systems involved in cognition and social behaviors is underway and may help identify targeted treatments in the future.

Genetics is not the entire cause of autism; for example, MZ twin concordance rates for autism are not 100%. Beginning in the 1970s, when a correlation between congenital rubella and autism was reported, researchers have continued to examine the role of various potential environmental, metabolic, and immunologic causes. One particularly controversial hypothesis implicated administration of the measles–mumps–rubella vaccine as a cause for autism. No conclusive scientific evidence, however, supports this hypothesis or any hypothesis of a combination of vaccines as a cause of autism (e.g., Miller & Reynolds, 2009). In addition, no conclusive evidence exists for a link between autism and mercury-containing preservatives used in the manufacture of vaccines (Miller & Reynolds, 2009).

Epidemiology

The Centers for Disease Control and Prevention (2012) recently reported a prevalence rate of one out of 88, a 78% increase over the past decade. Further, public agencies such as the U.S. Department of Education have identified autism as the largest growing low-incidence disability. No ethnic or racial boundaries exist in the incidence of autism, but boys are affected at least 4 times more often than girls. There is also documented disparity in age of diagnosis and access to specialized treatment interventions for minority or low-income families compared with White children (Fountain et al., 2011). Investigating correlates of the increase in autism prevalence, Chakrabarti and Fombonne (2005) found a disproportionate increase in the number of children with mild versus classic symptoms of autism. Overall, the authors concluded that although epidemiological studies of autism are flawed with methodological limitations, data on increased numbers of children with autism are likely to be reflecting (a) the use of a broader definition of autism, (b) changes in diagnostic criteria over time, and (c) an improved recognition of autism, especially in children without intellectual disability.

Comorbid Disorders

Individuals with ASD are at risk of comorbid disorders, with estimates of up to 72.5% of individuals affected (Memari, Ziaee, Mirfazeli, & Kordi, 2012). Intellectual disability occurs in the majority of individuals with autism but occurs in less than half of the total when the entire autism spectrum is included. About 20% to 30% of individuals with autism also have epilepsy (e.g., Amiet et al., 2008). In addition to intellectual disability and epilepsy, notable psychiatric comorbidities for individuals with ASD include depression, anxiety, obsessive–compulsive disorder, and bipolar disorder. Of the psychiatric disorders, anxiety and depression are the most common comorbidities, with reported frequency rates ranging greatly from 4% to 84% (Mazefsky, Conner, & Oswald, 2010). Overall, school psychologists should be aware of comorbidities, particularly depression and anxiety, and account for these when evaluating a child with confirmed or suspected ASD. The assessment of co-occurring (comorbid) emotional and behavior problems is discussed in Chapter 6.

The Role of Psychological Assessment

All children with ASD should receive a psychological assessment. Because of the time, effort, and costs associated with psychological assessment, it is critical that the clinician use a well-formulated approach to assessment that uses principles of evidence-based assessment (EBA) for ASD. The following sections identify and describe the defining principles of the comprehensive developmental approach (CDA) to ASD assessment as well as principles of the EBA movement. We advocate the use of the CDA as an overarching model to assessment that incorporates measures that meet the standards outlined by the EBA movement.

THE COMPREHENSIVE DEVELOPMENTAL APPROACH TO ASSESSMENT

Klin, Saulnier, Tsatsanis, and Volkmar (2005) outlined a valuable organizing strategy for assessing children and adolescents referred for diagnostic evaluation for the presence of ASD, the comprehensive developmental approach. Representing the *comprehensive* component of the CDA, Klin et al. (2005) argued that assessment of the individual's functioning should span a range of areas and contexts. The *developmental* aspect of the CDA posits that the individual's functioning should be compared with standards of both chronological and mental age expectations. The inclusion of both normative (i.e., chronological age) and ipsative (i.e., mental age) standards of interpretation is a key feature of the CDA, designed to assist with diagnostic decision making as well as guiding recommendations for intervention.

Principles of Psychological Assessment From a Comprehensive Developmental Approach

The CDA assumes that individuals with suspected or confirmed ASD will likely present with wide variability across domains of psychological functioning and present with inconsistency with respect to performance across multiple settings and varied contexts. The assumption of intraindividual heterogeneity emphasizes the need for assessment to identify key resources and critical deficits relevant to improving the child's adaptation. That is, the CDA is designed to identify areas of strength that may prove useful to help remediate or accommodate areas of significant weakness. The CDA articulates six principles of assessment: (a) assessment of multiple areas of functioning, (b) adoption of a developmental perspective, (c) emphasis on variability of skills, (d) emphasis on variability across settings, (e) emphasis on functional adjustment, and (f) evaluation of delays and deviance (Klin et al., 2005).

First, the CDA emphasizes assessment of various areas of functioning, such as social communication, cognition, language, and functional or adaptive adjustment, in a comprehensive diagnostic evaluation of ASD. Second, in light of the frequent co-occurrence of intellectual disability with ASD, the CDA frames interpretation in terms of normative comparisons but also compares functioning across domains with respect to overall developmental level. Comparing functioning, particularly social and communicative functioning, with developmental level is also necessary to evaluate several diagnostic criteria (e.g., peer relationships that fall well below developmental level). Third, the CDA assumes variability in the profile of children with ASD and advises against overgeneralization of "splinter" skill areas; it also calls for an understanding of the limitations of the interpretation of general summary scores. Fourth, the CDA emphasizes the idiosyncratic responsiveness of students with ASD and the importance of the clinician documenting contexts in which individual performance is maximized as well as contexts in which individual performance is impeded. It is important to describe facilitating or impeding circumstances in the assessment report to assist educators with programming decision making. Fifth, the CDA emphasizes the importance of documenting functional adjustment across domains and potentially linking core deficits with functional impairment.

Finally, the CDA emphasizes the assessment of both *delays* in development (i.e., comparing the individual's performance with normative expectations) and *deviance* in development (i.e., documenting behavior not typically observed during any stage of development). The guiding principle of documenting delays and deviance holds practical importance for the selection and use of assessments. For example, cognitive delays should be identified with the use of a standardized and appropriately normed measure of intelligence. Deviant behavior observed with autism, such as unusual sensory experiences, echolalic speech, or hand flapping, exists at a low base rate in the general population such that measures are not typically normed for such behaviors. Therefore, "autism specific" instrumentation that is standardized but not normed with the general population should be used to document deviant behavior.

Guiding Principles and Standards of Evidence-Based Assessment

The CDA should help the practitioner organize and interpret assessment data from an interdisciplinary perspective. Specific selection and use of assessment measures in the CDA should be informed by principles of EBA. The philosophical stance of using scientific evidence to guide practice has affected various professions, such as the evidence-based practice movement in special education, the evidence-based medicine movement, and empirically supported therapies or evidence-based practice movement in psychology. In the field of psychology, various study groups have articulated similar goals to inform the use and interpretation of psychological assessment. As a result, the term *evidence-based assessment* was introduced by Mash and Hunsley (2005) and adopted and operationalized by others.

General Tenets of Evidence-Based Assessment

The basic tenet of EBA is that psychologists should use assessment measures that are supported by a sound empirical knowledge base. Of course, the overall goal of EBA is easier to articulate than to operationalize or realize. For example, the varied purposes of psychological assessment, such as screening, diagnosis, treatment planning, and treatment monitoring, offer a challenge for EBA (e.g., Mash & Hunsley, 2005). Of course, no measure is suited to all assessment purposes. In addition to the varied purposes of assessment, the seemingly straightforward goal of defining standards to determine whether an assessment procedure constitutes an EBA is similarly challenging. Varied aspects of a measure's technical adequacy, for example, should be considered when judging its standing as evidence based. No absolute criteria exist when judging characteristics such as test development, norming, various types of reliability evidence, and validity evidence. For example, an assessment measure is neither valid nor invalid; rather, a measure may be supported as valid for specific uses, for instance, as a general population screener for the presence of ASD for children between the ages of 18 and 24 months. Measures described in this chapter are considered EBAs. Chapter 2 describes the important psychometric characteristics to consider when evaluating the usefulness of a test or screening instrument.

Additional Considerations for Assessment

In addition to the guiding principles informing assessment from the CDA and the EBA model, other guidelines are important when conducting assessments with individuals either diagnosed with an ASD or suspected of having an ASD. The comprehensive component of the CDA requires involvement of multiple disciplines, which aligns well with school-based assessment practice. Assessment practice should also involve input from various stakeholders, particularly parents, caregivers, and teachers. Given the social, communicative, sensory, and behavioral symptoms that characterize

ASD, specific assessment techniques and strategies are recommended to maximize assessment.

Interdisciplinary Approach

Because of the complexity of symptoms and potential for pervasive delays across various domains of functioning, interdisciplinary evaluations are recommended for students with ASD. Involvement of multiple disciplines, such as psychology and communication sciences, is desirable to document cognitive, developmental, language, communicative, and behavioral functioning in individuals. For school-based practice, interdisciplinary teams typically involved in evaluation should be available for collaboration and consultation throughout the assessment process. Interdisciplinary collaboration is important for comparing clinical observations, findings, and impressions prior to sharing evaluation findings with caregivers (Klin et al., 2005).

Involvement of Parents, Caregivers, and Teachers

As important members of the interdisciplinary team, parents and teachers should be closely involved in the evaluation for various reasons. First, parental participation is necessary to collect developmental information that may guide differential diagnosis (e.g., onset of symptoms). Involvement of parents and teachers is also important to "demystify" the evaluation process by allowing discussion of observations during procedures and offering justification for tests and methods used in the evaluation (Klin et al., 2005). Parent and teacher involvement also develops relational and conceptual groundwork for the presentation of findings, team-based decision making, and eligibility determination. Discussion of functioning, diagnosis, and special education classification, if appropriate, will occur with parents and teachers understanding the rationale for diagnostic conclusions and recommendations for intervention. Chapter 10 focuses on how school professionals can support families of children with ASD.

General Recommendations to Maximize Assessment

The complex presentation of the child with confirmed or suspected ASD often yields challenges during formal and informal assessment procedures. Definitive recommendations about maximizing performance for all children with ASD are inappropriate because of the heterogeneity that exists in this group; however, several general principles apply. Reinforcement strategies that may work well with a larger population of children may not work as well for children with ASD. For example, children with ASD may be less motivated by social reinforcement (e.g., saying, "Great work!") to attend to and perform tasks; therefore, tangible reinforcement, such as access to a preferred toy or activity, may work well. Because of difficulties with attention and sensory processing, children with ASD will require a setting that is free from distractions, such as a testing room that is quiet and perhaps free from windows, extra furniture, or artwork. Evaluators must also be aware of the level of verbal and social response required for testing tasks and should consider interspersing social and nonsocial or verbal and nonverbal tasks throughout the evaluation.

ASSESSMENT METHODS AND PROCEDURES BASED ON THE COMPREHENSIVE DEVELOPMENTAL APPROACH AND EVIDENCE-BASED ASSESSMENT FRAMEWORK

Until relatively recently, autism and related disorders were diagnosed primarily through subjective clinical opinion without the use of objective measures (Ozonoff, Goodlin-Jones, & Solomon, 2005). These circumstances have changed as replicable and statistically sound measures have become available to large numbers of professionals. The CDA and EBA framework work well with school-based assessment practice because of practitioners' access to children in their natural environment and the ability to develop evaluation plans targeting individual student strengths and weaknesses. Ozonoff et al. (2005) noted that a developmental approach must be maintained during psychological assessment because autism characteristics can manifest differently across the age span. The school environment provides an ideal situation for observing developmental appropriateness and peer interactions with structured, unstructured, and play opportunities. The school psychologist also has ideal access to observing the interplay between the child and their educational environment.

As articulated in the CDA, ASD assessment should incorporate multiple measures and an interdisciplinary approach that includes family involvement. No single test indicates whether a child meets diagnostic criteria; school psychologists must use various tools and sources of information to render sound diagnostic decisions. Further, a multidisciplinary approach is natural for school psychologists, with related service personnel being incorporated into the evaluation plan and integrating information provided from families about a child's early development and current functioning, strengths, and concerns. In the next section, we review several measures targeting suspected autism behaviors, which can elicit patterns and expressions that are different from those expected in typically developing children. Additional domains and measures for an ASD assessment are also introduced and reviewed, including cognitive, adaptive, language, motor, and academic measures.

Autism-Specific Measures

Autism Diagnostic Observation Schedule

The Autism Diagnostic Observation Schedule (ADOS; Lord, Rutter, DiLavore, & Risi, 2001) is consistently identified as the gold standard for ASD diagnostic assessment. The ADOS is a standardized, semistructured measure of communication, social interaction, and play designed for use with individuals from toddler to adult over a 30- to 45-minute testing session. Toddlers must have a nonverbal developmental age of at least 12 months. On the basis of the child's responses to "social presses" from the examiner (Le Couteur, Haden, Hammal, & McConachie, 2008), observations are made regarding social behavior, restricted and repetitive behavior, and nonverbal and verbal communication. Examiners use observations to derive scores that are summed to yield an algorithm score that renders a decision regarding whether an individual meets a cutoff score for a diagnosis of autism or ASD. The ADOS demonstrates excellent interrater reliability, internal consistency, and test–retest reliability, as well as excellent diagnostic validity for autism and other disorders.

Recently, revised diagnostic algorithms were developed for toddlers, children using five or more single words, and for children under age 5 using phrase speech (Gotham, Risi, Pickles, & Lord, 2007; Luyster et al., 2009). To administer the ADOS, Lord et al. (2001) noted that examiners should be experienced clinicians and obtain extensive training, either in-person or through an equivalent DVD training package. When administering the ADOS initially, school psychologists should involve another professional to observe the test administration, take notes, and share input into the scoring decision making. In addition, and most important, school psychologists should be knowledgeable about ASD. The ADOS and its revision, the ADOS–2 (Lord et al., 2012), which includes updated protocols, revised algorithms, and a toddler module, are recommended as part of the assessment process.

Autism Diagnostic Interview—Revised

The Autism Diagnostic Interview—Revised (ADI–R; Rutter, Le Couteur, & Lord, 2003) is a standardized interview conducted with parents or caregivers to assist in the diagnosis of ASD. Like the ADOS, the ADI–R is regarded as a gold standard diagnostic measure for ASD. The ADI–R focuses on the three core symptom areas of autism: social communication, reciprocal social interactions, and restricted, repetitive, and stereotyped behavior and interests. The interview is designed for parents or caregivers of children and adults with a mental age of 2 and above (Rutter, Le Couteur, & Lord, 2003). On the basis of information obtained from the respondent, items are scored and transformed into an algorithm that yields a diagnostic decision about the presence of autism. Respondents must possess good knowledge of the individual's functioning between ages 4 and 5 and be able to provide examples of behaviors and interactions with others.

Administration and scoring typically takes 1½ to 2½ hours. For school psychologists to administer the ADI–R for clinical purposes, extensive training is required, either face-to-face or through training materials from the publishers. The ADI–R demonstrates strong psychometric properties (e.g., Rutter, Le Couteur, & Lord, 2003). Although the ADI–R provides the most reliable parent interview information, training all school psychologists to administer it presents a challenge. School districts should consider using the ADOS and ADI–R in the context of an autism assessment to allow for a well-trained and experienced team to conduct diagnostic evaluations.

Social Communication Questionnaire

The Social Communication Questionnaire (SCQ; Rutter, Bailey, & Lord, 2003) is a parent-report questionnaire designed for individuals ages 4 and above with a mental age over 2 years. Although developed for screening, the SCQ is based on the ADI–R and shares content, yielding fairly good correspondence with the parent measure (e.g., Ozonoff et al., 2005). Oosterling et al. (2010), however, found that the SCQ produced a high number of false positives for preschoolers, and they recommended that the ADOS be used for assessing very young children suspected of ASD. Also, the format of the SCQ does not allow for details that can be provided in a semistructured interview. Because school psychologists must take a developmental and family-based approach in assessing ASD, a comprehensive parent interview should be common practice; the SCQ could be used in this context to identify critical areas for follow-up inquiry and evaluation.

Autism Rating Scales

Rating scales and questionnaires are a common part of a school psychologist's assessment toolbox across all disabilities; however, particular caution is warranted in the area of ASD assessment. When used in conjunction with other gold standard measures, rating scales can provide useful information from multiple sources, as outlined in the CDA.

One such measure is the Childhood Autism Rating Scale 2 (CARS2)— Standard Version (CARS2–ST) and High-Functioning Version (CARS2–HF; Schopler, Reichler, & Renner, 2010). A parent questionnaire, the CARS2–QPC, provides data to be used by a professional (e.g., school psychologist) in conjunction with assessment, interview, and direct observations for scoring the CARS2. The CARS2–ST was designed for children below 6 years of age and those possessing cognitive or language difficulties. The CARS2–ST consists of 15 areas derived from the original scale. The CARS2–HF consists of similar domains and can be used for assessing verbally fluent children 6 years of age and older with average or above intellectual ability. Wilkinson (2010) indicated that items are reflective of current research on characteristics of high-functioning individuals with ASD. The CARS2–HF modified six areas; for example, "imitation" in the standard form was changed to "social–emotional understanding." For the CARS2–HF, a clinical sample included groups of individuals with an IQ of 80 or above with other diagnoses. The CARS2 has demonstrated high internal consistency and good interrater reliability. Wilkinson (2010) also noted that the CARS2 should be considered one tool in the multidisciplinary evaluation and that practitioners must have a good understanding of the scoring criteria.

The Autism Spectrum Rating Scales (ASRS; Goldstein & Naglieri, 2009) is separated from other autism rating scales in terms of sampling procedures. The ASRS is a norm-referenced measure designed to assist in identification of children and adolescents suspected of having an ASD. The ASRS used a normative sample (n = 3,800) and a clinical sample (n= 1,250) with a variety of disabilities, including ASD. The ASRS features validity scales, similar to traditional behavior rating scales, which include a positive impression, negative impression, and inconsistency index. The ASRS is designed for children and adolescents ages 2 to 18, with a parent and teacher form. ASRS scoring is similar to that of familiar behavior rating scales for school psychologists, with T scores of 70 or higher indicating high levels of ASD behavioral concerns (Simek & Wahlberg, 2011).

The Social Responsiveness Scale (SRS; Constantino & Gruber, 2005) is a brief quantitative measure of ASD symptoms in 4- to 18-year-old children and youth, which is designed to be completed by an adult (teacher and/or parent) who is familiar with the child. The SRS measures ASD symptoms in the domains of social awareness, social information processing, reciprocal social communication, social anxiety or avoidance, and stereotypic behavior or restricted interests. The SRS is an efficient tool for capturing the more subtle aspects of social impairment associated with ASD (e.g., pervasive developmental disorder not otherwise specified) and reflects the level of severity. The SRS may be used as an effective screening tool in clinical or educational settings; however, results derived from rating scales should not replace clinical assessment and must be integrated with information from different sources. A revised version of the SRS, the SRS–2 (Constantino, & Gruber, 2012), was recently published. The SRS–2 includes two *DSM–5*–compatible subscales that allow comparison of symptoms with the new *DSM–5* ASD diagnostic criteria. Chapter 2 illustrates the use of the SCQ, ASRS, and SRS–2 in screening and identification of students at risk of ASD.

Some other common rating scales for ASD assessment include the Asperger Syndrome Diagnostic Scale (ASDS; Myles, Bock, & Simpson, 2001) and the Gilliam Autism Rating Scale—Second Edition (GARS–2; Gilliam, 2006). These measures provide summary scores, with higher scores indicating elevated symptomatology. The ASDS may be useful in developing recommendations or in a school-based reevaluation where eligibility has been established and is not in question (Hammond & Murphy, 2012); however, the ASDS is not recommended for diagnostic assessment.

The GARS–2 is designed as a screening tool and diagnostic aid for individuals with autism between the ages of 3 and 22. Pandolfi, Magyar, and Dill (2010) noted questionable psychometric properties for the GARS–2 and thus conducted a factor analysis on the standardization sample. They found the GARS–2 to have limited clinical utility, and further found that the Autism Index should be interpreted with caution. For school psychologists, the GARS–2 might hold limited potential utility for reevaluation or for helping plan and determine IEP goals but not for initial diagnosis or eligibility. The GARS–2 provides a brief parent checklist, investigating early symptoms in the areas of language, social communication, and play. The parent component could be used in a school setting as part of a parent interview to establish the early history required for eligibility; however, the GARS–2 checklist does not substitute for the thorough interview required for initial diagnosis or eligibility decision making.

Additional Domains of Functioning

The CDA emphasizes that a variety of constructs and areas of functioning are essential in ASD assessment, including social communication and cognitive and adaptive adjustment. In the CDA, assessment of delays in development, such as cognitive delays documented by a standardized instrument, is necessary to complement evaluation of unusual development, such as observation or clinical history obtained through autism-specific measures. Additional domains of assessment, including cognitive functioning, adaptive behavior, language and social communication, academic functioning, are discussed in Chapters 4 and 5.

Cognitive Functioning

Wechsler Scales

The Wechsler Intelligence Scale for Children—Fourth Edition (WISC–IV; Wechsler, 2003) and its predecessors have been used in the context of autism assessment for many years, particularly for higher functioning individuals.

The WISC–IV is considered an appropriate measure of cognitive abilities because it possesses excellent psychometric properties and features a knowledge base for individuals with ASD. In the manual, for example, high-functioning individuals with autism ($n = 19$) were found to demonstrate a difference between two WISC–IV indices, with perceptual reasoning abilities better developed than verbal comprehension abilities. A larger discrepancy between nonverbal and verbal abilities (i.e., 18 standard score points) was found for a sample of children on the Wechsler Preschool and Primary Scale of Intelligence—Third Edition (WPPSI–III; Wechsler, 2002). The use of a single score for intellectual ability is inappropriate for children with ASD, and intellectual test performance should not be used for purposes of differential diagnosis.

Kaufman Assessment Battery for Children—Second Edition

Another cognitive measure, the Kaufman Assessment Battery for Children—Second Edition (KABC–2; Kaufman & Kaufman, 2004), espouses a different approach to measuring cognitive functioning by adopting Cattell-Horn's (Carroll, 1993) and Luria's (1970) theories of intelligence. The KABC–2 yields a Fluid Crystallized Index (FCI), which includes a measure of acquired knowledge, whereas the Mental Processing Index (MPI), based on Luria's theory, excludes a measure of acquired knowledge (Kaufman, Lichtenberger, Fletcher-Janzen, & Kaufman, 2005). The measure also yields a Nonverbal Intelligence Index (NVI) score.

In a sample of children with autism, not ASD ($n = 38$), the overall scores on the FCI ($M = 66.9$), MPI ($M = 68.1$), and NVI ($M = 68.6$) were fairly similar (Kaufman & Kaufman, 2004). Children with autism also demonstrated a relative strength on the Learning scale of the KABC–2, which consists of two subtests, Atlantis and Rebus, in which children are taught and asked to recall names associated with pictures and symbols. Both subtests involve a form of teaching through immediate feedback following incorrect responses (Atlantis) and continuous repeating of symbols and their associated words (Rebus). For application in the classroom, both of these subtests can also be administered later in the testing as part of a delayed recall. The Delayed Recall scale produced the highest standard scores in children with autism. Kaufman et al. (2005) argued for the importance of this result, suggesting that the KABC–2 may identify a strength for students with ASD that may go undetected by other scales.

Stanford–Binet

The Stanford–Binet Intelligence Scales, Fifth Edition (SB5; Roid, 2003) should also be considered as a standardized cognitive measure for ASD assessment. In particular, Roid and Tippen (2008) indicated that the expanded nonverbal version of the SB5 would be useful in assessing individuals with autism. The SB5 possesses excellent reliability (Roid, 2003), and the large standardization sample included a small sample of individuals with autism. The SB5 uses a routing procedure that consists of a verbal and nonverbal subtest to determine appropriate testing start points. Roid and Tippen noted that the routing procedure is intended to provide a more precise assessment of cognitive ability in a shorter period, which may benefit students with ASD. On the negative side, however, the SB5 features "testlets," which incorporate frequent changes in task demands, potentially hindering performance for students with ASD who have difficulties with tolerating such changes.

Nonverbal Cognitive Measures

Cognitive measures that are less reliant on language, such as the Leiter–R (Roid & Miller, 1997) and the Universal Nonverbal Intelligence Test (UNIT; Bracken & McCallum, 1998), should be considered when individuals with ASD present with significant language deficits. Language deficits are not equivalent to cognitive delays; therefore, a measure relying heavily on language may yield an inaccurate picture of cognitive functioning. Thus, a measure such as the Leiter (1979) has often been used in research and clinical settings for children with ASD. Tsatsanis et al. (2003) investigated the concurrent validity of the Leiter–R with the Leiter and found that in a sample of children with autism ($n = 26$), scores were comparable. Because of concerns for children with autism understanding the required gestures for directions, Tsatsanis et al. modified standardized testing procedures and used simple verbal directives.

The UNIT does not feature an autism sample, yet the test was designed for individuals with communication impairments, including developmental disabilities (Bracken & McCallum, 1998). There is limited research on the use of the UNIT with children with ASD. It is of note that the UNIT uses all nonverbal gestures to supplement verbal directives. Thus, instead of the receptive language needed for traditional cognitive tests, inferring information from gestures is required, which is often an inherent challenge for individuals with ASD. Overall, school psychologists must consider the benefits and potential limitations of a nonverbal cognitive measure in ASD assessment.

Adaptive Behavior

Regardless of cognitive functioning, practitioners should consistently assess adaptive behavior skills in children suspected of ASD. The Vineland Adaptive Behavior Scales, Second Edition (Vineland–II; Sparrow, Cicchetti, & Balla, 2005) is an individually administered measure of adaptive behavior for age birth through 90. There are three versions, including two survey forms for parents (interview and rating scale), an expanded interview, and a teacher rating form. Sparrow et al. (2005) noted that the Vineland–II now covers a broad range of adaptive domains corresponding with the *DSM–IV–TR*. Similar to other measures, the Vineland–II provides an overall Adaptive Behavior Composite (ABC) standard score and three domain scores: Communication, Daily Living, and Socialization. Motor skills are assessed for children ages 3 to 6. The Vineland–II was normed on a large sample that included a clinical sample of children with autism. For the verbal group ($n = 46$), the ABC mean was 65.7, whereas for the nonverbal group ($n = 31$) the mean was 50.7. Sparrow et al. reported similar profiles for both groups, with socialization being the most relatively impaired area. The parent interview format allows for examples and a detailed understanding of the child's functional limitations and strengths. The Vineland–II also allows school psychologists to work with the family, obtain valid information on adaptive functioning through an open-ended format, and identify adaptive strengths and weaknesses that may facilitate identifying and tracking IEP goals.

School psychologists should also consider the Adaptive Behavior Assessment System—Second Edition (ABAS–2; Harrison & Oakland, 2003), a normed measure of adaptive behavior for birth to age 89. The ABAS–2 consists of a parent and teacher rating scale for 0 to 5 years or 2 to 5 years and for 5 to 21 years on both. The ABAS–2 is based on the *DSM–IV–TR* and special education classification systems (Harrison & Oakland, 2003) and yields a General Adaptive Composite score (GAC) and three domain scores: Conceptual, Social, and Practical. The ABAS–2 included an autism sample for each form. For a group of young children with autism (3–5 years; $n = 62$), the mean GAC standard score was 68.

Language Functioning

Another essential component of ASD assessment is working with a speech–language pathologist (SLP) in assessing receptive, expressive, and pragmatic language. Standardized measures, such as the Peabody Picture Vocabulary Test—IV (Dunn & Dunn, 2007) and the co-normed Expressive Vocabulary Test—2 (Williams, 2007), provide a basic understanding of the child's receptive and expressive language. The Clinical Evaluation of Language Fundamentals—Fourth Edition (Semel, Wiig, & Secord, 2003), typically administered by SLPs, provides a more comprehensive evaluation of language and can assist with determining eligibility for language services and with program planning. In addition, for higher functioning individuals, pragmatic language assessment is essential when considering language delays. The Test of Pragmatic Language (2nd ed.; Phelps-Terasaki & Phelps-Gunn, 2007) is a norm-referenced measure that can assist with understanding nuances in pragmatic language that might not be evident in a traditional language assessment. Chapter 5 of this volume describes the verbal and nonverbal pragmatic aspects of language and assessment of social communication skills.

SLPs and school psychologists will each collect data relevant to language and communicative functioning in the context of the CDA. For example, the ADOS activities and structure may supplement a standardized language evaluation or protocol. Because of the nature of formal language assessment (e.g., testing occurring in a well-controlled situation), pragmatic impairments may not be detected until the social components of communication are emphasized, such as during the ADOS. Thus, school psychologists should share results with SLPs and vice versa; collaboration may also extend to observation and administration of the ADOS to assist in determining eligibility or diagnosis (Hammond & Murphy, 2012). Using the ADOS–2 to assess the child's use of communicative functions is discussed in Chapter 5.

Motor Functioning

Motor functioning may also be delayed for individuals with ASD and should constitute an area of assessment in the CDA. Motor deficits have a significant impact on writing skills in the academic setting. The Beery–Buktenica Developmental Test of Visual–Motor Integration (6th ed.; Beery VMI–6; Beery & Beery, 2010) is a brief assessment of visual–motor and graphomotor abilities for individuals ages 2 to 18. School psychologists may administer this test, or the Beery VMI–6 may constitute a component of a school-based occupational therapist's evaluation. Through the use of geometric forms, children who dislike graphomotor tasks, such as handwriting, may be more likely to engage in the Beery VMI–6 copying tasks than in writing demands in academic contexts.

Academic Functioning

In the school and clinical settings, school psychologists should gather information related to academic skills for program planning and as a component of eligibility decision making (i.e., educational impact). For an ASD assessment, academic functioning can be measured using standardized achievement tests, curriculum-based measurement (CBM), and behavior observations. Also, the increase in universal screening and frequent progress monitoring provides school psychologists with a variety of sources to understand patterns of reading, writing, and math development. Ozonoff et al. (2005) noted that children with ASD might demonstrate strengths in rote academic skills, such as math calculation, and weaknesses in applied academic skills, such as reading comprehension. School psychologists should use their understanding of the academic curriculum and the child's developmental level to determine which norm-referenced achievement test is the most appropriate. Currently, the Kaufman Test of Educational Achievement—Second Edition (Kaufman & Kaufman, 2005), the Wechsler Individual Achievement Test—Third Edition (Wechsler, 2009), and the Woodcock–Johnson III Normative Update Tests of Achievement (Woodcock, McGrew, Schrank, & Mather, 2007) have been revised and meet EBA standards for the assessment of academic functioning. In addition, school psychologists can use CBM data, either from the teacher-administered, school-administered, or individually designed measures, to assist in educational planning. Measures that are derived from the curriculum will allow for ongoing tracking of academic progress on interventions or specially designed instruction in the case of an IEP.

CONCLUSION

Given the recent prevalence estimates for ASD, school psychologists will inevitably assess students with suspected or confirmed ASD. We recommend that such an assessment be based on two guiding models: the CDA and EBA guidelines. Specifically, we advocate school-based psychological assessment practice that (a) is comprehensive in coverage, (b) is grounded in interpretation based on the student's developmental level, (c) involves multiple disciplines, (d) includes involvement and input from the family, (e) incorporates multiple sources of input, and (f) uses measures that are well-established psychometrically. School-based assessment aligns well with the principles outlined in the chapter, and we identified a set of measures that provide sound evidence in support of their use with students with suspected or confirmed ASD. The school psychologist is well-positioned to provide critically important assessment data for the purposes of initial diagnosis and eligibility decision making, as well as generating and monitoring progress on various educational goals.

REFERENCES

Amaral, D. G., Schumann, C. M., & Nordahl, C. W. (2008). Neuroanatomy of autism. *Trends in Neurosciences, 31*, 137–145. doi:10.1016/j.tins.2007.12.005

American Psychiatric Association. (2000). *Diagnostic and statistical manual of mental disorders* (4th ed., text rev.). Washington, DC: Author.

American Psychiatric Association. (2013). *Diagnostic and statistical manual of mental disorders* (5th ed.). Washington, DC: Author.

Amiet, C., Gourfinkel-An, I., Bouzamondo, A., Tordjman, S., Baulac, M., Lechat, P., & Cohen, D. (2008). Epilepsy in autism is associated with intellectual disability and gender: Evidence from a meta-analysis. *Biological Psychiatry, 64,* 577–582. doi:10.1016/j.biopsych.2008.04.030

Beery, K. E., & Beery, N. A. (2010). *The Beery–Buktenica Developmental Test of Visual–Motor Integration (6th ed.): Administration, scoring, and teaching manual.* Minneapolis, MN: Pearson.

Betancur, C. (2011). Etiological heterogeneity in autism spectrum disorders: More than 100 genetic and genomic disorders and still counting. *Brain Research, 1380,* 42–77. doi:10.1016/j.brainres.2010.11.078

Bracken, B. A., & McCallum, R. S. (1998). *Universal Nonverbal Intelligence Test.* Rolling Meadows, IL: Riverside.

Carroll, J. B. (1993). *Human cognitive abilities: A survey of factor analytic studies.* New York, NY: Cambridge University Press.

Centers for Disease Control and Prevention. (2012). *Prevalence of autism spectrum disorders—Autism and Developmental Disabilities Monitoring Network, United States, 2008.* Retrieved from http://www.cdc.gov/mmwr/preview/mmwrhtml/ss6103a1.htm

Chakrabarti, S., & Fombonne, E. (2005). Pervasive developmental disorders in preschool children: Confirmation of high prevalence. *The American Journal of Psychiatry, 162,* 1133–1141. doi:10.1176/appi.ajp.162.6.1133

Constantino, J. N., & Gruber, C. P. (2005). *Social Responsiveness Scale.* Los Angeles, CA: Western Psychological Services.

Constantino, J. N., & Gruber, C. P. (2012). *Social Responsiveness Scale, Second Edition.* Torrance, CA: Western Psychological Services.

Courchesne, E., & Pierce, K. (2005). Why the frontal cortex in autism might be talking only to itself: Local over-connectivity but long-distance disconnection. *Current Opinion in Neurobiology, 15,* 225–230. doi:10.1016/j.conb.2005.03.001

Dunn, L. M., & Dunn, D. M. (2007). *Peabody Picture Vocabulary Test* (4th ed.). Minneapolis, MN: Pearson.

Fountain, C., King, M. D., & Bearman, P. S. (2011). Age of diagnosis for autism: Individual and community factors across 10 birth cohorts. *Journal of Epidemiology and Community Health, 65,* 503–510. doi:10.1136/jech.2009.104588

Gilliam, J. E. (2006). *Gilliam Autism Rating Scale—Second Edition.* Austin, TX: PRO-ED.

Goldstein, S., & Naglieri, J. A. (2009). *Autism Spectrum Rating Scales.* North Tonawanda, NY: Multi-Health Systems.

Gotham, K., Risi, S., Pickles, A., & Lord, C. (2007). The Autism Diagnostic Observation Schedule: Revised algorithms for improved diagnostic validity. *Journal of Autism and Developmental Disorders, 37,* 613–627. doi:10.1007/s10803-006-0280-1

Hammond, R. K., & Murphy, M. A. (2012, February). *Comorbidity and differential diagnosis in ASD: An investigation of assessment practices.* Paper presented to the Jefferson County Public School Psychologists, Louisville, KY.

Harrison, P. L., & Oakland, T. (2003). *Adaptive Behavior Assessment System* (2nd ed.). San Antonio, TX: Psychological Corporation.

Individuals With Disabilities Education Improvement Act of 2004, 20 U.S.C. § 1400 (2004).

Kaufman, A. S., & Kaufman, N. L. (2004). *Kaufman Assessment Battery for Children, Second Edition, manual (KABC–II)*. Circle Pines, MN: American Guidance Service.

Kaufman, A. S., & Kaufman, N. L. (2005). *Kaufman Test of Educational Achievement, Second Edition, manual (KTEA–II)*. Circle Pines, MN: American Guidance Service.

Kaufman, A. S., Lichtenberger, E. O., Fletcher-Janzen, E., & Kaufman, N. L. (2005). *Essentials of KABC–II assessment*. Hoboken, NJ: Wiley.

Klin, A., Saulnier, C., Tsatsanis, K., & Volkmar, F. R. (2005). Clinical evaluation in autism spectrum disorders: Psychological assessment within a transdisciplinary framework. In F. R. Volkmar, R. Paul, A. Klin, & D. Cohen (Eds.), *Handbook of autism and pervasive developmental disorders* (3rd ed., pp. 772–798). Hoboken, NJ: Wiley.

Le Couteur, A., Haden, G., Hammal, D., & McConachie, H. (2008). Diagnosing autism spectrum disorders in pre-school children using two standardised assessment instruments: The ADI-R and the ADOS. *Journal of Autism and Developmental Disorders, 38*, 362–372. doi:10.1007/s10803-007-0403-3

Leiter, R. G. (1979). *Instruction manual for the Leiter International Performance Scale*. Wood Dale, IL: Stoelting.

Lord, C., Rutter, M., DiLavore, P. C., & Risi, S. (2001). *Autism Diagnostic Observation Schedule Manual*. Los Angeles, CA: Western Psychological Services.

Lord, C., Rutter, M., DiLavore, P. C., Risi, S., Gotham, K., & Bishop, S. L. (2012). *Autism Diagnostic Observation Schedule, Second Edition*. Torrance, CA: Western Psychological Services.

Lord, C., Rutter, M., & Le Couteur, A. (1994). Autism Diagnostic Interview—Revised: A revised version of a diagnostic interview for caregivers of individuals with possible pervasive developmental disorders. *Journal of Autism and Developmental Disorders, 24*, 659–685. doi:10.1007/BF02172145

Luria, A. R. (1970, March). The functional organization of the brain. *Scientific American, 222*(3), 66–78.

Luyster, R., Gotham, K., Guthrie, W., Coffing, M., Petrak, R., Pierce, K., . . . Lord, C. (2009). The Autism Diagnostic Observation Schedule—Toddler Module: A new module of a standardized diagnostic measure for autism spectrum disorders. *Journal of Autism and Developmental Disorders, 39*, 1305–1320. doi:10.1007/s10803-009-0746-z

Mash, E. J., & Hunsley, J. (2005). Evidence-based assessment of child and adolescent disorders: Issues and challenges. *Journal of Clinical Child and Adolescent Psychology, 34*, 362–379. doi:10.1207/s15374424jccp3403_1

Mazefsky, C. A., Conner, C. M., & Oswald, D. P. (2010). Association between depression and anxiety in high-functioning children with autism spectrum disorders and maternal mood symptoms. *Autism Research, 3,* 120–127. doi:10.1002/aur.133

Memari, A., Ziaee, V., Mirfazeli, F., & Kordi, R. (2012). Investigation of autism comorbidities and associations in a school-based community sample. *Journal of Child and Adolescent Psychiatric Nursing, 25,* 84–90. doi:10.1111/j.1744-6171.2012.00325.x

Miller, L., & Reynolds, J. (2009). Autism and vaccination—The current evidence. *Journal for Specialists in Pediatric Nursing, 14,* 166–172. doi:10.1111/j.1744-6155.2009.00194.x

Myles, B. S., Bock, S. J., & Simpson, R. L. (2001). *Asperger Syndrome Diagnostic Scale (ASDS).* Austin, TX: PRO-ED.

Oosterling, I., Rommelse, N., De Jonge, M., Van der Gaag, R., Swinkels, S., Roos, S., . . . Buitelaar, J. (2010). How useful is the Social Communication Questionnaire in toddlers at risk of autism spectrum disorder? *Journal of Child Psychology and Psychiatry, 51,* 1260–1268. doi:10.1111/j.1469-7610.2010.02246.x

Ozonoff, S., Goodlin-Jones, B. L., & Solomon, M. (2005). Evidence-based assessment of autism spectrum disorders in children and adolescents. *Journal of Clinical Child and Adolescent Psychology, 34,* 523–540. doi:10.1207/s15374424jccp3403_8

Pandolfi, V., Magyar, C. I., & Dill, C. A. (2010). Constructs assessed by the GARS–2: Factor analysis of data from the standardization sample. *Journal of Autism and Developmental Disorders, 40,* 1118–1130. doi:10.1007/s10803-010-0967-1

Phelps-Terasaki, D., & Phelps-Gunn, T. (2007). *Test of Pragmatic Language—Second Edition (TOPL–2).* Torrance, CA: Western Psychological Services.

Roid, G. H. (2003). *Stanford–Binet Intelligence Scales—Fifth Edition, examiner's manual.* Rolling Meadows, IL: Riverside.

Roid, G. H., & Miller, L. J. (1997). *Leiter International Performance Scale—Revised.* Wood Dale, IL: Stoelting.

Roid, G. H., & Tippin, S. M. (2008). Assessment of intellectual strengths and weaknesses with the Stanford–Binet Intelligence Scales—Fifth Edition (SBV). In J. A. Naglieri & S. Goldstein (Eds.), *Practitioner's guide to assessing intelligence and achievement* (pp. 127–152). Hoboken, NJ: Wiley.

Rutter, M., Bailey, A., & Lord, C. (2003). *Social Communication Questionnaire.* Los Angeles, CA: Western Psychological Services.

Rutter, M., Le Couteur, A., & Lord, C. (2003). *Autism Diagnostic Interview—Revised.* Los Angeles, CA: Western Psychological Services.

Schopler, E., Reichler, R. J., & Renner, B. R. (2010). *Childhood Autism Rating Scale, Second Edition (CARS2).* Los Angeles, CA: Western Psychological Services.

Semel, E., Wiig, E. H., & Secord, W. A. (2003). *Clinical evaluation of language fundamentals—Fourth edition (CELF-4).* San Antonio, TX: Pearson.

Simek, A. N., & Wahlberg, A. C. (2011). Test review: Autism Spectrum Rating Scales. *Journal of Psychoeducational Assessment, 29,* 191–195. doi:10.1177/0734282910375408

Sparrow, S. S., Cicchetti, D. V., & Balla, D. A. (2005). *Vineland Adaptive Behavior Scales* (2nd ed.). Minneapolis, MN: Pearson.

Tsatsanis, K. D., Dartnall, N., Cicchetti, D., Sparrow, S. S., Klin, A., & Volkmar, F. R. (2003). Concurrent validity and classification accuracy of the Leiter and Leiter–R in low-functioning children with autism. *Journal of Autism and Developmental Disorders, 33,* 23–30. doi:10.1023/A:1022274219808

Wechsler, D. (2002). *WPPSI–III technical and interpretive manual.* San Antonio, TX: Psychological Corporation.

Wechsler, D. (2003). *Technical and interpretive manual for the Wechsler Intelligence Scale for Children* (4th ed.). San Antonio, TX: Psychological Corporation.

Wechsler, D. (2009). *The Wechsler Individual Achievement Test—Third Edition (WIAT–III).* San Antonio, TX: Pearson.

Wilkinson, L. (2010). *Best practice autism review: The Childhood Autism Rating Scale, Second Edition (CARS2).* Retrieved from http://bestpracticeautism.blogspot.com/2010/11/best-practice-autism-review-childhood.html

Williams, K. T. (2007). *Expressive Vocabulary Test* (2nd ed.). San Antonio, TX: Pearson.

Woodcock, R. W., McGrew, K. S., Schrank, F. A., & Mather, N. (2007). *Woodcock–Johnson III Tests of Achievement Normative Update.* Rolling Meadows, IL: Riverside.

Yeargin-Allsopp, M., Rice, C., Karapurkar, T., Doernberg, N., Boyle, C., & Murphy, C. (2003). Prevalence of autism in a U.S. metropolitan area. *JAMA, 289,* 49–55. doi:10.1001/jama.289.1.49

4

COGNITIVE, NEUROPSYCHOLOGICAL, ACADEMIC, AND ADAPTIVE FUNCTIONING

LINDA C. CATERINO

The evaluation of children suspected of having a diagnosis of autism is a complex and comprehensive undertaking. It involves not only a determination of whether a child meets the recognized diagnostic criteria but also an understanding of the child's cognitive processes, academic achievement, and adaptive behavior, as well as communication and social–emotional skills, so that an effective treatment plan can be developed.

This chapter focuses on the assessment of cognitive, neuropsychological, academic, and adaptive behavior skills. Current evaluation instruments, together with recent research regarding their use with autism spectrum disorder (ASD), are discussed. Chapter 3 describes various cognitive, achievement, and adaptive behavior measures in the context of a comprehensive developmental approach to assessment.

http://dx.doi.org/10.1037/14338-005
Autism Spectrum Disorder in Children and Adolescents: Evidence-Based Assessment and Intervention in Schools, L. A. Wilkinson (Editor)

COGNITIVE ASSESSMENT

Comprehensive assessments of children with suspected autism typically include a measure of the child's cognitive abilities. Allen, Robins, and Decker (2008) found that school psychologists used a cognitive measure in 94% of their evaluations of children who present with possible autism. Information about cognitive abilities can be useful in determining the child's potential and can provide insight into their patterns of intellectual strengths and weaknesses.

At one time it was thought that all children with autism were intellectually disabled (ID), but this is no longer the case (Edelson, 2006). Recent research has indicated that only 55% of children with ASD (Baird et al., 2006) and 70.4% of those specifically diagnosed with autism (Frombonne, 2005) have IQ scores in the ID range. In addition to an IQ score, cognitive assessments can yield information regarding visual perception, language, and attention, as well as working memory, processing speed, and abstract reasoning processes. According to Klin, Saulnier, Tsatsanis, and Volkmar (2005), cognitive functioning is one of the most important factors in determining the level of severity of symptomatology in social and communication domains and in assessing the child's potential for self-sufficiency and other future outcomes.

Measures

The Wechsler Preschool and Primary Scale of Intelligence—Third Edition (WPPSI–III; Wechsler, 2002) is normed on children from 2 years, 6 months to 7 years, 3 months. Administration time is from 45 to 60 minutes. A full scale IQ score is derived, as well as Verbal, Performance, Processing Speed, and General Language composite scores. Although there are 14 possible subtests in the WPPSI–III, only four subtests are used to yield the Full Scale, Verbal, and Performance scale quotients for children up to 3 years, 11 months, whereas seven subtests are used for children older than 4 years of age. Although only 21 children with a diagnosis of autism were included in the standardization sample, the group with autism scored significantly lower than matched controls on all composite and subtest scores, with the exception of Block Design and Object Assembly. In addition, Performance IQ score was higher than Verbal IQ. The conceptual demands of the WPPSI–III, especially some of the subtests (e.g., Matrix Reasoning and Picture Concepts), may be difficult for young children with autism to comprehend, and the use of timed tasks in all of the Wechsler scales may be stressful for children with autism.

The Wechsler Intelligence Scale for Children—Fourth Edition (WISC–IV; Wechsler, 2003) can be administered to children from 6 years, 0 months to 16 years, 11 months. The WISC–IV consists of 10 core subtests and five supplemental subtests. It yields a Full Scale IQ score, as well as scaled scores in Verbal Comprehension, Perceptual Reasoning, Working Memory, and Processing Speed. It usually takes about 80 minutes to administer. There were only 19 children diagnosed with autism in the standardization sample with the mean Full Scale IQ score being 76.4. These children scored significantly lower on all composites and on all required subtests, with the exception of Block Design. The highest subtests were Block Design, Matrix Reasoning, and Picture Concepts, and the lowest subtests were Comprehension, Symbol Search, and Coding (Wechsler, 2003). Although the sample size was quite small, this study suggests that children with autism may perform better on nonverbal tasks than on subtests that measure verbal or processing speed skills.

Early research using previous revisions of the WISC also found that individuals with ASD demonstrated higher nonverbal skills than verbal skills (e.g., Asarnow, Tanguay, Bott, & Freeman, 1987). However, Miller and Ozonoff (2000) found no significant difference between Verbal and Performance IQ scores using the WISC–III (Wechsler, 1991). Mayes and Calhoun (2003), also using the WISC–III, discovered that although preschool children with ASD did show greater strength in nonverbal skills, this pattern did not continue across the life span, and by elementary school age this nonverbal–verbal discrepancy was not evident, especially for children with IQ scores above 80.

It now appears that only about one half to three quarters of individuals with autism have verbal–nonverbal discrepancies (e.g., Gilchrist et al., 2001). This finding could be influenced by differences in diagnostic criteria (e.g., inclusion of children with Asperger's disorder in the autistic sample). It may also be attributed to differences in versions of the WISC; for example, in contrast to Miller and Ozonoff (2000), Lincoln, Hanzel, and Quirmbach (2007), using the WISC–IV, found a significant discrepancy (18.5 points) between the Perceptual Reasoning Index and the Verbal Comprehension Index. Mayes and Calhoun (2008) found that children with high-functioning autism (HFA) scored significantly higher on the General Ability Index than on the Full Scale IQ (113 vs. 101). They earned above-normal scores on the Perceptual Reasoning and Verbal Comprehension Indexes and below-normal scores on the Working Memory and Processing Speed Indexes of the WISC–IV.

In Mayes and Calhoun's (2008) study, the untimed, motor-free visual reasoning subtests of Matrix Reasoning and Picture Concepts, both new to the WISC–IV, were found to be the highest of the nonverbal subtests, and Coding had the lowest mean subtest score. The authors suggested that the use of the WISC–IV may be more advantageous to children with autism who are strong in visual reasoning than to those who may have difficulty with visual–motor skills and problems working under a time constraint. They also found that children with HFA performed significantly lower on the Comprehension subtest than they did on the Similarities and Vocabulary subtests, suggesting a weakness in social reasoning, as well as language comprehension.

Their findings are consistent with other studies of subtest analysis, which have found a pattern of relatively higher scores on Block Design, especially for males (Koyama, Kamio, Inada, & Korita, 2009) and lower scores on Comprehension (e.g., Lincoln et al., 2007), Symbol Search, and Coding (Lichtenberger, 2004). The weak central coherence theory (see Chapter 1, this volume) is suggested as a rationale for the higher performance on the Block Design subtest because individuals with autism may perform better on tasks that require analysis than on global tasks. However, this theory has come under scrutiny in recent years (Burnette et al., 2005).

The Stanford–Binet Intelligence Scales, Fifth Edition (SB5; Roid, 2003) can be used with individuals from 2 to 85+ years of age. The test requires 45 to 75 minutes to administer. The SB5 yields a Full Scale IQ score, a Nonverbal IQ score, and a Verbal IQ score, as well as five factor scales: (a) Fluid Reasoning, (b) Knowledge, (c) Quantitative Reasoning, (d) Visual–Spatial Processing, and (e) Working Memory. The reliability of the test is excellent, with internal consistency coefficients of .95 to .98 across all age ranges. It includes several manipulatives and can be interesting and entertaining even for young children.

Mayes and Calhoun (2003), in a study using the SB5 in a sample of children with ASD who were 3 to 7 years of age, found that nonverbal IQ scores were higher than verbal IQ scores. Carpentieri and Morgan (1994), using the SB4 (Thorndike, Hagen, & Sattler, 1986), found that the verbal scores of children with autism were significantly lower than those of children with ID with the same IQ score. In their study, the Comprehension and Absurdities subtests were the weakest, and the Quantitative Reasoning subtest was the strongest. In another study, children with autism scored lowest on the Absurdities subtest and highest on the Pattern Analysis subtest (Harris, Handelman, & Burton, 1990). The SB5 also offers an Abbreviated Battery IQ, which is useful for screening purposes; nonverbal subtests can be administered alone so that a nonverbal IQ can be calculated for children with communication difficulties.

The Kaufman Assessment Battery for Children—Second Edition (KABC–2; Kaufman & Kaufman, 2004) is designed for children from 3 to 18 years of age. Administration time ranges from 30 to 70 minutes. The KABC–2 yields three different IQ scores: the Mental Processing Index (based on the Cattell–Horn–Carroll model; McGrew, 2005), the Fluid Crystallized Index (based on Luria's processing theory; Luria, 1973), and the Nonverbal Intelligence Index, which does not include any language-related tasks. The KABC–2 includes five scales: Sequential Processing, Simultaneous

Processing, Learning Ability, Planning Ability, and Knowledge. The authors reported that a small sample of 38 children (32 boys and six girls) diagnosed with autism were included in the standardization sample. The children with autism scored significantly lower on all IQ measures (Kaufman & Kaufman, 2004). A relative strength on the Learning Ability scale indicates that these children can learn new information, both language-related and visual, and retain it after an interval of 20 minutes.

The highest subtest scores were on the visual tests of Gestalt Closure, Triangles, and Atlantis, and the lowest subtest scores were on the Riddles, Verbal Knowledge, and Rover subtests, all of which require a high level of executive functioning and deductive reasoning. Although the KABC–2 does not include a specific assessment of the child's ability to understand social situations, the Face Recognition subtest, which measures the child's ability to remember faces, has demonstrated some ability to distinguish between children with autism and typical children (Klin et al., 1999). The KABC–2 can be especially useful for the assessment of children with ASD because it is an engaging test that is less dependent on acquired knowledge, and it includes teaching and demonstration items.

There are other cognitive measures that can be used with children with ASD, such as the Woodcock–Johnson III Tests of Cognitive Abilities (WJ III COG; Woodcock, McGrew, & Mather, 2001), the Differential Ability Scales—II (DAS–II; Elliott, 2007), and the Cognitive Assessment System (CAS; Naglieri & Das, 1997). The first two tests are derived from the Cattell–Horn–Carroll model of intelligence and possess excellent reliability and validity characteristics. The DAS–II can be administered to children from 2½ to almost 18 years of age, and the WJ III COG is designed for individuals from 2 to 90 years of age. The CAS is based on the PASS model of planning, attention, simultaneous, and successive processes. One study using the CAS (Gutwirth, 1996) found that children with ASD scored more poorly on the CAS than typical children and those with other disabilities, and these children showed the most difficulty on successive tasks. Two tests for preschoolers and those functioning in this range include the Bayley Scales of Infant and Toddler Development, Third Edition (Bayley, 2005) and the Mullen Scales of Early Learning (Mullen, 1995). There is research indicating that children with ASD score lower on these measures than do typical children (e.g., Akshoomoff, 2006). Because of page limitations, and/or the lack of research with ASD populations, these tests are not discussed further.

Nonlanguage Tests

Because many children with autism have significant language difficulties, it may be necessary to also use ability tests that do not require verbal expression and, instead, focus on visual perceptual skills. The examiner should be aware, however, that although nonlanguage tests do provide IQ scores, these scores may not be a comprehensive measure of the child's abilities. Nonlanguage tests include the Leiter International Performance Scale—Revised (Leiter–R; Roid & Miller, 1997), Raven's Progressive Matrices (RPM; Raven, Raven, & Court, 2004), the Naglieri Test of Nonverbal Abilities (NNAT; Naglieri, 1997), and the Universal Nonverbal Intelligence Test (UNIT; Bracken & McCallum, 1998). Both the NNAT and the UNIT can be used with children from 5 to almost 18 years of age. Because no studies using the NNAT or the UNIT with an ASD sample were found, these tests are not discussed in this chapter.

The Leiter–R (Roid & Miller, 1997) is designed for individuals from 2 years to 20 years, 11 months of age. It consists of the Visualization and Reasoning battery and the Attention and Memory battery. Composite scores can be obtained for Fluid Reasoning, Fundamental Visualization, Spatial Visualization, Attention, and Memory. There is also a full scale IQ score, as well as four social–emotional rating scales (Examiner, Parent, Self, and Teacher). Administration time is 90 minutes, although a brief screener can be completed in 25 minutes. Although no children with autism were included in the norm group, Tsatsanis et al. (2003) found that children with ASD performed better on the Fundamental Visualization composite than on the Fluid Reasoning composite. The Leiter–R is a colorful and interesting test with little emphasis on timed tasks, so it may be useful in autism assessment. The Leiter–3 (Roid, Miller, Pomplun, & Koch, 2013) has just recently been published; more research will need to be completed on this new instrument to determine its utility in the assessment of children with autism.

The Raven's Progressive Matrices present the examinee with a series of visual stimuli each having a missing element and a choice of multiple stimuli that can complete the pattern. There are several versions of the test, including Raven's Standard Progressive Matrices, Raven's Coloured Progressive Matrices, and Raven's Advanced Progressive Matrices. The RPM can be presented in person or by computer. M. Dawson, Soulières, Gernsbacher, and Mottron (2007) discovered that although individuals with autism were able to respond more quickly to the RPM items, they made as many mistakes as those without autism. Interestingly, their scores on the RPM were, on average, 30 to 70 percentile points higher than on the WISC–III. Fugard, Stewart, and Stenning (2011) found that poor social skills but better attention switching predicted a higher Advanced Progressive Matrices score; higher self-reported social skills scores predicted better performance on visuospatial items than on verbal–analytic items.

Despite this wide variety of cognitive assessment instruments, there are still some children with mental ages below 2 years for whom none of the instruments may be appropriate. The psychologist may then use nonstandardized tasks, such as puzzles, language tasks, and Piagetian tasks to roughly determine the child's developmental level.

Psychologists who administer cognitive measures should be aware of the special challenges in assessing children with autism. Many children with ASD have difficulty attending to tasks that are not of their own choosing. They may have problems understanding instructions and may show overactive or impulsive behavior, as well as poor cooperation. Psychologists should be familiar with test administration prior to beginning the evaluation procedure because there may be little, if any, time to review specific subtest instructions during the administration. They should also be cognizant of the child's level of stamina and avoid administering too many tests in a single day. Frequent breaks or rest periods may be needed. They also should be attentive to any loss of concentration and continue to prompt the child to attend as needed.

If the psychologist does not feel confident that the standardized ability tests accurately capture the child's full cognitive potential, he or she may choose to administer the tests in a "testing the limits" manner: The psychologist may administer items under different circumstances that the child missed or did not respond to—for example, without time limits or with the use of tangible reinforcements. Scores obtained using this method, however, cannot be used as a standardized IQ score but may provide nonstandardized information regarding the child's abilities.

When reporting test results, psychologists should note that in many cases the cognitive scores obtained may be more of a measure of minimal performance than optimal ability, and they should provide information regarding what skills the child may fluently demonstrate and what tasks may be too difficult at the time, rather than focusing only on a total IQ score. Although an intellectual score or profile may not be considered as the defining factor in a diagnosis of autism, it does provide a framework for further assessment and may form the basis for treatment planning. Moreover, the use of certain cognitive test instruments with broad age ranges may allow the examiner to track the child's development over time.

NEUROPSYCHOLOGICAL ASSESSMENT

Neuropsychological assessment encompasses the measurement of *executive functioning*, which comprises the skills necessary for purposeful, goal-directed behavior, including impulse control, response inhibition, planning, goal selection, initiation of activity, set maintenance, perseveration, cognitive flexibility, and use of feedback and working memory. Executive functioning deficits may be manifested in inappropriate social behavior; difficulty in devising, following, and shifting plans; organizational problems; difficulty initiating tasks; distractibility; memory difficulties; and carelessness. Several researchers have found that executive functioning plays a significant part in ASD (e.g., Hill, 2004; Verté, Geurts, Roeyers, Oosterlaan, & Sergeant, 2006). Williams, Goldstein, and Minshew (2006a) found that the neuropsychological skills that best discriminated between children with autism and typical children were sensory, perceptual, motor, complex language, and complex memory. There are numerous neuropsychological instruments, but due to space constraints, this chapter is limited to discussion of just a few of the available measures.

Attention

Attention is the ability to concentrate on a particular stimulus. *Selective attention* involves inhibiting responses to distracting stimuli, and *sustained attention* is the ability to attend over time. Rimland (1964) originally proposed that attention was the core deficit in autism, and current researchers have found that children with autism perform poorly on measures of attention (e.g., Calhoun & Mayes, 2005; Mayes & Calhoun, 2003). Research has indicated that children with ASD exhibit difficulties in both visual and auditory attention (Corbett & Constantine, 2006), as well as selective attention (e.g., Courchesne, Lincoln, Yeung-Courchesne, Elmasian, & Grillon, 1989). Mayes and Calhoun (1999), using a sample of 143 children with autism, found that 93% had significant attention problems; however, these children could also hyperfocus for long periods on preferred activities. Williams, Goldstein, and Minshew (2006b) found that attention did not discriminate between autistic and typical groups and concluded that problems for children with autism are most evident when they are confronted with complex information or higher order tasks that require integration of information.

The prevalence of attention-deficit/hyperactivity disorder (ADHD) symptoms in individuals with a primary clinical diagnosis of ASD ranges between 20% and 85% in clinical samples (e.g., Sinzig, Morsch, Bruning, Schmidt, & Lehmkuhl, 2008). Continuous performance tests may be used to obtain a measure of the child's ability to attend to auditory or visual stimuli. Corbett and Constantine (2006), using an early version of the Integrated Visual and Auditory Continuous Performance Test Plus (Sandford & Turner, 1993–2007), found that children with ASD showed significant deficits in visual and auditory attention and in impulsivity compared with typical children and those with ADHD. However, this test has been criticized for poor test–retest reliability and for being too difficult for younger children (Strauss, Sherman, & Spreen, 2006). Gordon's Diagnostic System (GDS; Gordon, McClure, & Aylward, 1996) has more published research and a longer history of use in clinical settings than any other continuous performance test (Harrington, 2004). Mayes and Calhoun (2007), in a study using a large clinical sample ($n = 866$) and 149 typical children ages 6 to 16, found that children with autism scored significantly more poorly on the GDS than did typical children but that their performance was not significantly different from youth with ADHD.

Memory

Because memory is a complex concept that includes many specific types, research in this area has been inconsistent. Some studies have shown that for individuals with autism, verbal memory may be impaired (Pennington et al., 1997; Toichi & Kamio, 1998). A study by Hermalin and O'Conner (1970) indicated that although children with autism recall random words as well as do typical children, their recall did not improve relative to typical children when semantic meaning was added. Tager-Flusberg (1991) found that although children with ASD benefit when clues are given to them, they do not create their own semantic, syntactic, or temporal sequences to facilitate retrieval. Williams, Goldstein, and Minshew (2006b) also suggested that children with autism may have difficulty with complex memory tasks in both visual and verbal domains because they do not initiate organizing strategies or use contextual cues.

Other studies have suggested that the visual–spatial memory skills of children with autism may be intact. For example, Ameli, Courchesne, Lincoln, Kaufman, and Grillon (1988) did not find any impairment in visual recognition memory for children with autism. Others have found that children with autism could appropriately recall pictures of everyday scenes and objects (e.g., Gepner, de Gelder, & de Schonen, 1996). Although children with autism have been reported to possess adequate spatial memory (when defined as recall of a location of a picture on a page; e.g., Williams, Goldstein, Carpenter, & Minshew, 2005), there is also evidence to suggest that they may also have difficulty remembering visual sequences (e.g., Minshew, Goldstein, & Siegel, 1997).

In terms of delayed memory, children with autism have been found to perform as well as matched control participants on a delayed-response visual discrimination task (Prior & Chen, 1976), on a delayed match-to-sample visual memory task (Barth, Fein, & Waterhouse, 1995), and on a delayed recall of a visual design (i.e., on the Rey–Osterrieth Complex Figure Test; Minshew & Goldstein, 2001). Memory for faces has been found to be difficult for children with autism compared with both typical and ID children (e.g., Boucher, Lewis, & Collis, 1998; Klin et al., 1999). Hauck, Fein, Maltby, Waterhouse, and Feinstein (1998) found that children with autism had difficulty with facial memory tasks and that their scores correlated positively with scores of social ability on the Vineland Adaptive Behavior Scales (Sparrow, Balla, & Cicchetti, 1984) Communication, Daily Living, and Socialization domains.

The Wide Range Assessment of Memory and Learning, Second Edition (WRAML2; Sheslow & Adams, 2003), is designed for individuals from 5 to 90 years of age. It provides a Verbal Index score, a Visual Index score, an Attention/Concentration Index score, and a General Memory Index score, as well as a score for an abbreviated screening scale. More research has been conducted on the first edition of the WRAML than on the WRAML2; for example, Williams et al. (2006b) administered the WRAML to 38 children with autism and 38 matched controls from 8 to 16 years of age. They found that children with ASD showed deficits in memory for both complex visual and verbal information and spatial working memory but had relatively intact associative learning ability, recognition, verbal working memory, memory for location, and delayed recall. Principal components analysis of the WRAML subtests administered to children with ASD indicated a very different ability structure from that demonstrated by the typically developing control group and from that of the normative sample for the WRAML.

The California Verbal Learning Test—Children's Version (CVLT–C; Delis, Kramer, Kaplan, & Ober, 1994) measures verbal learning and memory using a multiple-trial list-learning paradigm. It is designed for children 5 to 16 years of age and requires the individual to remember two word lists. Minshew and Goldstein (1993) compared the performance of 21 children with autism with that of 21 typical children on the CVLT–C and found that children with autism scored worse on 30 of the 33 variables, including free recalls, intrusion errors, semantic cluster, and global cluster ratios, and concluded that children with autism may not be able to formulate efficient organizational recall strategies.

Cognitive Flexibility

Cognitive inflexibility is one of the most frequently reported executive functioning difficulties in children with ASD (Geurts, Verté, Oosterlaan, Roeyers, & Sergeant, 2004; Sinzig et al., 2008). The Wisconsin Card Sorting Test (WCST; Heaton, Chelune, Talley, Kay, & Curtis, 1993) measures perseveration and cognitive flexibility. It is designed for individuals from 6½ to 89 years of age and can be administered in a one-to-one format or by computer. The WCST requires the examinee to sort up to 128 stimulus cards. After 10 correct responses, a shift occurs, and the child must develop new sorting algorithms according to color, form, or number. Thus, the child must first determine the correct sorting principle on the basis of feedback, maintain this set, and then be able to adapt when the sorting principle changes.

Ozonoff (1995) found the original WCST to be highly reliable for use with children with ASD and noted that these children performed better on the computer-administered test than on the traditional administration. Several researchers (e.g., Ciesielski & Harris, 1997) have found that children with ASD demonstrate a high rate of perseverative errors on the WCST. Kaland, Smith, and Mortensen (2008) found that a group of individuals diagnosed with HFA performed more poorly than did typical peers on all categories of the WCST, although the differences were not statistically significant, except for the failure to maintain set category, which they interpreted as a deficit in focused attention.

The Trail Making Test, Parts A and B (TMT–A, TMT–B; Reitan & Wolfson, 1985) assesses attention, speed, and cognitive flexibility. It requires the examinee to connect encircled numbers and letters in alternating order under timed conditions. Minshew, Goldstein, Muenz, and Payton (1992) found that TMT–A scores were significantly different for adolescents with autism than for matched typical peers. Ciesielski and Harris (1997) found that youth with autism took much longer on the TMT–B, and their error rate was higher than that of typical children.

Planning

Planning is defined by Hill (2004) as a complex, dynamic operation in which a sequence of planned actions must be constantly monitored, reevaluated, and updated. G. Dawson and Watling's (2000) research indicated that lack of motor planning appears to be a major factor in autism. The Tower of London–Drexel University—2nd Edition (TOLDX–2; Culbertson & Zillmer, 2005) provides a measure of planning ability, procedural memory, information processing, and ability to inhibit prepotent responses in individuals from 7 to 80 years of age. It consists of 10 problems that require the child to move objects from one position to another in a set number of moves. Research regarding the performance of children with autism on the TOLDX–2 has been mixed. Geurts et al. (2004) found no difference in performance accuracy between children with HFA, children with ADHD, and typical children, except for the longer amount of time taken by the HFA group. However, Zinke et al. (2010) found that children with HFA performed more poorly on the TOLDX–2 task, solving fewer problems correctly.

The Tower of Hanoi (TOH; Borys, Spitz, & Dorans, 1982) is a similar task that involves moving disks onto three rods in a certain order. Research has indicated that individuals with ASD also perform poorly on the TOH compared with children with ADHD, Tourette's syndrome, and learning disabilities and compared with children in typically developing control groups. Poorer performance on the TOH was also associated with higher scores for stereotypic, ritualized behaviors and interests on the Autism Diagnostic Interview—Revised (ADI–R; Rutter, Le Couteur, & Lord, 2008) or the Autism Diagnostic Observation Schedule (ADOS; Lord, Rutter, DiLavore, & Risi, 1999; e.g., Bennetto, Pennington, & Rogers, 1996), with these deficits being stable over time (Ozonoff & McEvoy, 1994).

The Delis–Kaplan Executive Function System (D–KEFS; Delis, Kaplan, & Kramer, 2001) can be administered to individuals from 8 through 89 years of age. It has nine subtests that can be used singly or in combination. Kleinhans, Akshoomoff, and Delis (2005) administered the Color–Word Interference test, the Trail Making test, the Verbal Fluency test, and the Design Fluency test from the D–KEFS to 12 adults and adolescents with HFA and found that this group scored significantly below average on the composite measure of executive functioning. They noted that complex verbal tasks that require cognitive switching and efficient lexical retrieval strategies were the most difficult for the individuals with HFA but that cognitive inhibition was intact.

The Developmental Neuropsychological Assessment—Second Edition (NEPSY–II; Korkman, Kirk, & Kemp, 2007) measures several neuropsychological abilities. It was normed on children 3 to 16 years, 11 months, of age. The NEPSY–II assesses six domains: (a) Attention and Executive Functioning, (b) Language, (c) Memory and Learning, (d) Sensorimotor Functioning, (e) Social Perception, and (f) Visuospatial Processing. It offers 32 subtests that the examiner can tailor to the specific examinee. In addition to tests of memory and executive functioning, the NEPSY–II also includes tests of theory of mind (which assess the ability to recognize the feelings and thoughts of others) and affect recognition (which measure the ability to recognize feelings expressed on faces), both of which should be useful for the autistic population. The test has good validity and reliability.

Research using the first edition of the NEPSY (Korkman, Kirk, & Kemp, 1998) showed that children with ASD have difficulty on tasks of attention and memory, especially memory for faces (Korkman et al., 2007). Hooper, Poon, Marcus, and Fine (2006), using the NEPSY with an HFA group and a typical group, revealed significant differences for Phonological Processing, Auditory Attention, Response Set, Speeded Naming, Comprehension of Instruction, and Narrative Memory; however, these differences were not significant after controlling for IQ. The HFA group also showed significantly lower scores on the Arrows subtest.

The NEPSY–II manual includes a clinical study with a small group of individuals with autism ($n = 23$). The authors reported that the autistic group scored significantly lower than the norm group in all domains. On the Attention and Executive Functioning domain, measures of sorting, cognitive flexibility, and auditory attention were impaired, whereas measures of impulse control were relatively intact. Specific impairments were noted on the Memory for Designs, Memory for Faces, Narrative Memory, and Word List Interference subtests. In the Language domain, all scores were lower for the autistic group compared with the control group. Affect Recognition and Theory of Mind were also impaired in the group with ASD. Scores on the Visuospatial Processing domain, Arrows, Design Copying, and Picture Puzzles subtests were lower in the group with autism, but scores on the Block Construction and Geometric Puzzles subtests were not significantly different between the clinical and control groups. The lowest scores on all subtests were found on the Animal Sorting, Comprehension of Instructions, Narrative Memory, and Word List Interference subtests. Other low scores were obtained on Phonological Processing, Memory for Designs, Delayed, and Visuomotor Precision subtests.

The Behavior Rating Inventory of Executive Function (BRIEF; Gioia, Isquith, Guy, & Kenworthy, 2000) is a parent and teacher rating scale designed for children from 5 to 18 years of age. The BRIEF yields a global measure of executive functioning (Global Executive Composite) and two indexes: Behavior Regulation and Metacognition. Gilotty, Kenworthy, Sirian, Black, and Wagner (2002) found a negative relationship between executive functioning and adaptive behavior. Parents rated 35 children diagnosed with ASD with the BRIEF and the Vineland Adaptive Behavior Scales (VABS; Sparrow, Balla, & Cicchetti, 1984) and found that the Initiate and Working Memory domains of the BRIEF were negatively correlated with most of the VABS domains. The Communication and Socialization scales of the VABS were also negatively correlated with several areas of executive functioning as measured by the BRIEF. The BRIEF–Preschool Version (Gioia, Espy, & Isquith, 2003) can be used for young children from 2 years to 5 years, 11 months of age.

Neuropsychologists typically use subtests from various instruments to assess specific skills. For example, they may administer short-term memory tasks from the NEPSY–II, WRAML2, or D–KEFS and then compare the child's performance on each instrument. Using specific neuropsychological tests allows the evaluator to more fully explore a particular cognitive process. Cognitive and neuropsychological assessments provide important information regarding the child's verbal and nonverbal problem solving, concept formation, reasoning, learning style, and memory skills (Klin, Jones, Schultz, & Volkmar, 2005), all of which can be helpful in treatment planning.

ACADEMIC ASSESSMENT

Children with autism are reported to have a relatively high rate of learning difficulties. Mayes and Calhoun (2006), using a large sample of 949 children, found that 67% of children with autism with normal intelligence had a learning disability. In general, decoding has been found to be a relative strength for children with ASD, whereas reading comprehension and writing have been shown to be relative weaknesses (e.g., Mayes & Calhoun, 2003; Minshew, Goldstein, Taylor, & Siegel, 1994). Math performance appears to be related to general cognitive development (Mayes & Calhoun, 2006), and high functioning children with autism may score at an average level in computation (Minshew et al., 1994).

The Psychoeducational Profile—Third Edition (PEP–3; Schopler, Lansing, Reichler, & Marcus, 2005) is made up of 10 subtests, six of which measure developmental abilities in communication and motor skills and four that assess maladaptive behaviors. The PEP–3 yields three composite scores: Communication, Motor, and Maladaptive Behaviors. There is also a Caregiver Report, which has three subtests including Problem Behaviors, Personal Self-Care Skills, and Adaptive Abilities. The test can be useful for basic curricular planning for children 2 years, 7 months to 6 years of age and for older children who are functioning in this age range. The test provides examiner flexibility and can be engaging and interesting for children with ASD.

The Woodcock–Johnson III (WJ III; Woodcock et al., 2001) is a comprehensive achievement test designed for individuals ages 2 to 90. It has 22 subtests that assess reading, math, written expression, and general knowledge. The test is highly reliable, and the Standard Battery typically takes 60 to 70 minutes. Although the WJ III is commonly used in psychoeducational evaluations, no studies specifically regarding the WJ III with children with autism were found. However, the National Center for Special Education Research (2006) conducted a study of preschoolers with disabilities and found that 3-year-old preschoolers with autism scored above the population mean for all preschool students with disabilities on the Letter Identification subtest of the WJ III. In contrast, scores of the preschoolers with autism were lower on the Applied Problems subtest, suggesting that initial reading scores are less affected for preschoolers with autism than are math scores.

Most studies of academic achievement in children with autism have used the Wechsler Individual Achievement Test—Third Edition (WIAT–III; Wechsler, 2009). Although the WIAT–III is the most current test in this series, most of the research has been conducted with previous editions of the battery. Mayes and Calhoun (2008) found that mean standard scores for children with ASD on the WIAT–II (Wechsler, 2001) for Word Reading, Reading Comprehension, and Math subtests were not significantly different from the norm or from each other; however, they were significantly different from the mean score on the Written Expression subtest. Children with HFA showed problems with both handwriting and expressing their thoughts in writing. In another study by the same authors (Mayes & Calhoun, 2006), 60% of children with ASD demonstrated learning disabilities in written expression, with learning disability rates for other areas being much lower (e.g., reading 6%, math 23%, spelling 9%).

In addition to standardized tests of achievement, the academic performance of the child with autism can also be assessed using response to intervention (RTI) techniques; however, the use of standardized tests seems to be more favored by evaluators. A survey by Allen et al. (2008) found that only 18.8% of the school psychologists asked reported that their school districts used RTI in determining eligibility for ASD special education services. When the participants were directly asked whether RTI is an appropriate model for determining special education eligibility under the ASD category, only 28.2% responded affirmatively.

ADAPTIVE FUNCTIONING

Adaptive functioning involves daily living skills, including communication, self-care, socialization, independent living skills, and community functioning. In addition to gathering information regarding the child's cognitive and executive functioning abilities, it is critical that the school psychologist evaluate the child's daily functioning. Allen and colleagues (2008) reported that adaptive behavior scales are routinely (87% of the time) administered in autism evaluations. Tomanik, Pearson, Loveland, Lane, and Shaw (2007) found that the use of an adaptive behavior measure (e.g., the Vineland Adaptive Behavior Scales) significantly improved the diagnostic accuracy of other assessment instruments for autism (i.e., ADI–R and ADOS).

The Vineland Adaptive Behavior Scales, Second Edition (Vineland–II; Sparro, Cicchetti, & Balla, 2005), includes a Survey Interview Form administered by the examiner and a Parent/Caregiver Rating Form, an Expanded Interview Form, and a Teacher Rating Form. The Vineland–II yields scores in the following domains: Communication, Daily Living, Socialization, Motor Skills, and Maladaptive Behavior, as well as 11 subdomains. The standardization sample included 77 individuals with autism. Significant differences were obtained between this group and age-matched typical peers in the Adaptive Behavior Composite scores, Interpersonal Relationships, Play and Leisure Time, and Expressive Language subscales.

The Vineland–II may be helpful in discriminating between children with autism and those with ID. Research using the first edition of the Vineland indicated that individuals with autism demonstrated a more uneven profile than did children with ID. Children with autism also scored more poorly on interpersonal skills than did individuals with Down syndrome (Rodrigue, Morgan, & Geffken, 1991) or other developmental delays (Volkmar, Szatmari, & Sparrow, 1993). Relative strengths were noted in Daily Living and Motor skills with deficits in Socialization and, to a lesser extent, in Communication (Volkmar et al., 1993). Carter et al. (1998) reported special population norms for the Vineland for individuals with ASD who were mute or had limited verbal skills. They found that young children with autism had higher standard scores than older individuals with autism across all domains. In the Communication domain, younger verbal children with autism were least impaired, and older mute individuals with autism were most impaired. Verbal individuals achieved higher scores in Daily Living Skills than mute individuals.

Perry, Flanagan, Geier, and Freeman (2009) used the Vineland–II in a large sample of young children (mean age = 51.7 months) with varying cognitive levels. They found that IQ scores were higher than the Vineland–II Adaptive Behavior Composite score among high functioning children, but the opposite pattern was found for children with lower IQ scores. In a comparison of children with autism and ID, the former were found to have lower scores in Socialization and Communication. Akshoomoff (2006) found that Vineland–II Communication and Socialization scores were strongly correlated with Expressive Language scores on the Mullen Scales of Early Learning and that Communication scores were significantly correlated with the Mullen Receptive Language score.

In a study with older children with ASD (ages 7–18 years), Klin et al. (2007) found that their ASD group scored 1 to 2 standard deviations below the norm for communicative adaptive skills and 2 to 3 standard deviations below the norm for interpersonal skills. Although they did not find a strong negative correlation between autism symptoms as measured by ADOS and the Vineland–II, they did find a negative relationship between age and Vineland–II scores, suggesting that youth with autism become increasingly more impaired relative to their same age peers as they age. McGovern and Sigman (2005) found parent-reported improvements in Daily Living Skills and Socialization, but not in Communication, as their children transitioned from middle school to adolescence and young adulthood. Youth with higher IQs showed greater improvement than did lower functioning children. Similar findings were noted by Freeman, Del'Homme, Guthrie, and Zhang (1999), who found that children with autism improved in all areas of adaptive behavior (Communication, Daily Living Skills, and Socialization) as a function of age and IQ. Interestingly, although Communication and Daily Living Skills were related to initial IQ, improvement on the Social Skills domain of the Vineland–II was independent of initial total IQ scores; Nonverbal IQ was the best predictor of growth in Communication. The Vineland–II should be useful in assessing gains in adaptive skills over time.

Another measure of adaptive behavior is the Adaptive Behavior Assessment System—Second Edition (Harrison & Oakland, 2003). This instrument provides rating forms for the parent and teacher, as well as a self-rating form for adults. There are three separate Adaptive domain scores—Conceptual, Social, and Practical—and a General Adaptive Composite (GAC). Individuals with autistic disorder were included in the standardization group, and they demonstrated significant deficits in the GAC, as well as in the adaptive domains and each skill area compared with age-matched controls, with the greatest discrepancy being in Communication, Health and Safety, Leisure, and Social subscales. Functional Pre-Academics scores of the ASD group, although significantly below that of the control group, was a relative strength for young children (under 6 years) with autism. The Scales of Independent Behavior—Revised (Bruininks, Woodcock, Weatherman, & Hill, 1996) is another measure of adaptive behavior; however, no research was found using this scale with the ASD population.

CONCLUSION

The assessment of children with autism requires an integration of information from a variety of sources. The evaluation should be comprehensive and move beyond just a dichotomous classification regarding the presence or absence of autism to a description of the child's functioning in all areas—cognitive, neuropsychological, academic, adaptive, linguistic, and socioemotional. By doing so, appropriate interventions can be developed. It should be kept in mind that although a formal evaluation procedure describes the child's performance at a specific point, the evaluation procedure should continue as an evolving process, and the child's skill development should be continually assessed.

REFERENCES

Akshoomoff, N. (2006). Use of the Mullen Scales of Early Learning for the assessment of young children with autism spectrum disorders. *Child Neuropsychology, 12*, 269–277. doi:10.1080/09297040500473714

Allen, R. A., Robins, D., & Decker, S. L. (2008). Autism spectrum disorders: Neurobiology and current assessment practices. *Psychology in the Schools, 45*, 905–917. doi:10.1002/pits.20341

Ameli, R., Courchesne, D., Lincoln, A., Kaufman, A., & Grillon, C. (1988). Visual memory processes in high-functioning individuals with autism. *Journal of Autism and Developmental Disorders, 18*, 601–615. doi:10.1007/BF02211878

Asarnow, R. F., Tanguay, P. E., Bott, L., & Freeman, B. J. (1987). Patterns of IQ in nonretarded autistic and schizophrenic children. *The Journal of Child Psychology and Psychiatry, 28*, 273–280. doi:10.1111/j.1469-7610.1987.tb00210.x

Baird, G., Simonoff, E., Pickles, A., Chandler, S., Loucas, T., Meldrum, D., & Charman, T. (2006). Prevalence of disorders of the autism spectrum in a population cohort of children in South Thames. *The Lancet, 368,* 210–215. doi:10.1016/S0140-6736(06)69041-7

Barth, C., Fein, D., & Waterhouse, L. (1995). Delayed match-to-sample performance in autistic children. *Developmental Neuropsychology, 11,* 53–69. doi:10.1080/87565649509540603

Bayley, N. (2005). *Bayley Assessment Scales of Infant and Toddler Development* (3rd ed.). San Antonio, TX: Harcourt.

Bennetto, L., Pennington, B., & Rogers, S. (1996). Intact and impaired memory functions in autism. *Child Development, 67,* 1816–1835. doi:10.2307/1131734

Borys, S. V., Spitz, H. H., & Dorans, B. A. (1982). Tower of Hanoi performance of retarded young adults and nonretarded children as a function of solution length and goal state. *Journal of Experimental Child Psychology, 33,* 87–110. doi:10.1016/0022-0965(82)90008-X

Boucher, J., Lewis, V., & Collis, G. (1998). Familiar face recognition in relatively able autistic children. *The Journal of Child Psychology and Psychiatry, 39,* 171–181. doi:10.1111/1469-7610.00311

Bracken, B., & McCallum, S. (1998). *Universal Nonverbal Intelligence Test.* Odessa, FL: PAR.

Burnette, C. P., Mundy, P. C., Moore, J. A., Sutton, S. K., Vaughan, A. E., & Charak, D. (2005). Weak central coherence and its relation to theory of mind and anxiety in autism. *Journal of Autism and Developmental Disorders, 35,* 63–73. doi:10.1007/s10803-004-1035-5

Calhoun, S., & Mayes, S. (2005). Processing speed in children with clinical disorders. *Psychology in the Schools, 42,* 333–343. doi:10.1002/pits.20067

Carpentieri, S., & Morgan, S. (1994). Brief report: A comparison of patterns of cognitive functioning of autistic and nonautistic retarded children on the Stanford–Binet—Fourth Edition. *Journal of Autism and Developmental Disorders, 24,* 215–223. doi.org/10.1007/BF02172098

Carter, A. S., Volkmar, A. R., Sparrow, S. S., Wang, J.-J., Lord, C., Dawson, G., . . . Schopler, E.. (1998). The Vineland Adaptive Behavior Scales: Supplementary norms for individuals with autism. *Journal of Autism and Developmental Disorders, 28,* 287–302. doi:10.1023/A:1026056518470

Ciesielski, K., & Harris, R. (1997). Factors related to performance failure on executive tasks in autism. *Child Neuropsychology, 3,* 1–12. doi:10.1080/09297049708401364

Corbett, B. A., & Constantine, L. J. (2006). Autism and Attention Deficit Hyperactivity Disorder: Assessing attention and response control with the Integrated Visual and Auditory Continuous Performance Test. *Child Neuropsychology, 12,* 335–348. doi:10.1080/09297040500350938

Courchesne, E., Lincoln, A., Yeung-Courchesne, R., Elmasian, R., & Grillon, C. (1989). Pathophysiological findings in nonretarded autism and receptive developmental language disorder. *Journal of Autism and Developmental Disorders, 19,* 1–17. doi:10.1007/BF02212714

Culbertson, C., & Zillmer, E. (2005). *Tower of London* (2nd ed.). Chicago, IL: MHS.

Dawson, G., & Watling, R. (2000). Interventions to facilitate auditory, visual, and motor integration in autism. *Journal of Autism and Developmental Disorders, 30,* 415–421. doi:10.1023/A:1005547422749

Dawson, M., Soulières, I., Gernsbacher, M. A., & Mottron, L. (2007). The level and nature of autistic intelligence. *Psychological Science, 18,* 657–662. doi:10.1111/j.1467-9280.2007.01954.x

Delis, D., Kaplan, E., & Kramer, J. (2001). *Delis Kaplan Executive Functioning System.* San Antonio, TX: Psychological Corporation.

Delis, D., Kramer, J. Kaplan, E., & Ober, B. (1994). *California Verbal Learning Test— Children's Version.* San Antonio, TX: Psychological Corporation.

Edelson, M. (2006). Are the majority of children with autism mentally retarded? A systematic evaluation of the data. *Focus on Autism and Other Developmental Disabilities, 21,* 66–83.

Elliott, C. (2007). *Differential Ability Scales* (2nd ed.). San Antonio, TX: Harcourt.

Freeman, B. J., Del'Homme, M., Guthrie, D., & Zhang, F. (1999). Vineland Adaptive Behavior Scale scores as a function of age and initial IQ in 210 autistic children. *Journal of Autism and Developmental Disorders, 29,* 379–384. doi:10.1023/A:1023078827457

Frombonne, E. (2005). Epidemiological studies of pervasive developmental disorders. In F. Volkmar, R. Paul, A. Klin, & D. Cohen (Eds.), *Handbook of autism and pervasive developmental disorders: Vol. 1. Diagnosis, development, neurobiology, and behavior* (3rd ed., pp. 42–69). Hoboken, NJ: Wiley.

Fugard, A. J. B., Stewart, M. E., & Stenning, K. (2011). Visual/verbal–analytic reasoning bias as a function of self-reported autistic-like traits: A study of typically developing individuals solving Raven's Advanced Progressive Matrices. *Autism, 15,* 327–340. doi:10.1177/1362361310371798

Gepner, B., de Gelder, B., & de Schonen, S. (1996). Face processing in autistics: Evidence for a generalized deficit? *Child Neuropsychology, 2,* 123–139. doi:10.1080/09297049608401357

Geurts, H. M., Verté, S., Oosterlaan, J., Roeyers, H., & Sergeant, J. A. (2004). How specific are executive functioning deficits in attention deficit hyperactivity disorder and autism? *The Journal of Child Psychology and Psychiatry, 45,* 836–854. doi:10.1111/j.1469-7610.2004.00276.x

Gilchrist, A., Green, J., Cox, A., Burton, D., Rutter, M., & Le Couteur, A. (2001). Development and current functioning in adolescents with Asperger Syndrome: A comparative study. *The Journal of Child Psychology and Psychiatry, 42,* 227–240. doi:10.1111/1469-7610.00714

Gilotty, L., Kenworthy, L., Sirian, L., Black, D., & Wagner, A. (2002). Adaptive skills and executive function in autism spectrum disorders. *Child Neuropsychology, 8,* 241–248. doi:10.1076/chin.8.4.241.13504

Gioia, G., Espy, K., & Isquith, P. (2003). *Behavior Rating Inventory of Executive Function—Preschool.* Odessa, FL: PAR.

Gioia, G., Isquith, P., Guy, S., & Kenworthy, L. (2000). *Behavior Rating Inventory of Executive Function*. Odessa, TX: PAR.

Gordon, M., McClure, F., & Aylward, G. (1996). *The Gordon Diagnostic System* (3rd ed.). DeWitt, NY: Gordon.

Gutwirth, B. (1996). *The relationship between cognitive processing profiles according to the PASS model: Planning, attention, simultaneous and successive processes, and childhood psychopathology* (Doctoral dissertation). Available from ProQuest Dissertations and Theses database. (UMI No. 9709089)

Harrington, R. (2004). *Review of the Gordon Diagnostic System*. The Buros Institute of Mental Measurements and the Board of Regents of the University of Nebraska, Lincoln (Accession no. 13191523).

Harris, S. L., Handelman, J. S., & Burton, J. L. (1990). The Stanford Binet profiles of young children with autism. *Special Services in the Schools, 6*, 135–143. doi.org/10.1300/J008v06n01_08

Harrison, P. L., & Oakland, T. (2003). *Adaptive Behavior Assessment System—2nd edition*. San Antonio, TX: Psychological Corporation.

Hauck, M., Fein, D., Maltby, N., Waterhouse, L., & Feinstein, C. (1998). Memory for faces in children with autism. *Child Neuropsychology, 4*, 187–198. doi:10.1076/chin.4.3.187.3174

Heaton, R., Chelune, G., Talley, J., Kay, G., & Curtis, G. (1993). *Wisconsin Card Sorting Test (WCST) manual—Revised and expanded*. Lutz, FL: Psychological Assessment Resources.

Hermalin, B., & O'Conner, N. (1970). *Psychological experiments with autistic children*. New York, NY: Pergamon.

Hill, E. (2004). Evaluating the theory of executive dysfunction in autism. *Developmental Review, 24*, 189–233. doi:10.1016/j.dr.2004.01.001

Hooper, S. R., Poon, K. K., Marcus, L., & Fine, C. (2006). Neuropsychological characteristics of school-age children with high functioning autism. *Child Neuropsychology, 12*, 299–305. doi:10.1080/09297040600737984

Kaland, N., Smith, L., & Mortensen, E. (2008). Brief report: Cognitive flexibility and focused attention in children and adolescents with Asperger syndrome or high-functioning autism as measured on the computerized version of the WCST. *Journal of Autism and Developmental Disorders, 38*, 1161–1165. doi:10.1007/s10803-007-0474-1

Kaufman, A., & Kaufman, N. (2004). *Kaufman Assessment Battery for Children* (2nd ed.). Circle Pines, MN: AGS.

Kleinhans, N., Akshoomoff, N., & Delis, D. (2005). Executive functions in autism and Asperger's Disorder: Flexibility, fluency, and inhibition. *Developmental Neuropsychology, 27*, 379–401. doi:10.1207/s15326942dn2703_5

Klin, A., Jones, W., Schultz, R. T., & Volkmar, F. R. (2005). The executive mind—From actions to cognition: Lessons from autism. In F. Volkmar, R. Paul, A. Klin,

& D. Cohen (Eds.), *Handbook of autism and pervasive developmental disorders* (3rd ed., pp. 682–703). Hoboken, NJ: Wiley.

Klin, A., Saulnier, C., Tsatsanis, K., & Volkmar, F. (2005). Clinical evaluation in autism spectrum. In F. Volkmar, P. Rheas, A. Klin, & D. Cohen (Eds.). *Handbook of autism and pervasive developmental disorders* (3rd ed., pp. 772–799). Hoboken, NJ: Wiley.

Klin, A., Saulnier, C. A., Sparrow, S. S., Cicchetti, D. V., Volkmar, F. R., & Lord, C. (2007). Social and communication abilities and disabilities in higher functioning individuals with autism spectrum disorders: The Vineland and the ADOS. *Journal of Autism and Developmental Disorders, 37,* 748–759. doi.org/10.1007/s10803-006-0229-4

Klin, A., Sparrow, S., de Bildt, A., Cicchetti, D., Cohen, D., & Volkmar, F. (1999). A normed study of face recognition in autism and related disorders. *Journal of Autism and Developmental Disorders, 29,* 499–508. doi:10.1023/A:1022299920240

Korkman, M., Kirk, U., & Kemp, S. (1998). NEPSY: A developmental neuropsychological assessment. San Antonio, TX: Psychological Corporation.

Korkman, M., Kirk, U., & Kemp, S. (2007). *NEPSY* (2nd ed.). San Antonio, TX: Harcourt.

Koyama, T., Kamio, Y., Inada, N., & Korita, H. (2009). Sex differences in WISC–III profiles with high functioning pervasive developmental disorders. *Journal of Autism and Developmental Disorders, 39,* 135–141. doi:10.1007/s10803-008-0610-6

Lichtenberger, E. A. (2004). Autism-spectrum disorders. In D. P. Flanagan & A. S. Kaufman (Eds.), *Essentials of WISC–IV assessment* (pp. 183–199). Hoboken, NJ: Wiley.

Lincoln, A. J., Hanzel, E., & Quirmbach, L. (2007). Assessing intellectual abilities of children and adolescents with autism and related disorders. In S. Smith & L. Handler (Eds.), *The clinical assessment of children and adolescents* (pp. 527–544). Mahwah, NJ: Erlbaum.

Lord, C., Rutter, M., DiLavore, P. C., & Risi, S. (1999). *Autism Diagnostic Observation Schedule—WPS Edition.* Los Angeles, CA: Western Psychological Services.

Luria, A. R. (1973). *The working brain.* London, England: Penguin Books.

Mayes, S. D., & Calhoun, S. L. (1999). Symptoms of autism in young children and correspondence with the DSM. *Infants and Young Children, 12,* 90–97. doi:10.1097/00001163-199910000-00011

Mayes, S. D., & Calhoun, S. L. (2003). Analysis of WISC–III, Stanford-Binet-IV, and academic achievement test scores in children with autism. *Journal of Autism and Developmental Disorders, 33,* 329–341. doi:10.1023/A:1024462719081

Mayes, S. D., & Calhoun, S. L. (2006). Frequency of reading, math, and writing disabilities in children with clinical disorders. *Learning and Individual Differences, 16,* 145–157. doi:10.1016/j.lindif.2005.07.004

Mayes, S. D., & Calhoun, S. L. (2007). Learning, attention, writing, and processing speed in typical children and children with ADHD, autism, anxiety, depression and oppositional defiant disorder. *Child Neuropsychology, 13,* 469–493. doi:10.1080/09297040601112773

Mayes, S. D., & Calhoun, S. L. (2008). WISC–IV and WIAT–II profiles in children with high-functioning autism. *Journal of Autism and Developmental Disorders, 38,* 428–439. doi:10.1007/s10803-007-0410-4

McGovern, C. W., & Sigman, M. (2005). Continuity and change from early childhood to adolescence in autism. *The Journal of Child Psychology and Psychiatry, 46,* 401–408. doi.org/10.1111/j.1469-7610.2004.00361.x

McGrew, K. S. (2005). The Cattell–Horn–Carroll theory of cognitive abilities: Past, present, and future. In D. P. Flanagan, J. L. Genshaft, & P. L. Harrison (Eds.), *Contemporary intellectual assessment: Theories, tests, and issues* (pp. 136–182). New York, NY: Guilford Press.

Miller, J. N., & Ozonoff, S. (2000). The external validity of Asperger disorder: Lack of evidence from the domain of neuropsychology. *Journal of Abnormal Psychology, 109,* 227–238. doi:10.1037/0021-843X.109.2.227

Minshew, N. J., & Goldstein, G. (1993). Is autism an amnesic disorder? Evidence from the California Verbal Learning Test. *Neuropsychology, 7,* 209–216. doi:10.1037/0894-4105.7.2.209

Minshew, N. J., & Goldstein, G. (2001). The pattern of intact and impaired memory functions in autism. *The Journal of Child Psychology and Psychiatry, 42,* 1095–1101. doi.org/10.1111/1469-7610.00808

Minshew, N. J., Goldstein, G., Muenz, L., & Payton, J. (1992). Neuropsychological functioning in non-mentally retarded autistic individuals. *Journal of Clinical and Experimental Neuropsychology, 14,* 749–761. doi:10.1080/01688639208402860

Minshew, N. J., Goldstein, G., & Siegel, D. (1997). Neuropsychologic functioning in autism: Profile of a complex information processing disorder. *Journal of the International Neuropsychological Society, 3,* 303–316.

Minshew, N. J., Goldstein, G., Taylor, H., & Siegel, D. (1994). Academic achievement in high functioning autistic individuals. *Journal of Clinical and Experimental Neuropsychology, 16,* 261–270. doi:10.1080/01688639408402637

Mullen, E. M. (1995). *Mullen Scales of Early Learning.* Minneapolis, MN: NCS Pearson.

Naglieri, J. A. (1997). *Naglieri Nonverbal Ability Test.* San Antonio, TX: Psychological Corporation.

Naglieri, J. A., & Das, J. P. (1997). *Cognitive Assessment System.* Itasca, IL: Riverside.

National Center for Special Education Research. (2006) *Preschoolers with disabilities: Characteristics, services and results.* Retrieved from http://ies.ed.gov/ncser/pdf/20063003.pdf

Ozonoff, S. (1995). Reliability and validity of the WCST in studies of autism. *Neuropsychology, 9,* 491–500. doi:10.1037/0894-4105.9.4.491

Ozonoff, S., & McEvoy, R. E. (1994). A longitudinal study of executive function and theory of mid development in autism. *Development and Psychopathology, 6,* 1081–1105.

Pennington, B., Rogers, S., Bennetto, L., Griffith, E., Reed, D., & Shyu, V. (1997). Validity tests of the executive dysfunction hypothesis of autism. In J. Russell (Ed.) *Autism as an executive disorder* (pp. 143–178). Oxford, England: Oxford University Press.

Perry, A., Flanagan, H., Geier, J., & Freeman, N. (2009). Brief report: The Vineland Adaptive Behavior Scales in young children with autism spectrum disorders at different cognitive levels. *Journal of Autism and Developmental Disorders, 39,* 1066–1078. doi:10.1007/s10803-009-0704-9

Prior, M. R., & Chen, C. S. (1976). Short term and serial memory. *Journal of Autism and Childhood Schizophrenia, 6,* 121–131. doi:10.1007/BF01538055

Raven, J., Raven, J. C., & Court, J. (2004). *Manual for Raven's Progressive Matrices and Vocabulary Scales.* San Antonio, TX: Harcourt Assessment.

Reitan, R., & Wolfson, D. (1985). *The Halstead–Reitan Neuropsychological Test Battery: Therapy and clinical interpretation.* Tucson, AZ: Neuropsychological Press.

Rimland, B. (1964). *Infantile autism.* New York, NY: Appleton-Century-Crofts.

Rodrigue, J. R., Morgan, S. B., & Geffken, G. R. (1991). A comparative evaluation of adaptive behavior in children and adolescents with autism, Down syndrome, and normal development. *Journal of Autism and Developmental Disorders, 21,* 187–196. doi:10.1007/BF02284759

Roid, G., Miller, L., Pomplun, M., & Koch, C. (2013). *The Leiter–3 International Performance Scale.* North Tonawanda, NY: Multi-Health Systems.

Roid, G., & Miller, L. J. (1997). *Leiter International Performance Scale—Revised.* Wood Dale, IL: Stoelting.

Roid, G. H. (2003). *Stanford–Binet Intelligence Scales* (5th ed.). Itasca, IL: Riverside.

Rutter, M., Le Couteur, A., & Lord, C. (2008). *Autism Diagnostic Interview (Revised).* Los Angeles, CA: Western Psychological Services.

Sandford, J., & Turner, A. (1993–2007). *Integrated Visual and Auditory Continuous Performance Test.* Richmond, VA: Braintrain.

Schopler, E., Lansing, M., Reichler, R., & Marcus, L. (2005). *Psychoeducational Profile: TEACCH Individualized Psychoeducational Assessment for Children with Autistic Spectrum Disorders* (3rd ed.). Austin, TX: PRO-ED.

Sheslow, D., & Adams, W. (2003). *Wide Range Assessment of Memory and Learning* (2nd ed.). Lutz, FL: PAR.

Sinzig, J., Morsch, D., Bruning, N., Schmidt, M., & Lehmkuhl, G. (2008). Inhibition, flexibility, working memory and planning in autism spectrum disorders with and without comorbid ADHD symptoms. *Child and Adolescent Psychiatry and Mental Health, 4,* 2–4. doi:10.1186/1753-2000-2-4

Sparrow, S., Balla, D., & Cicchetti, D. (1984). *Vineland Adaptive Behavior Scales*. Circle Pines, MN: AGS.

Sparrow, S., Cicchetti, D., & Balla, D. (2005). *Vineland Adaptive Behavior Scales* (2nd Ed.). Circle Pines, MN: AGS.

Strauss, E., Sherman, E., & Spreen, O. (2006). *A compendium of neuropsychological tests: Administration, norms and commentary*. New York, NY: Oxford University Press.

Tager-Flusberg, H. (1991). Semantic processing in the free recall of autistic children: Further evidence of a cognitive deficit. *British Journal of Developmental Psychology, 9*, 417–430. doi:10.1111/j.2044-835X.1991.tb00886.x

Thorndike, R. L., Hagen, E. P., & Sattler, J. M. (1986). *The Stanford–Binet Intelligence Scale, Fourth Edition*. Chicago, IL: Riverside.

Toichi, M., & Kamio, Y. (1998). Verbal memory in autistic adolescents. *Japanese Journal of Child and Adolescent Psychiatry, 39*, 364–373.

Tomanik, S. S., Pearson, D. A., Loveland, K. A., Lane, D. M., & Shaw, J. B. (2007). Improving the reliability of autism diagnoses: Examining the utility of adaptive behavior. *Journal of Autism and Developmental Disorders, 37*, 921–928. doi:10.1007/s10803-006-0227-6

Tsatsanis, K. D., Dartnall, N., Cicchetti, D., Sparrow, S. S., Klin, A., & Volkmar, F. R. (2003). Concurrent validity and classification accuracy of the Leiter and Leiter–R in low-functioning children with autism. *Journal of Autism and Developmental Disorders, 33*, 23–30. doi:10.1023/A:1022274219808

Verté, S., Geurts, H. M., Roeyers, H., Oosterlaan, J., & Sergeant, J. A. (2006). Executive functioning in children with an autism spectrum disorder: Can we differentiate within the spectrum? *Journal of Autism and Developmental Disorders, 36*, 351–372. doi.org/10.1007/s10803-006-0074-5

Volkmar, F. R., Szatmari, P., & Sparrow, S. S. (1993). Sex difference in pervasive developmental disorders. *Journal of Autism and Developmental Disorders, 23*, 579–591. doi:10.1007/BF01046103

Wechsler, D. (1991). *Wechsler Intelligence Scale for Children* (3rd ed.). San Antonio, TX: Psychological Corporation.

Wechsler, D. (2001). *Wechsler Individual Achievement Test* (2nd ed.). San Antonio, TX: Psychological Corporation.

Wechsler, D. (2002). *Wechsler Preschool and Primary Scale of Intelligence* (3rd ed.). San Antonio, TX: Psychological Corporation.

Wechsler, D. (2003). *Wechsler Intelligence Scale for Children* (4th ed.). San Antonio, TX: Psychological Corporation.

Wechsler, D. (2009). *Wechsler Individual Achievement Test—III*. San Antonio, TX: Pearson.

Williams, D. L., Goldstein, G., Carpenter, P. A., & Minshew, N. J. (2005). Verbal and spatial working memory in autism. *Journal of Autism and Developmental Disorders, 35*, 747–756. doi:10.1007/s10803-005-0021-x

Williams, D. L., Goldstein, G., & Minshew, N. J. (2006a). Neuropsychological functioning in children with autism: Further evidence for disordered complex information-processing. *Child Neuropsychology, 12,* 279–298. doi:10.1080/09297040600681190

Williams, D. L., Goldstein, G., & Minshew, N. J. (2006b). The profile of memory function in children with autism. *Neuropsychology, 20,* 21–29. doi:10.1037/0894-4105.20.1.21

Woodcock, R., McGrew, K., & Mather, N. (2001). *Woodcock–Johnson Tests of Cognitive Abilities* (3rd ed.). Itasca, IL: Riverside.

Zinke, K., Fries, E., Altgassen, M., Kirschbaum, C., Dettenborn, L., & Kliegel, M. (2010). Visuospatial short-term memory explains deficits in tower task planning in children with autism spectrum disorder. *Child Neuropsychology, 16,* 229–241.

5

LANGUAGE AND SOCIAL COMMUNICATION

DIANE TWACHTMAN-CULLEN
AND JENNIFER TWACHTMAN-BASSETT

Oliver Sacks (1989) defined language as "the symbolic currency [for the] exchange [of] meaning" (p. 39), a definition that clearly underscores its dynamic, functional, and purpose-driven nature while elevating it to its raison d'etre: communication. This definition provides a useful framework within which to discuss language development in children and adolescents with autism spectrum disorder (ASD), given that of the three aspects of language—syntactic (form), semantic (meaning), and pragmatic (function)—it is impairment in the latter social element that is the dominant feature of disordered language in this population. The pragmatic function is also the feature that drives the myriad uses that render language purposeful. For example, we can use language to obtain attention; to request and to comment; to ask and answer questions; to express opinions, thoughts, and feelings; to negotiate, explain, or elaborate; and to express frustration or joy, empathy or disdain. Language can ground us in the here and now or catapult us into the future.

http://dx.doi.org/10.1037/14338-006
Autism Spectrum Disorder in Children and Adolescents: Evidence-Based Assessment and Intervention in Schools, L. A. Wilkinson (Editor)

Through language, we can reflect on the past and imagine that which has not yet happened.

These are only some of the countless ways in which we can use language as the symbolic currency to express our intents, comprehend the intentions of others, and engage in the social reciprocity that makes possible the exchange of meaning. Add to this the social, largely unconscious, split-second decisions that go into vocabulary selection, the tailoring of one's message to suit the particular situation and audience, and the use of nonverbal features to support communication, and it becomes clear that language development is a multifaceted process that involves perceptual, cognitive, and social–cognitive learning—as well as ongoing interaction with mature language users—over a period of several years.

This chapter focuses predominantly on the verbal and nonverbal pragmatic aspects of communication, not only because of their relevance for individuals with ASD but also because pragmatic deficits often "fly under the radar" or are mischaracterized as behaviorally motivated. Verbal and nonverbal communication impairment is discussed as a function of underlying deficits in joint attention and theory of mind, with a view toward the impact these deficits have on concept development, word learning, and discourse. Evidence-based assessment practices and intervention strategies reflective of the language-learning research literature will also be addressed.

LANGUAGE DEVELOPMENT IN TYPICALLY DEVELOPING CHILDREN

To understand and appropriately address deviant language development, it is first necessary to understand how language develops in typical children. The first thing that must be said is that language development is a distinctly social phenomenon that begins with the birth cry and "ends" with the generative use of language to express a wide variety of functions and intents.

Early Models of Language Development

As early as 1927, behavioral psychologist Grace DeLaguna (1927/1963) captured the essence of language by addressing its raison d'etre—that is, its purposeful and interactive capabilities—when she wrote,

> Once we deliberately ask the question:—*What does speech do? What objective function does it perform in human life?*—the answer is not far to seek. Speech is the great medium through which human cooperation is brought about. It is the means by which the diverse activities of men

are coordinated and correlated with each other for the attainment of reciprocal ends. Men do not speak simply to relieve their feelings or to air their views, *but to awaken a response in their fellows and to influence their attitudes and acts* [emphasis added]. (pp. 19–20)

This description of language use captures the essence of symbolic communication: that it is intentional, dynamic, and reciprocal. Remarkably—in view of DeLaguna's (1927/1963) comments—the dominant view of language for most of the 20th century remained staunchly and unilaterally focused on the medium through which this social function was expressed (i.e., form and syntax and content and semantics).

Similarly, notwithstanding its acknowledgment of the existence of at least some functions of language, Skinner's *verbal behavior model* gave short shrift to them by requiring that only observable behavior be considered as capable of conveying the functions of communication. This view renders the concept of theory of mind and its focus on the internal mental states of the communicative partner null and void and denigrates the critical role of communicative intent and comprehension, because neither parameter is discernible except by inference.

Contemporary View

The so-called pragmatics revolution in the latter part of the 20th century ushered in sweeping changes in the way language had theretofore been viewed and championed the long-awaited focus on the social uses of language and their capacity to "influence [the] attitude and acts" (DeLaguna, 1927/1963, pp. 19–20) of others. This conceptualization of language not only highlighted the importance of the functions of communication but also underscored the dominant role of the interactive partner in the language-learning process by putting consideration of his or her intentional mental states front and center. Furthermore, it elevated context and experience to central roles in social-language learning. Given the nature of the communication deficits in ASD, the social–pragmatic view of language would seem to offer an ideal framework for examining language-use issues in children and adolescents with ASD.

The Social–Pragmatic View of Language Development

The *social–pragmatic view* of language development holds that in mature speakers language use is intentional, reciprocal, and representational (i.e., symbolic; Twachtman-Cullen, 2000). That said, the road to intentionality does not "begin" with the child per se but rather evolves as a function of the transactions between the child and the mature language user. How does this occur? Seminal research has demonstrated that, even without specific intent, the infant's earliest behaviors are designed to influence others (Bates, 1976; Bates, Camaioni, & Volterra, 1975), and those others, in turn, are necessary partners in the language-learning process because it is their task to "read in" or attribute intentionality to the infant's behaviors, thus enabling him or her to establish meaning over time.

An example may help to illuminate this process. When very young infants cry, they do not intend to call their parents. They are simply "wired" to engage in this behavior whenever they go into a state of disequilibrium due to hunger, gastric discomfort, or other types of discomfort. Similarly, adults are wired to interpret infant behavior as communicative and, as such, to respond to infants' distress signals. Over the course of several months and literally thousands of such interactions, the infant comes to learn that his or her voice is a powerful tool to summon the parent and to have his or her needs met. At this point—the point at which the child makes the connection between his or her behavior and the parent's response—the behavior becomes intentional. Accounting for individual differences, this milestone event takes place in the latter part of the first year of life, typically somewhere between 10 and 12 months of age, and as is discussed later, it is an important precursor to symbolic communication (Twachtman-Cullen, 2008). The essential point to be made is that intentionality is not a unilateral event that occurs within the infant but rather a dyadic (two-way) transactional event in which the infant and adult mutually influence one another in the context of shared experiences.

Figure 5.1, the circle of social-language learning, is Diane Twachtman-Cullen's conceptualization of the language-learning process. It illustrates the interplay among the "key players" in social-language learning. Specifically, early exploration and experiential learning contribute to the child's developing understanding of the world and over time lead to more refined dyadic interactions—for example, to reciprocal (back-and-forth) social routines such as pat-a-cake and peek-a-boo. These "games of infancy" provide rich opportunities for affect sharing and for the child to learn about important aspects of language use such as reciprocity, role taking, and anticipation. Furthermore, these dyadic interactions lead to the triadic interactions known as *joint attention* (Leekam & Ramsden, 2006), in which the child and adult share attention regarding a third entity. This shared focus—joint attention—serves as the foundation for conceptual development, word learning, and eventually conversational discourse. Finally, it is no accident that context occupies a central position in the schematic in Figure 5.1, because it is considered an essential element in the development of social communication in children. All of these elements are discussed later in greater detail, with a view toward where this process goes awry in ASD.

Figure 5.1. The circle of social-language learning. This intervention protocol "mirrors" the language-learning process by providing a strong foundation, working within a context, and following an orderly pattern of skill development.

ELEMENTS OF SOCIAL-LANGUAGE LEARNING

Language learning is largely a social process fueled by experience. As such, children with ASD are at a distinct disadvantage when it comes to social-language development.

Exploration and Experiential Learning

It is well known that children with ASD have circumscribed interests and prefer sameness, both of which militate against the active environmental exploration and rich experiential learning that is so important in concept building. For example, the child with autism who spends his time spinning the wheel of a toy car learns little about the affordances of that car that would lead to a broad-based conceptual understanding of it. Instead, his stereotypic action leads to a stilted, restrictive idea of "car-ness," if you will. That said, research demonstrates, however, that experiential learning activities fuel brain development (Bell & Fox, 1994; Greenough & Black, 1992; Schwartz & Begley, 2002) and are therefore vitally important to learning about the world, forming concepts, and learning language. And, as seen in Figure 5.1, experiential learning sets the stage for the dyadic interactions (as in the games of infancy) that eventually lead to joint attention (Leekam & Ramsden, 2006) and the theory of mind knowledge that is foundational to symbolic communication. Because experience is an important component of social-language learning, its impoverishment in children with ASD places them at a distinct disadvantage when it comes to social communication.

Joint Attention and Theory of Mind

Joint attention and theory of mind are pivotal, interrelated aspects of social cognition. Both are linked to the concept of intentionality and hence are foundational to language development and meaningful word use. As noted, joint attention, considered a core deficit in autism (Kasari, Fannin, & Goods, 2012), is operationalized in triadic interactions. This can occur through eye gaze alternation, facial expressions, and protodeclarative (social-referencing) pointing in which the child checks back to see whether the adult is looking at the same thing. Because protodeclarative pointing is used to direct another's attention, it is one of the earliest indicators of the child's emerging theory of mind because it demonstrates the child's awareness that people "see" things differently. It is important to underscore that joint attention is not a passive process in which two people happen to be looking at the same thing at the same time, but rather a dynamic one in which each partner shares awareness of the other's experience (Hobson, 2005). Indeed, it is this shared awareness—the knowledge of "being on the same wavelength" with another—that makes joint attention truly *joint*.

There is a great deal of research that demonstrates deficits in joint attention in individuals with ASD (Leekam, 1993; Lewy & Dawson, 1992; Mundy, Sigman, Ungerer, & Sherman, 1986). Hence, children with ASD do not typically engage in the social behaviors of gaze shifting, offering or "showing" gestures, or protodeclarative (social) pointing reflective of joint attention (Happé, 1996). When these behaviors do develop, they are not only delayed but also used less frequently than is seen in typically developing youngsters (Kasari et al., 2012).

What makes these observations and findings compelling is that they have direct implications for language development. For example, Landa, Holman, Sullivan, and Cleary (2005) found that toddlers with autism who had better joint attention skills prior to treatment made greater gains in language after treatment. Likewise, Siller and Sigman (2002) found that children with autism who exhibited stronger joint attention skills in their younger years had better language development when they reached adolescence. Importantly, the same relationship between joint attention ability and language outcomes seen in children with autism is also seen in typically developing children (Tomasello, 2003; Tomasello & Farrar, 1986; Tomasello & Todd, 1983). This suggests that the social-language learning process proceeds according to the same rules in both typically developing children and those with ASD (Twachtman-Cullen & Twachtman-Reilly, 2007).

The implications for intervention should be obvious. *Theory of mind*—or the ability to attribute internal mental states such as thoughts and feelings to others (Twachtman-Cullen, 2008)—is inextricably intertwined with joint attention. Theory of mind knowledge is indicated by the use of italicized mental state terms in the following statements: She *thinks* she fooled me; he *knows* that bothered me. In each of these statements the speaker infers what is going on in another person's mind, a process that enables him or her to make sense of the person's verbal and nonverbal behavior. Because this process deals with "shades of gray" (educated guesses), it is an area of weakness in individuals with ASD.

Research has demonstrated a brain-based link between joint attention and theory of mind. Specifically, Williams, Waiter, Perra, Perrett, and Whiten (2005) found that the attribution of mental states and joint attention share a common neural substrate in the brain. Furthermore, Tomasello (2003) linked intentionality to theory of mind and word learning, stating that the latter "is a process of skill learning that builds upon a deep and pervasive understanding of other persons and their intentional actions (i.e., social cognition in general) that is available to children by the time language acquisition begins" (p. 123).

Ironically, one of the best examples to illustrate the role of joint attention and theory of mind in social communication comes from observing a child in which these skills are lacking. Several years ago Diane Twachtman-Cullen was consulting on behalf of a 4-year-old preschool child with high-functioning autism.[1] Michael had been receiving discrete trial therapy since the age of 3. Hence, he not only had lots of words in his lexicon but also had developed an obsessive interest in them. Indeed, Michael's favorite pastime in his preschool classroom was writing, saying, and reading words. His vocabulary development, from the perspective of both number and sophistication of words, was well beyond that of typically developing preschool children. Even so, Michael rarely used his words to communicate his wants and needs. Being a self-sufficient little boy, if he wanted something on a high shelf, he would simply drag a chair to where it was and obtain it himself. As impressive as his problem-solving skills were from the perspective of independent functioning, they were a red flag regarding Michael's social-language development.

---

[1]The identifying features of this case have been changed to preserve the anonymity of the individual involved.

To gain more information regarding Michael's ability to exercise basic pragmatic functions such as obtaining attention or requesting, I (Diane Twachtman-Cullen) instructed his teacher to place a preferred item—a tub of plastic letters—on a high shelf while Michael watched. Predictably, on seeing the letters, Michael dragged a chair over to the shelf so that he could climb onto it and obtain the tub of letters. As I had also previously instructed, his teacher stopped him from getting on the chair saying, "I'll get you what you want, Michael." The child ignored her and walked away, only to return a short time later to stare at the tub of letters. He made no attempt to get his teacher's attention, and repeated prompts by her seemed only to increase his anxiety. He would look up at the letters, pace, and then look up at them again. A few times, he would point to the object while staring at it intently, never checking to see whether anyone else was looking in his direction. After several minutes of this behavior, Michael seemed to give up, and walked across the room dejectedly.

What happened next was the equivalent of a pragmatic "aha" experience: Michael had not given up his quest for the plastic letters at all. On the contrary, he went to the easel, picked up a marker and—outside of our visual range—wrote the word *HELP*. Clearly, Michael not only had the concept of what he needed in mind but he also had the word to express it. What was missing, however, was the shared awareness—joint attention—and theory of mind knowledge that would have enabled him to recognize and act on his teacher's "need to know" his specific intent. Moreover, although Michael did point to the desired object, unlike the protodeclarative point to direct attention cited earlier, he used a *protoimperative* point as an instrumental, self-referenced strategy to obtain something for himself. There was neither eye gaze alternation nor "checking back" behavior to determine his teacher's attentional focus. Indeed, what underscores the profound importance of the role played by joint attention and theory of mind in communication is the stark contrast between Michael's lack of intentionality (joint attention and theory of mind knowledge) and his linguistic sophistication. To wit, he did not write the word *letters* but instead used the more abstract and interactive term *help*.

To summarize, this example illustrates how the lack of joint attention and theory of mind knowledge adversely affects the child's ability to communicate his intents even when he has the vocabulary to do so. In addition, Michael's behavior offers a priori evidence that notwithstanding a sophisticated lexicon, he did not understand the basic idea of communication—that it requires not only a sender (Michael) but also a receiver (his teacher)—both of whom must share awareness of the other's attentional focus for it to occur. With this in mind, the question is, How important is the number of words in a child's lexicon—or their level of sophistication—if he or she is unable to use those words as "the symbolic currency for the exchange of meaning" (Sacks, 1989, p. 39)?

Nonverbal Aspects of Communication

It is important to underscore the difference between gestures that are used for instrumental purposes and social gestures that are, by nature, interactive. The former are used for behavior regulation—for example, Michael's pointing to the object as an end in itself, without checking to see whether his teacher shared his focus of attention. These gestures are often within the behavioral repertoire of children and adolescents with ASD (Wetherby, 1986). Social *gestures*, however, are those that involve others, such as using pointing to simply engage with another. For example, if a child points to an elephant at the circus, alternating her gaze between the animal and another person, it is assumed that she is doing so to share her focus of interest, not as a request for the elephant (Kasari et al., 2012). Affect sharing and accompanying facial expressions during such interactions are nonverbal aspects of joint attention.

Research has found that children with ASD have difficulty with both the comprehension and use of nonverbal signals (i.e., gestures, eye gaze, and facial expressions; Mundy et al., 1986). Indeed, lack of gesture use has been identified as a defining symptom of ASD in young children (Camaioni, Perucchini, Muratori, & Milone, 1997). Concomitant with the paucity of gesture use by children with ASD is their difficulty in "reading" gestures and facial expressions, a skill that is crucial to inferring the internal mental states of others and responding appropriately.

Pioneering research into eye gaze patterns offers clues to possible underlying causes for the difficulties in understanding and using gestures. Klin and Jones (2008) used eye-tracking equipment to review preferential viewing patterns in a 15-month-old infant, who would later receive a confirmatory diagnosis of autism, and two matched control participants. Eye gaze patterns for the child with autism revealed a strong preference for physical as opposed to social contingency. This pattern was reversed in the control subjects. In another eye-tracking experiment designed to determine fixation patterns with respect to people, Klin and Jones reported the following: "As predicted, the infant with autism showed viewing preference for the mouth region rather than the eye region of the face" (p. 43). The eye region is the area most associated with social cues, whereas the mouth region is thought to reflect physical contingency. These results are consistent with earlier findings that examined the viewing patterns of older individuals with autism (Klin, Jones, Schultz, Volkmar, & Cohen, 2002). The deleterious effect that inattention to social cues has on overall social learning was revealed in a follow-up case control study by Jones, Carr, and Klin (2008) in which they found that "the lack of preferential attention to the eyes actually had predictive value for the level of social impairment in two-year-olds with autism" (Twachtman-Cullen, 2010, p. 47).

The findings of these research studies, and others demonstrating the difficulty that children with autism have in orienting to social versus nonsocial stimuli (Leekam, López, & Moore, 2000), have far-reaching implications for social learning. They also offer a plausible explanation for the lack of interest in and attention to gestures and other nonverbal cues that individuals with ASD manifest. Moreover, the preference for physical contingency driving the atypical viewing patterns would likely also interfere with the child's interest and engagement in socially motivated joint attention interactions, thus disrupting the "social fit" between adult and child that drives social-language learning.

In addition to limited gesture use, children with ASD also have difficulty coordinating verbal and nonverbal means of communication to effectively communicate their messages (Wetherby et al., 2004). Thus, comprehensive assessment of social-language skills in children and adolescents with ASD must include both verbal and nonverbal means of communication regardless of the child's level of linguistic skill development.

THE INTERRELATED PROCESSES OF CONCEPT DEVELOPMENT AND WORD LEARNING

Concept development and word learning are two critical components of an interrelated process because, according to Bloom (2000), the concept (mental representation) is the word's meaning. Clearly, one cannot learn a word without forming the concept, because true word learning—which implies understanding and use of the word—requires comprehension of its associated concept (meaning; Bloom, 2000). That said, there are important differences regarding concept development in individuals with ASD that have implications for word learning.

Minshew, Meyer, and Goldstein (2002) found that in individuals with autism there is "a dissociation between concept formation and concept identification" (p. 333), such that these individuals have greater difficulty with the former higher order skill than with the latter lower level task. This finding likely reflects the greater strengths in procedural knowledge (underlying concept identification) and the weaknesses in declarative knowledge (underlying concept formation) that are found in individuals with autism (Minshew, Goldstein, & Siegel, 1995; Minshew, Goldstein, Taylor, & Siegel, 1994). Taken together, these findings help to explain the oft-cited observation that an individual with autism has or knows lots of words—and can identify them in discrete trials—but does not use them to communicate wants and needs. Could it be that he or she has not formed the concept but has only learned to identify the word? To illustrate, a child may be able to identify (point to) a picture of a modem across several trials. (He may even be able to recite the label *modem* when shown a picture.) Notwithstanding, lacking the concept (meaning) of what a modem is, he will not be able to use the word in a meaningful way. That brings us to the subject of how words are learned.

The social–pragmatic view of word learning holds that words are learned in the context of social interactions and, further, that intention reading—afforded by joint attention and theory of mind knowledge—is an integral part of the process (Tomasello, 2001). Indeed, Tomasello (2001) stated,

> The prototypical case of word learning is assumed to be the learning of an object label in an ostensive context: an adult intends that a child learn a word and so "shows" her its referent (e.g., by holding up or pointing) in temporal contiguity with the utterance. . . . I argue that learning new words is dependent on young children's ability to perceive and comprehend adult intentions, and they do this using a wide array of social-pragmatic cues. (p. 114)

Tomasello (2001) went on to cite verbs as "prototypical" of words that are learned through social interaction as opposed to within ostensive naming contexts. Indeed, research has demonstrated that children learn verbs more easily when they are used immediately prior to an event rather than when they are used in conjunction with an ongoing event (Bloom, 2000; Tomasello & Kruger, 1992). Interestingly, this normative process is often reversed with respect to children and adolescents with ASD. For example, where an adult might say to a typical child, "Give the toy to Sally," it is common to hear an adult say to a child with ASD, "Good job giving the toy to Sally."

Another important consideration in word learning is that not all words are "created equal" in terms of when and how they are acquired: Nouns are acquired before adjectives and verbs (Bates & Goodman, 2001). The manner in which different classes of words are acquired also differs based on the nature of each. For example, many nouns can be learned in ostensive (clear or explicit) contexts because they typically refer to whole objects (e.g., cup, shoe). Verbs and adjectives, however, are typically learned in nonostensive (vague or ambiguous) contexts according to the nature of each (Tomasello, 1992; Tomasello & Kruger, 1992). Specifically, verbs are experience based and hence not easily represented in pictures. Moreover, when pictures are used to depict verbs, the child is required to zero in on a small aspect of the whole—for example, an arm throwing—to understand the portion that captures the action. Given the difficulties that individuals with ASD have in determining relevance, there is no guarantee that they will be able to make the appropriate connection between the action depicted and the verb *throw*. Adjectives can be both transient and relative (e.g., what is big in one context may be small in another), making them a "moving target" in static picture formats. In our experience, these factors are rarely considered in vocabulary selection.

Bloom (2000) offered an excellent, research-based summary regarding the processes at work in word learning that put it squarely in the social–pragmatic "camp":

> Children's word learning actually draws extensively on their understanding of the thoughts of others—on their theory of mind. Theory of mind underlies how children learn the entities to which words refer, intuit how words relate to one another, and understand how words can serve as communicative signs. (p. 56)

Children with ASD, then, may actually "prove the rule," meaning that their difficulties with social cognition likely lead to the types of intention-reading deficits they manifest. This is not to say that the language-learning rules do not apply but rather that experiences that drive meaning and lead to joint attention and intention-reading need to be "titrated" to fit the complex learning needs of children and adolescents with ASD.

THREE INTERRELATED ASPECTS OF PRAGMATICS

Before discussing social–pragmatic assessment issues and guidelines for intervention, it is important to first consider the three features of pragmatics that govern language development. The first and best known of these concerns the purposes or functions of communication—that is, "the use of speech acts to express intentionality in order to accomplish a given purpose (i.e., function)" (Twachtman-Cullen, 2000, p. 229). The second feature of pragmatics concerns the ability to make social judgments about the communication partner's needs, and the third one relates to the rules of discourse by which speakers (co)operate. Each of these is discussed in greater detail next.

Pragmatic Functions of Communication

The pragmatic functions of communication vary in their levels of complexity. For the most part, the basic-level functions, many of which serve instrumental purposes, are typically unimpaired in more able children and adolescents. These functions include, but are not limited to, requesting, protesting (i.e., rejecting or saying *no*), giving basic information, and/or answering simple questions. Higher level functions, however, require greater social understanding and, as such, pose greater difficulty for all children and adolescents on the spectrum, even those without intellectual impairment. These include, but are not limited to, the more social functions of obtaining attention, commenting or complimenting, opining, negotiating, and using irony or sarcasm. The ability to use these functions of communication—and to understand the intentions of others when they use them—requires not only a working knowledge of the social world (amassed through experience) but also an evolving understanding of the mental states (thoughts, feelings, and intentions) of the communicative partner.

Less able children and adolescents with ASD often have considerable difficulty with even basic-level pragmatic functions. As a result, they may use aberrant behavior instead of appropriate means to express them. For example, a child who is unable to request a desired food item appropriately (through words, pointing, picture card, or other symbol) may simply take the item off the plate of another child. This is sometimes referred to as *stealing*, a characterization that belies the lack of understanding of the pragmatic communication deficit underlying the act—the inability to appropriately request the item through symbolic means. Likewise, children and adolescents who are unable to protest appropriately by saying or in some way indicating *no* may push items off the table or drop to the floor to opt out. When such behavior is viewed separate and apart from its intent—as the means by which to reject something in the absence of more appropriate means—it is often judged as a willful act of noncompliance rather than as a red flag signaling pragmatic impairment. The result of this mischaracterization is to treat the symptom (pushing food off the table or dropping to the floor) without regard to its cause (the inability to appropriately exercise the pragmatic function of protesting). When this occurs, the inappropriate behavior is perpetuated (or escalated), and the pragmatic impairment goes untreated.

Presuppositions

A second area of pragmatics is an intention-reading "minefield" for even more able verbal individuals with ASD (Twachtman-Cullen, 1998) because it requires that they make *presuppositions* (social judgments) about their communication partners' listening needs (Bates, 1976). Broadly conceived, these judgments enable speakers to tailor their messages to suit the situation and audience, and they involve both verbal (vocabulary selection) and nonverbal (gestures, facial expressions, tone of voice, etc.) elements. Presuppositions are heavily rooted in theory of mind knowledge because making appropriate social judgments requires an understanding that the contents of other people's minds not only differ from one's own but also that it must be taken into account in determining what to say and how to say it.

To make the presuppositions that inform message content, the speaker must make inferences about the information their communication partners already have in order to determine the specific input they need to understand the message. The information gleaned from these inferences is then used to make adjustments in the content of messages. Although neurotypical speakers make these judgments and consequent adjustments effortlessly and in real time, this area of pragmatics is fraught with difficulty for individuals with ASD.

Children and adolescents with ASD evidence presuppositional difficulty in many different ways. For example, in the absence of an understanding of the informational needs of the communication partner, they might start a conversation "in the middle" without providing sufficient background information to ground the listener in the subject. In addition, they are often redundant, failing to appreciate what the listener already knows. They also have difficulty adding new information germane to the topic to extend the conversation appropriately.

The use of metaphorical language (i.e., using an utterance that holds a private, idiosyncratic meaning for the speaker) by individuals with ASD offers a priori evidence that they are not only unaware that their listeners do not share their informational base but they are also unknowledgeable regarding its importance. For example, a child with ASD who had been given a cookie at the mall a week ago as her mother said, "There you go," may use that same phrase to request a cookie weeks later, unmindful that her mother does not share her frame of reference and thus would be unable to understand the message's intent.

Presuppositional knowledge also enables neurotypical speakers to adjust the form, content, and delivery style of their messages to suit the specific person or persons for whom they are intended. For example, they would use a different style of speech when speaking to a stranger than to a family member. Similarly, presuppositional knowledge enables neurotypical speakers to adjust their messages to suit the situational context. Hence, one would use a different style of speech and more informal language at a sports event than in a hospital waiting room or at a formal dinner. Individuals with ASD do not typically make these adjustments in the form, style, or content of their messages, given the social–cognitive decision making required. Indeed, problems with presuppositional information—rooted as they are in theory of mind knowledge—are likely at the heart of the untoward comments that individuals with ASD sometimes make. Consider, for example, the adolescent who on receiving a tie for his birthday says, "That's the ugliest tie I ever saw." We would argue that this remark is not rooted in rudeness, as is often thought to be the case, but rather reflects a lack of knowledge regarding the mental states (and sensibilities) of others.

Rules of Conversational Discourse

The third area of pragmatics is one that has relevance for children and adolescents with ASD who are at a discourse or conversational level in language development. It is discussed only briefly here so that its implications for assessment and intervention can be understood in later sections of this chapter. Like presuppositions, the four conversational maxims or rules that govern discourse—quantity, quality, relevance, and clarity (Grice, 1975)—are heavily rooted in theory of mind knowledge, because to abide by these rules, speakers must have knowledge of the mental states of their communication partners. Moreover, the ability to engage in reciprocal conversational exchanges requires an "instinctive" understanding of the rules by which speakers cooperate in discourse. This is no easy task because these rules are unwritten, unconsciously applied, and largely unrecognized—unless something goes awry.

For example, conversational partners may not be aware of the rule governing the *quantity* of information—the rule to say just the right amount to get the message across—unless one of the speakers is overly verbose or gives too little information. Or they may be unaware of the rule of *quality*—the rule that governs the truth value of utterances—until they learn that the information provided bears no resemblance to reality. Violations to the rule of quality occur when the speaker lies, confabulates (gives false information that the speaker nonetheless believes to be true), or otherwise misinforms. Finally, conversational partners may be unaware of the rules of *relevance* (the need to provide information pertinent to the subject) or *clarity* (the need to make the message understandable) until the speaker violates either the former by veering off topic and making tangential comments or the latter by failing to give the information needed to promote comprehension. These conversational maxims can be used as yardsticks to determine the level of discourse competence and specific areas of weakness in verbal children and adolescents with ASD. They can also serve as springboards for need-based intervention.

ASSESSMENT CONSIDERATIONS

Assessing the social-communication skills of children and adolescents with ASD can be challenging. For one thing, formal tests may be beyond the capabilities of children with ASD who also have intellectual impairments. For another, youngsters with ASD may not readily comply with the demands and inflexibility of formal testing. It should also be noted that formal test instruments are unable to fully capture the dynamic, functional, and interactive nature of communication. Acknowledging this, Booth (2012) stated that, notwithstanding the availability of some standardized measures, "assessment of pragmatic language and social communication requires a skilled clinician who recognizes the need for direct, unstructured interaction with the client" (p. 47). Ironically, formal tests for more able children and adolescents may actually yield false positive results. Specifically, these youngsters may be able to score well on tests that require them to explain aspects of pragmatics even though they are unable to apply that knowledge in real-world situations. Taking all of these factors into consideration, assessment of the social-communication impairments in children with ASD requires a combination of procedures involving careful observation, information gathering, and both formal and informal evaluation.

Determining What to Assess

Throughout this chapter we have chosen to focus on pragmatic impairment. We have argued that the nature and type of pragmatic difficulty seen in ASD are direct results of the weaknesses in joint attention and theory of mind knowledge that are at the heart of intention reading and which help to inform concept development, word learning, and discourse. Hence, the main focus of assessment in this section is on the social–pragmatic areas of need discussed in this chapter. We leave to others the discussion of ways to evaluate language form (syntax and grammar) and content (semantics).

Information Gathering

A clinical interview of the child's parents and relevant school personnel is an essential part of any assessment process. The interview becomes even more important, however, for youngsters with ASD, given the oft-reported inconsistency in skill use across settings. If the examiner is not able to directly speak to parents, information from these important caregivers can be obtained through a written questionnaire. The interview or questionnaire should target information regarding how the child communicates basic wants and needs, the extent to which the child initiates communication, the degree and type of prompting required, and the different means of communication available to the child. It is also important to obtain information regarding the presence of joint attention behaviors such as eye gaze alternation and pointing or giving to share interest and attention.

Another useful means of information gathering is direct observation of the child in natural settings (e.g., classroom, lunch room, at home, if possible). The information gleaned from observation may illuminate differences in communication patterns across settings and in the circumstances under which the individual initiates joint attention and communication. The observer may also obtain useful information regarding the consistency of skill use and the level of prompting used by adults. Observation periods need not be lengthy, but they should be scheduled at the times and in the settings in which the child or adolescent has opportunities to use his or her communication skills.

Assessment of Pragmatic Functions and Elements of Discourse

Informal assessment of the child's comprehension and use of the pragmatic functions of communication can occur in motivating joint action routines—for example, using bubbles, playing with a cause–effect toy, or in a gross motor activity—structured to elicit functional communication such as obtaining attention, requesting, answering, and commenting. If greater structure is desired, the Autism Diagnostic Observation Schedule, Second Edition (ADOS–2; Lord, Lyuster, Gotham, & Guthrie, 2012; Lord, Rutter, et al., 2012) can also be used to assess the child's use of communicative functions; this instrument contains not only a variety of motivating materials and activities useful for this purpose but also guidelines for the systematic observation and coding of skills. Although designed specifically to diagnose ASD, the ADOS–2 can also be used to measure gesture use, conversational elements, quality of social overtures, and other functional, social-communication skills. When the ADOS–2 is used for this purpose, selected tasks can be given and assessed informally.

The ADOS–2 also provides an excellent vehicle for assessing progress in specific skill areas over time, because there are no restrictions on the frequency of administration. Although training is needed for an individual to become proficient with the ADOS–2, more and more school districts are investing in this instrument and training packages. Finally, although the ADOS–2 can be administered to children and adults of all ages and functioning levels, Jennifer Twachtman-Bassett has found it to be particularly useful for assessment of communication skills in less able children with ASD.

As discussed earlier, the conversational maxims can be used to judge the extent to which verbal children and adolescents abide by the rules of discourse in their conversational interactions. Hence, clinicians should determine whether individuals with ASD violate the rule of quantity by giving too much information—perhaps by speaking nonstop on a subject of interest—or too little information by failing to extend the conversation or take conversational turns. They should also assess the quality of messages to determine whether they contain confabulatory information perhaps secondary to obsessive interests. In addition, clinicians should also obtain information on the individual's grasp of relevance by observing the degree to which he or she is able to stick to the topic under discussion without veering off on a tangent.

Last, the clarity of messages should be assessed to determine the extent to which they are understandable to conversational partners.

To summarize, obtaining pragmatic communication samples across a variety of situations and conversational partners can yield valuable information regarding violations to discourse rules that can be used to inform intervention. Moreover, these language samples can also reveal important information regarding the individual's grasp of presuppositional and other theory of mind knowledge.

Formal Assessment Instruments

Notwithstanding the cautionary note regarding the use of formal instruments sounded earlier, there are some recently developed formal tests that do capture some of the higher level pragmatic impairments in more able children with ASD. When used in conjunction with informal procedures, they can yield important information. Jennifer Twachtman-Bassett has found both the elementary and adolescent versions of the Social Language Development Test (SLDT; Bowers, Huisingh, & LoGiudice, 2008, 2010) useful for assessing aspects of theory of mind and the individual's ability to read nonverbal cues. Indeed, her extensive use of the SLDT (both with children with and without autism) has revealed the subtests on which children with ASD consistently perform poorly. The first of these is the Making Inferences subtest. Here, the child is shown a picture and asked, "Pretend you are this person, what are you thinking?" The child is then asked to state the specific visual cues (e.g., facial expression, gestures) of the person in the picture that led to his or her inference. The Interpersonal Negotiation and Problem-Solving subtests on the elementary and adolescent versions of the SLDT, respectively, are also consistent in revealing impaired performance in children with ASD. In both subtests, the individual is presented with a picture depicting a socially based problem that involves a conflict between two peers. In each case, the individual is required to explain how he or she would solve the problem in a manner that reflects an appreciation of the perspectives of both peers in the picture.

To summarize, assessing the social-communication difficulties in children and adolescents with ASD is a complex process that requires attention to many aspects of pragmatic functioning. Although there are other instruments available that tap into this area of functioning, space constraints do not permit their inclusion here. The important thing to keep in mind is that language *in use* cannot easily be tapped by static tests of language development. Hence, formal testing should always be supplemented by observation, case history information, and informal procedures. Standardized measures of language development are reviewed in Chapter 3.

GUIDELINES FOR INTERVENTION

Although it is beyond the scope of this chapter to provide detailed information regarding specific intervention programs, we do offer a general plan for "constructing" social communication skills, as seen in Figure 5.2, as well as guidelines for intervention that are applicable to children and adolescents with ASD across functioning levels. Evidence-based intervention strategies and program models are discussed in Chapter 7.

Our intention in using the house illustration is to underscore that intervention for social-language learning should mirror the normative process of language development, particularly because, as noted earlier, research has shown that the principles governing social-language learning apply to both typically developing children and those with ASD. Hence, as Figure 5.2 indicates, language intervention should be "rooted" in contextually based experiences that help to fuel meaning. Furthermore, work on concept building and word learning, sentence development, and discourse must not only rest on a solid foundation of joint attention and intention-reading but must also follow one upon the other, just as the second floor and attic are built on top of the first floor in a house.

The schematic of the house to symbolize social-language intervention also enables one to understand what can happen when treatment approaches ignore developmental principles. Consider again the case of Michael discussed

Figure 5.2. A general plan for "constructing" social communication skills. The figure depicts the key elements in the social-language learning process and the centrality of context.

earlier. Michael's language intervention program did not begin with the foundational skill of joint attention but rather with the "first floor" language target of words. That left Michael not only unable to use the words in his lexicon but also unable to move up the symbolic "ladder," given the absence of the foundational skill of joint attention from which intentionality emerges.

Unfortunately, Michael's situation is not unique. The prodigious use of echolalia by many children with ASD often blinds interventionists to their weaknesses in comprehension. If verbal output alone is viewed as representative of overall social-language development, clinicians may be tempted to begin language intervention at the sentence or discourse level. This is the intervention equivalent of beginning house construction with the second floor or attic, an effort less productive than building a "house of cards." The message, then, is to begin social-language intervention where the learner is (Twachtman-Cullen, 2008). With these cautionary notes in mind, the following intervention guidelines are offered:

- *Provide contextually based activities.* Although one-to-one advance priming can be helpful in some cases, intervention activities should be embedded in a context that helps to support meaning. Out-of-context drills may create "skills" in the short term; however, application of those skills in a different, real-world context is often problematic (Kasari et al., 2012; Minshew et al., 2002).

- *Actively engage the individual.* Provide motivating activities to actively engage the child or adolescent in the intervention process, because according to Schwartz and Begley (2002), "only an attending brain" (p. 224) can derive benefit from experiences. Over the years, we have observed many children with ASD "going through the motions" as intervention is "applied" irrespective of their attentional focus. Bloom (2000) distinguished between input and intake when he stated, "It is not how often the adult says the word that matters; it is how often the child processes it" (p. 90). If meaningful learning is to occur, the child must be actively engaged.

- *Adhere to word-learning constraints.* Because different classes of words (nouns vs. verbs vs. adjectives) are learned in different ways, intervention efforts should be tailored to the ways in which words are learned. For example, teaching verbs in a Simon Says format, play routine, or other action-oriented milieu designed for adolescents makes far more sense than having youngsters identify verbs in a static naming task.

- *Build in generalization.* Because the generalization of skills across activities, settings, and people is especially problematic for individuals with ASD, interventionists should build in generalization early on in the intervention program. This can be done by embedding language-learning targets in meaningful activities, training others to also provide intervention activities, and providing a variety of contexts in which intervention targets can be used. For example, if the child or adolescent is working on the pragmatic functions of communication or the rules of discourse, he or she should have opportunities to use language targets across activities (e.g., in a snack routine, at lunch, during physical education), people (e.g., the speech-language pathologist, classroom teacher, office assistant), and settings (e.g., classroom, lunch, recess).

It is our contention that pragmatically based communication deficits require pragmatically based intervention. These guidelines are designed to help clinicians create a social-language learning milieu that will support meaning and provide rich opportunities for language use.

REFERENCES

Bates, E. (1976). *Language and context.* New York, NY: Academic Press.

Bates, E., Camaioni, L., & Volterra, V. (1975). The acquisition of performatives prior to speech. *Merrill-Palmer Quarterly, 21,* 205–226.

Bates, E., & Goodman, J. C. (2001). On the inseparability of grammar and the lexicon: Evidence from acquisition. In M. Tomasello & E. Bates (Eds.), *Language development: The essential readings* (pp. 134–162). Oxford, England: Blackwell.

Bell, M. A., & Fox, N. A. (1994). Brain development over the first year of life: Relations between EEG frequency and coherence and cognition and affective behaviors. In G. Dawson & K. Fischer (Eds.), *Human behavior and the developing brain* (pp. 314–345). New York, NY: Guilford Press.

Bloom, P. (2000). *How children learn the meanings of words.* Cambridge, MA: MIT Press.

Booth, L. (2012). Speech, language, and communication assessment. In C. A. Saulnier & P. E. Ventola (Eds.), *Essentials of autism spectrum disorders evaluation and assessment* (pp. 39–58). Hoboken, NJ: Wiley.

Bowers, L., Huisingh, R., & LoGiudice, C. (2008). *Social Language Development Test—Elementary (SLDT–E).* East Moline, IL: LinguiSystems.

Bowers, L., Huisingh, R., & LoGiudice, C. (2010). *Social Language Development Test—Adolescent (SLDT–A).* East Moline, IL: LinguiSystems.

Camaioni, L., Perucchini, P., Muratori, F., & Milone, A. (1997). Brief report: A longitudinal examination of the communicative gestures deficit in young children with autism. *Journal of Autism and Developmental Disorders, 27*, 715–725. doi:10.1023/A:1025858917000

DeLaguna, G. A. (1963). *Speech: Its function and development*. Bloomington, IN: Indiana University Press. (Originally published in 1927)

Greenough, W. T., & Black, J. E. (1992). Induction of brain structure by experience: Substrates for cognitive development. *Developmental Behavioral Neuroscience, 24*, 155–200.

Grice, H. (1975). Logic and conversation. In D. Davidson & G. Harmon (Eds.), *The logic of grammar* (pp. 41–58). Encino, CA: Dickinson.

Happé, F. G. E. (1996). *Autism: An introduction to psychological theory*. Cambridge, MA: Harvard University Press.

Hobson, R. P. (2005). What puts the jointness into joint attention? In N. Eilan, C. Hoerl, T. McCormack, & J. Roessler (Eds.), *Joint attention: Communication and other minds: Issues in philosophy and psychology* (pp. 185–204). New York, NY: Oxford University Press. doi:10.1093/acprof:oso/9780199245635.003.0009

Jones, W., Carr, K., & Klin, A. (2008). Absence of preferential looking to the eyes of approaching adults predicts level of social disability in 2-year-old toddlers with autism spectrum disorder. *Archives of General Psychiatry, 65*, 946–954. doi:10.1001/archpsyc.65.8.946

Kasari, C., Fannin, D. K., & Goods, K. S. (2012). Joint attention intervention for children with autism. In P. A. Prelock & R. J. McCauley (Eds.), *Treatment of autism spectrum disorders: Evidence-based intervention strategies for communication and social interactions* (pp. 139–161). Baltimore, MD: Brookes. doi:10.1016/j.jaac.2012.02.019

Klin, A., & Jones, W. (2008). Altered face scanning and impaired recognition of biological motion in a 15-month-old infant with autism. *Developmental Science, 11*, 40–46. doi:10.1111/j.1467-7687.2007.00608.x

Klin, A., Jones, W., Schultz, R., Volkmar, F., & Cohen, D. (2002). Visual fixation patterns during viewing of naturalistic social situations as predictors of social competence in individuals with autism. *Archives of General Psychiatry, 59*, 809–816. doi:10.1001/archpsyc.59.9.809

Landa, R., Holman, K., Sullivan, M., & Cleary, J. (2005). Language and social change in toddlers with ASD: Early intervention [Abstract]. *Proceedings of the International Meeting For Autism Research, 87*.

Leekam, S. R. (1993). Children's understanding of mind. In M. Bennett (Ed.), *The development of social cognition: The child as psychologist* (pp. 26–61). New York, NY: Guilford Press.

Leekam, S. R., López, B., & Moore, C. (2000). Attention and joint attention in preschool children with autism. *Developmental Psychology, 36*, 261–273. doi:10.1037/0012-1649.36.2.261

Leekam, S. R., & Ramsden, C. A. H. (2006). Dyadic orienting and joint attention in preschool children with autism. *Journal of Autism and Developmental Disorders*, *36*, 185–197. doi:10.1007/s10803-005-0054-1

Lewy, A. L., & Dawson, G. (1992). Social stimulation and joint attention in young autistic children. *Journal of Abnormal Child Psychology*, *20*, 555–566. doi:10.1007/BF00911240

Lord, C., Lyuster, R. J., Gotham, K., & Guthrie, W. (2012). *Autism Diagnostic Observation Schedule, Second Edition (ADOS–2) manual (Part II): Toddler Module*. Torrance, CA: Western Psychological Services.

Lord, C., Rutter, M., DiLavore, P. C., Risi, S., Gotham, K., & Bishop, S. L. (2012). *Autism Diagnostic Observation Schedule, Second Edition (ADOS–2) manual (Part I): Modules 1–4*. Torrance, CA: Western Psychological Services.

Minshew, N. J., Goldstein, G., & Siegel, D. J. (1995). Speech and language in high-functioning autistic individuals. *Neuropsychology*, *9*, 255–261. doi:10.1037/0894-4105.9.2.255

Minshew, N. J., Goldstein, G., Taylor, H. G., & Siegel, D. J. (1994). Academic achievement in high functioning autistic individuals. *Journal of Clinical and Experimental Neuropsychology*, *16*, 261–270. doi:10.1080/01688639408402637

Minshew, N. J., Meyer, J., & Goldstein, G. (2002). Abstract reasoning in autism: A dissociation between concept formation and concept identification. *Neuropsychology*, *16*, 327–334. doi:10.1037/0894-4105.16.3.327

Mundy, P., Sigman, M., Ungerer, J., & Sherman, T. (1986). Defining the social deficits of autism: The contribution of nonverbal communication measures. *The Journal of Child Psychology and Psychiatry*, *27*, 657–669. doi:10.1111/j.1469-7610.1986.tb00190.x

Sacks, O. (1989). *Seeing voices: A journey into the world of the deaf*. Berkeley, CA: University of California.

Schwartz, J. M., & Begley, S. (2002). *The mind and the brain: Neuroplasticity and the power of mental force*. New York, NY: Regan Books.

Siller, M., & Sigman, M. (2002). The behaviors of parents of children with autism predict the subsequent development of their children's communication skills. *Journal of Autism and Developmental Disorders*, *32*, 77–89. doi:10.1023/A:1014884404276

Tomasello, M. (1992). *First verbs: A case study of early grammatical development*. New York, NY: Cambridge University Press. doi:10.1017/CBO9780511527678

Tomasello, M. (2001). Perceiving intentions and learning words in the second year of life. In M. Tomasello & E. Bates (Eds.), *Language development: The essential readings* (pp. 132–158). Oxford, England: Blackwell. doi:10.1017/CBO9780511620669.007

Tomasello, M. (2003). *Constructing a language: A usage-based theory of language acquisition*. Cambridge, MA: Harvard University Press.

Tomasello, M., & Farrar, M. J. (1986). Joint attention and early language. *Child Development*, *57*, 1454–1463. doi:10.2307/1130423

Tomasello, M., & Kruger, A. (1992). Joint attention on actions: Acquiring verbs in ostensive and non-ostensive contexts. *Journal of Child Language, 19,* 311–333. doi:10.1017/S0305000900011430

Tomasello, M., & Todd, J. (1983). Joint attention and lexical acquisition style. *First Language, 4,* 197–211. doi:10.1177/014272378300401202

Twachtman-Cullen, D. (1998). Language and communication in high-functioning autism and Asperger syndrome. In E. Schopler, G. B. Mesibov, & L. J. Kunce (Eds.), *Asperger syndrome or high-functioning autism?* (pp. 199–225). New York, NY: Plenum Press. doi:10.1007/978-1-4615-5369-4_10

Twachtman-Cullen, D. (2000). More able children with autism spectrum disorders: Sociocommunicative challenges and guidelines for enhancing abilities. In A. M. Wetherby & B. M. Prizant (Eds.), *Autism spectrum disorders: A transactional developmental perspective* (pp. 225–249). Baltimore, MD: Brookes.

Twachtman-Cullen, D. (2008). Symbolic communication: Common pathways and points of departure. In K. D. Buron & P. Wolfberg (Eds.), *Educating learners on the autism spectrum: Preparing highly qualified educators* (pp. 88–113). Shawnee Mission, KS: AAPC.

Twachtman-Cullen, D. (Spring 2010). Pioneering research into abnormalities of social engagement. *Autism Spectrum Quarterly.* Higganum, CT: Starfish Specialty Press.

Twachtman-Cullen, D., & Twachtman-Reilly, J. (2007). Communication and language issues in less able school-age children with autism. In R. L. Gabriels & D. E. Hill (Eds.), *Growing up with autism: Working with school-age children and adolescents* (pp. 73–94). New York, NY: Guilford Press.

Wetherby, A. M. (1986). Ontogeny of communicative functions in autism. *Journal of Autism and Developmental Disorders, 16,* 295–316. doi:10.1007/BF01531661

Wetherby, A. M., Woods, J., Allen, L., Cleary, J., Dickinson, H., & Lord, C. (2004). Early indicators of autism spectrum disorders in the second year of life. *Journal of Autism and Developmental Disorders, 34,* 473–493. doi:10.1007/s10803-004-2544-y

Williams, J. H. G., Waiter, G. D., Perra, O., Perrett, D. I., & Whiten, A. (2005). An fMRI study of joint attention experience. *NeuroImage, 25,* 133–140. doi:10.1016/j.neuroimage.2004.10.047

6

CO-OCCURRING EMOTIONAL AND BEHAVIOR PROBLEMS

KARLA J. DOEPKE, BREA M. BANKS, JENNIFER F. MAYS,
LAURYN M. TOBY, AND STEVEN LANDAU

Children with autism spectrum disorder (ASD) frequently have co-occurring psychiatric conditions, with estimates as high as 70% to 84% (Leyfer et al., 2006; Simonoff et al., 2008). Psychiatric disorders are not only common in this population but they are also frequently multiple, with 30% to 40% of these children meeting criteria for more than two disorders (Leyfer et al., 2006; Matson & Nebel-Schwalm, 2007; Simonoff et al., 2008). Among these, the most common diagnoses are anxiety disorders, attention-deficit/hyperactivity disorder (ADHD), and disruptive behavior disorders, with rates significantly higher than would be expected from the general child population. Other co-occurring conditions that present with higher base rates than expected by chance alone include obsessive–compulsive disorder and depressive disorders.

This work was supported in part by a grant from The Autism Program of Illinois awarded to Karla J. Doepke.

http://dx.doi.org/10.1037/14338-007
Autism Spectrum Disorder in Children and Adolescents: Evidence-Based Assessment and Intervention in Schools, L. A. Wilkinson (Editor)

Despite the complexity of the diagnostic picture, teachers and school support personnel are called on to provide evidence-based treatment (EBT) to these children. This chapter provides a strategy for considering the various explanations for co-occurrence of the more prevalent comorbid disorders, highlighting potential moderators that may affect treatment and integrating evidence-based interventions used successfully with children with ADHD, disruptive behavior disorders, anxiety, and depression into practical strategies for treating children with ASD and the co-occurring disorders. Specifically, general diagnostic and assessment considerations are discussed. For each disorder, the unique symptom picture is described, highlighting distinctive risk factors while taking into account both qualitative and quantitative distinctions of symptomatology. Practical strategies for multidimensional assessment of these disorders in the school-age population are suggested.

Following this, a general framework is proposed for integrating strategies that are successful in working with children with ASD with what we currently know regarding EBTs for the co-occurring conditions. A brief review of EBTs for children diagnosed with the comorbid disorders is presented, and examples that use school-based strategies translated from treatment research vis-à-vis the unique learning styles of children with ASD are provided. Implications for the incorporation of others (e.g., physicians, families) to improve treatment outcomes are highlighted.

The presence of co-occurring disorders in children with ASD may sometimes be obscured because the child's symptoms of autism are so salient that many professionals who work with these children and adolescents (e.g., psychologists, speech–language therapists) view additional problems as part of the child's unique typography of autism symptoms. Take, for example, the symptom of inattention. Should children with ASD who present with gaze aversion be considered severely inattentive and comorbid for the predominantly inattentive subtype of ADHD? Or perhaps children with ASD could be viewed as presenting with social phobia if their inattention presents as hypervigilance to social stimuli in the environment. In this case, correctly identifying the comorbid condition that accounts for the symptom of inattention is paramount in identifying the most efficacious treatments.

In general, accurate, reliable diagnosis of comorbid psychiatric disorders in children with ASD and understanding the unique symptoms associated with these co-occurring disorders is critical in designing effective treatments for these children. The presence of comorbid disorders may cause significant clinical impairment and, if recognized as manifestations of the presence of another psychiatric disorder rather than only isolated behaviors attributable to ASD, may lead to a more focused and more comprehensive intervention.

THEORETICAL EXPLANATIONS

Numerous theoretical explanations have been suggested for this co-occurrence phenomenon, and each is probably correct for some cases. First, as described by Caron and Rutter (1991), overlapping diagnostic criteria in the taxonomy may provide clues to the high rates of comorbidity seen in this population. Indeed, many symptoms of ASD also appear in criteria sets for other distinct disorders (e.g., failure to develop peer relationships at appropriate developmental level). The more severe the autism disorder, the more likely multiple and diverse diagnostic criteria will be satisfied.

Second, different manifestations of a particular problem could rightfully be labeled the same despite involving behaviors that have markedly different functions. For example, the hallmark behavioral indicator of oppositional defiant disorder (ODD) involves temper tantrums. Many children with ASD have tantrums; are they comorbid for ODD because of this nominally similar characteristic?

Third, one disorder may represent an early manifestation of another disorder. For example, ritualistic behaviors characteristic of ASD sometimes become more complex and routinized with age. Are these initial behaviors actually early signs of obsessive–compulsive disorder?

Fourth, two or more disorders may co-occur because they share common risk factors or an overlap of risk factors. For example, genetic links have been identified in some individuals with autism, as well as some with depression. Is it possible that for some presentations there is an underlying genetic risk factor that predisposes the individual to develop both disorders?

Fifth, the co-occurrence of disorders may be the result of one disorder causing a second disorder as its sequelae. For example, children functioning at the high end of the autism spectrum are at increased risk of the development of adolescent depression as they become more keenly aware of their interpersonal differences.

Finally, comorbid disorders may be the true syndrome, and the pure single disorders may actually be different subtypes of the more complex disorder. For example, is it possible that the predominantly inattentive subtype of ADHD combined with Asperger's syndrome is the true prototype for children who function on the high end of the spectrum (Caron & Rutter, 1991)?

Methodological research issues inherent in diagnostic investigations may also contribute to the high rates of co-occurrence of psychiatric disorders seen in this population, especially when the prevalence rates are derived from clinic samples. As Berkson's (1946) bias predicts, if fewer than all children with a particular disorder are referred, clinic samples will always show an overrepresentation of cases with comorbidity. Specifically, the likelihood of referral of children with one disorder plus another disorder will be a function of the combined likelihood of the referral rate of each disorder. Thus, data collected on clinic-referred children with ASD may indicate inflated comorbidity. Whereas current comorbidity rates are indeed high for the ASD population, the need for epidemiological studies of community samples will provide a more accurate picture of the true nature of co-occurrence in this population.

To complete the clinical picture, potential moderators of risk of co-occurrence among children with ASD should be considered. For example, the severity of the ASD may serve a moderating function, with more classic cases of ASD involving those most impaired being more likely to have co-occurring psychiatric conditions. Alternatively, these classic cases may be least likely to receive a comorbid diagnosis because their ASD symptoms are so severe they are considered the explanation for their entire range of problems.

The age of a child with ASD may also moderate the risk of comorbidity, with older children being more likely to receive additional diagnoses because of the accumulation of impaired functioning over time. Children with ASD may also traverse different developmental pathways due to the presence or absence of particular co-occurring conditions. If so, which comorbid disorders will more likely moderate the outcome for the child? Most important, to what extent do comorbidity and case complexity inform treatment selection and moderate the child's response to intervention (Kazdin & Whitley, 2006)?

OTHER PIECES OF THE INTERVENTION PUZZLE

The presence of comorbid diagnoses is only a small part of what educators and other professionals need to know to design effective interventions. Until recently, little was known about the co-occurring presence of these disorders. Treatment of the symptoms of ASD per se is rarely, if at all, successful in ameliorating the problems and areas of impairment attributable to the presence of a secondary disorder. Thus, the question becomes, will current EBTs for other disorders work equally as well for children with ASD and co-occurring disorders? Perhaps, if the etiology, developmental course, and expression of these disorders were comparable, similar treatments might be expected to be effective.

Unfortunately, it is now clear that the symptoms of children with ASD are complicated by extreme heterogeneity and individual differences in the course of their disorder (Happé, Ronald, & Plomin, 2006). Research is providing increasing evidence that the presentation of co-occurring disorders may be as unique as the expression of autism itself (Sikora, Hartley, McCoy, Gerrard-Morris, & Dill, 2008.) Neither the putative risk factors nor the symptom pictures of these comorbid disorders in children with ASD are consistent with the prototype of the disorders in children without ASD. For example, neither IQ level nor any family factors that are identified as risk factors for the development of disorders in the general population have been found to serve as risk factors for children with comorbid ASD (Hartley, Sikora, & McCoy, 2008).

Similarly, there are quantitative and qualitative distinctions in the expression of symptoms in children with ASD. Although all children diagnosed with ASD exhibit social impairments, some are interested in social interaction but are inept with peers, whereas others completely shun human interaction. Therefore, even within the ASD diagnostic category, it is unlikely that children presenting with mild social difficulties would be at risk of similar comorbid disorders as their ASD counterparts with more significant social impairments.

General Diagnostic Considerations

Reliable clinical diagnosis involves gathering information across multiple settings from a variety of sources using standardized interviews, behavioral checklists, ratings by others, self-reports, observations, and standardized assessments integrated with clinical judgment. Beginning with broadband diagnostic tools, professionals can screen for a range of symptoms and then follow up with narrow-band assessments in specific areas of concern. Further, it is essential to take a developmental perspective, considering the child's level of cognitive and adaptive functioning. Multitiered screening and a comprehensive developmental approach to assessment are described in Chapters 2 and 3 of this volume, respectively.

Although there is no current gold standard tool for diagnosing psychopathology in children with ASD, the Autism Comorbidity Interview—Present and Lifetime version (ACI–PL; Leyfer et al., 2006), based on versions of the Kiddie Schedule for Affective Disorders and Schizophrenia (Ambrosini, 2000; Chambers et al., 1985; Kaufman et al., 1997), provides a promising starting point. The *Diagnostic and Statistical Manual of Mental Disorders* (5th ed.; *DSM–5*; American Psychiatric Association, 2013) acknowledges that comorbidity is the rule rather than the exception for children with ASD, indicating that approximately 70% of individuals meet criteria for one comorbid mental disorder and 40% meet criteria for two or more disorders. In addition, the *DSM–5* indicates that comorbidity does not cluster around one specific disorder but may involve a range of conditions, including intellectual impairment, language impairment, externalizing behavior disorders, and internalizing disorders.

The ACI–PL provides for assessment of the full range of presenting symptoms for psychopathology in a child. As such, the ACI–PL includes items that refer to relevant symptoms for ASD, such as significant increases in agitation, self-injury, and temper outbursts, while it also asks detailed questions about symptoms of the disorder and their application to the child. Although useful, this scale only gathers information from parent informants, but to complete the diagnostic picture, information from others (self and teachers) is also important. Because it is relatively new, the reliability and validity of the instrument has only been assessed with high functioning children with autism.

Identifying core symptoms and their stability over time and across environments is a key consideration in diagnosis; however, in the ASD population, the diagnostic picture may still be obscure. Discriminating ASD from ADHD, anxiety disorders, and disruptive behavior disorders is particularly difficult given the overlapping presentation of these disorders (Gadow, DeVincent, & Pomeroy, 2006; Hartley & Sikora, 2009; Sikora et al., 2008). For example, both ASD and ADHD involve difficulties with peer interaction, social communication, and range of interests that hold attention (Clark, Feehan, Tinline, & Vostanis, 1999; Gadow et al., 2006). In addition, symptoms of inattention and hyperactivity, core characteristics of ADHD, are also evident in a high percentage of children with ASD. Specifically, recent studies have indicated that 50% to 80% of children with ASD also meet criteria for ADHD (Frazier et al., 2001; Gadow et al., 2006). A significant change in the *DSM–5* is the removal of the *DSM–IV–TR* (American Psychiatric Association, 2000) hierarchical rules prohibiting the concurrent diagnosis of ASD/pervasive developmental disorder (PDD) and ADHD. The *DSM–5* recommends that when the criteria for both ASD and ADHD are met, both diagnoses should be given.

Similarly, discriminating ASD from anxiety disorders is difficult due to symptom correspondence. As with ASD, anxiety disorders often include preoccupations with topics, rigid routines, repetitive activities and behaviors, and social withdrawal; thus, the presence of these behaviors may be poor indicators for differential diagnosis. Recent studies have found 42% to 84% of children with ASD also met criteria for one or more anxiety disorders (Simonoff et al., 2008).

Although disruptive behaviors are considered only associated or secondary impairments among the symptoms of ASD, conduct problems such as temper tantrums, aggression, noncompliance, and self-injurious behaviors are frequently part of the clinical description of ASD. Therefore, symptom overlap between ASD and disruptive behavior disorders also makes differential diagnoses a complex problem for professionals. The wide range in rates of disruptive behavior disorders in individuals with ASD (2%–68%; Mazurek, Kanne, & Miles, 2012) is indicative of this diagnostic conundrum.

Classic symptoms of depressive disorders, including increased irritability, withdrawal, changes in sleeping or eating habits, and difficulties making decisions are also found in individuals with ASD (Lainhart, 1999; Lainhart & Folstein, 1994). Although there is no general consensus on the rates of comorbid depression in the ASD population, with rates ranging from 1.4% to 58% (Ghaziuddin, Tsai, & Ghaziuddin, 1992; Ghaziuddin, Weidmer-Mikhail, & Ghaziuddin, 1998; Lainhart 1999), it is widely agreed that depression appears in children with ASD at the higher range of functioning on the spectrum (e.g., pervasive developmental disorder not otherwise specified, Asperger's syndrome).

Because the purpose of assessment is to guide treatment, it is more informative for professionals to look not at diagnostic categories per se but rather at the unique symptom picture of each child, and thus, tailor treatments not based on labels but on specific characteristics and areas of impairment. We advocate moving away from the taxonomic perspective and instead focusing on areas of impairment across multiple domains of functioning.

General Assessment Considerations for Co-Occurring Conditions

Because of the heterogeneity of the ASD population, it is important to approach assessment of comorbidity understanding that there are several potential moderating factors to consider. First, the severity of autism affects the presentation of symptoms and levels of impairment. Specifically, individuals with more classic autism are at increased risk of comorbid disruptive behavior disorders (Dominick, Davis, Lainhart, Tager-Flusberg, & Folstein, 2007). In contrast, individuals at the higher end of the autism continuum are at increased risk of comorbid anxiety and depression (Kim, Szatmari, Bryson, Streiner, & Wilson, 2000).

The severity of autism characteristics may also affect qualitative differences in the presentation of symptoms. For example, similar internalizing symptoms are noted among higher functioning children with ASD and children without ASD (White, Oswald, Ollendick, & Scahill, 2009); however, qualitative differences in symptoms are evident in those diagnosed with more classic forms of ASD, with these children exhibiting more acting-out behaviors rather than classic internalizing symptoms (Lainhart, 1999).

The severity of the child's autism-related symptomology may present unique obstacles to the accurate identification of comorbid conditions. For example, because a diagnosis of ASD is often accompanied by communication difficulties, the child may lack the ability to accurately report his or her own symptoms. As a result, diagnostic interviews and rating scales are often completed by significant others in the child's life. Children with more sophisticated language skills may be able to complete self-report measures; however, clinical experience has shown that even these must be interpreted with caution. Many self-report measures ask about abstract experiences or require comprehension skills that go beyond the child's cognitive development and are particularly difficult for individuals on the autism spectrum. For example, children with ASD may endorse the symptom of having a racing heart (a symptom of anxiety), but when asked, may indicate that they have a racing heart when they run but not in any other situation.

In addition to the severity of autism characteristics, the level of cognitive development may also affect the presentation of comorbid symptoms. Specifically, lower cognitive abilities have been linked to disruptive behaviors in children with ASD, which may be associated with both lower language and cognitive ability levels (Davis, Saeed, & Antonacci, 2008; Lecavalier 2006; Mazurek et al., 2012).

For individuals with ASD, deficits in social cognition (e.g., lack of theory of mind and social perspective taking) may also affect the individual's ability to recognize and infer mental states in him- or herself, as well as to understand that others may have thoughts and feelings that are different from his or her own (Guttman-Steinmetz, Gadow, & DeVincent, 2009). These deficits likely contribute to disruptive behaviors and inept social behaviors, especially when coupled with language impairments (Werner, Dawson, Munson, & Osterling, 2006).

Qualitative differences in symptom presentation may also be moderated by age. For example, in a study comparing the ADHD subtypes in children with PDD and children with other clinic referral problems, the results indicated an age-related trend with differential patterns of co-occurring symptoms in the PDD group (Gadow et al., 2006). The co-occurring psychiatric symptoms were more pronounced in older than younger children with ASD, suggesting older children with PDD who exhibit ADHD symptoms are more adversely affected by comorbid psychiatric symptoms than their younger counterparts.

General Assessment Strategies

A multi-informant multimethod strategy will aid in providing a comprehensive picture of a child's strengths and areas of concern to identify relevant targets for treatments. Specifically, it is recommended that professionals gather information across multiple settings from parents, teachers, other relevant caretakers, the child, and peers (if appropriate) by using the full range of assessment tools (e.g., rating scales, interviews, self-report measures, direct observation). In addition to the severity of autistic symptoms, it is also important to assess the child's developmental level and cognitive and language skills to complete the clinical picture. The assessment of cognitive functioning is discussed in Chapter 4 and language and social communication in Chapter 5.

Rating Scales

Broadband rating scales (e.g., Child Behavior Checklist; Achenbach & Rescorla, 2001) that provide a normative perspective are useful for screening and identifying issues in an individual that merit further evaluation. Narrow-band rating scales (e.g., Children's Depression Inventory—2; Kovacs, 2010) similarly provide a normative perspective but measure symptoms specific to a disorder and are useful in diagnostic evaluation. Ratings by others are typically considered more reliable indicators of externalizing behavioral issues, whereas self-ratings may be more sensitive to internalizing concerns but should be interpreted with caution in this population.

Interviews

Structured and semistructured interviews (e.g., Diagnostic Interview Schedule for Children IV; Shaffer, Fisher, Lucas, Dulcan, & Schwab-Stone, 2000) conducted with the child's parent, teacher, or the child, yield information regarding the current perception of the problems, possible contextual factors, and the impact of these difficulties, as well as giving a historical perspective. Structured interviews have a formalized, limited set of prompts that assess specific factors related to difficulties and provide a normative perspective. In contrast, semistructured interviews are flexible, allowing the professional to ask more in-depth questions unique to the specific child's difficulties.

Direct Observations

Direct observations of behavior, one of the most common tools used by school psychologists, describe the behavior of individuals and groups of individuals as they function in real time. Direct observations provide the opportunity to identify contextual aspects in which the behavior is embedded, providing insight into the possible functional causes of behaviors. Direct observations may be conducted in naturalistic situations or in more contrived settings, allowing for the professional to exert control over some contextual variables (e.g., size of the group, complexity of the task).

Functional Behavior Assessment

Functional behavior assessment describes a systematic set of strategies used to identify the purposes of behaviors and the conditions in which these behaviors are likely or unlikely to occur. Functional behavior assessment consists of describing the behavior, identifying antecedent or consequent events that control the behavior, developing a hypothesis of the behavior, and testing the hypothesis. A functional behavior assessment may be particularly useful in conjunction with other assessments in determining how co-occurring symptoms may be contributing to a child's difficulties and thus provide insight into the most comprehensive treatment course.

Take, for example, the symptom of aggression. In children with ASD, aggression has often been conceptualized as an inappropriate form of communication (Carr & Durand, 1985). Aggression may communicate that the child wants something or wants to escape or avoid a situation. The contextual variables surrounding this behavior provide keys to determining the underlying causes. For example, a child with ASD and comorbid anxiety may exhibit aggression to escape an anxiety-provoking situation (e.g., a situation that requires speaking to others). Alternatively, a child with ASD and a comorbid disruptive behavior may exhibit aggression to gain control or to actively defy a request. Clearly, effective treatment will depend on accurately identifying the function of the behavior.

FROM ASSESSMENT TO TREATMENT

How does one go from knowing that a child with ASD has a comorbid disorder to effectively treating that condition? The following framework is suggested for use in integrating what we know about EBTs for psychosocial disorders with children in general and treatment strategies that are effective with children with ASD. This framework assumes that a careful assessment has been conducted and critical intervention variables have been identified (e.g., level of cognitive functioning, communication skills, severity and specificity of symptoms).

First, one should review the literature on evidence-based interventions for children of similar developmental level for the comorbid symptoms. For example, if a 15-year-old child with ASD is functioning at a 9-year-old developmental level and is also exhibiting symptoms of an anxiety disorder, the professional should review the literature for anxiety for elementary-aged children. Alternatively, if the child is functioning at a 13-year-old level (e.g., both linguistically and cognitively), the literature for evidence-based practices with adolescents may be pertinent. Although school personnel are equipped to implement psychosocial interventions, in the case of many comorbid conditions (e.g., ADHD, depression, anxiety), medication has been shown to be effective as well. Therefore, if the evidence indicates that pharmacological intervention may be helpful, one should work with the family in conjunction with a medical professional to identify potential appropriate pharmacological treatment in each individual case.

Second, one should identify strategies that have been helpful in teaching children with ASD in general and, specifically, those strategies that are most likely to be effective with the individual child (e.g., those that have proven successful in the past). Two major recent reviews of evidence-based practices for individuals with ASD from birth to 22 years of age (National Autism Center, 2009; National Professional Development Center on Autism Spectrum Disorders, 2009) indicated that the most successful interventions are behaviorally based, focus on pivotal behaviors (e.g., those behaviors that are likely to have broad impact across various domains, such as increasing motivation), and incorporate visual strategies.

Third, one should adapt EBTs for comorbid symptoms to the unique learning and behavioral style of the child with ASD. General suggestions for modifications include: (a) identify ways to motivate a child with ASD to make changes, (b) choose intentional times to teach new skills, (c) provide interventions at the child's communicative level of understanding, (d) incorporate visual strategies wherever possible (making abstract concepts concrete), (e) provide ample times to practice with feedback, (f) practice in a variety of settings, (g) capitalize on intervention time by incorporating pivotal skills, and (h) incorporate self-monitoring techniques to promote independence in use of the new skills. Careful planning and accommodating treatments to the child's unique characteristics will lead to better outcomes.

Fourth, one should consider other factors in addition to treatment effectiveness, including the judgment and data-based clinical recommendations of qualified professional(s), the values (e.g., social validity) and preferences (e.g., treatment acceptability) of the individual with ASD and those who care for him or her, and the capacity of schools and families to deliver the treatment with fidelity (e.g., treatment integrity).

Fifth, one should devise a data-based plan to assess treatment effectiveness. EBTs for both autism and comorbid conditions are those that are most likely to work with children but do not provide guarantees that they will work for all children. Therefore, responsible professionals will evaluate each intervention carefully.

Finally, if the data indicate that the intervention is successful, one should make plans for maintenance of treatment gains. Alternatively, if the data indicate that interventions are not successful in effecting change, the treatment must be modified. Chapter 7 focuses on implementing evidence-based interventions in the classroom.

Assessing and Treating Autism Spectrum Disorder and Co-Occurring Attention-Deficit/Hyperactivity Symptoms

Symptoms of inattention and hyperactivity are hallmark symptoms of ADHD and have also been found in 30% to 60% of individuals with ASD (Ghaziuddin et al., 1998; Goldstein & Schwebach, 2004; Tsai, 2000). Although symptoms of overactivity appear to be quantitatively and qualitatively similar in children with ASD and their ADHD counterparts, the age of the individual appears to moderate the topography of the symptom of overactivity such that hyperactivity is present at younger ages but appears to diminish over time (Klin, Sparrow, Marans, Carter, & Volkmar, 2000). In contrast, symptoms of inattention remain stable across ages and lead to greater relative impairment in adolescents and young adulthood.

Researchers and practitioners have suggested that attention problems of children with ASD may differ qualitatively from those found in children with ADHD (Frazier et al., 2001; Ghaziuddin et al., 1992). Specifically, children with ASD are less likely to exhibit problems with sustained attention (Garretson, Fein, & Waterhouse, 1990) but rather have difficulties with focused (i.e., selective) attention (Frith & Happé, 1994). Some children with ASD, however, do exhibit classic ADHD symptoms (Noterdaeme, Amorosa, Mildenberger, Sitter, & Monnow, 2001; Perry, 1998). This points again to the heterogeneity of the ASD population and places responsibility on the professionals to determine not only the existence of symptoms but also the likely causes and functions of the resultant behaviors and their impact on impaired functioning as well.

Although not specifically normed for individuals with ASD, assessment methods commonly used in ADHD evaluations can be used to assess attention and overactivity symptoms. Specifically, interviews with parents and teachers provide their perceptions of the problems, possible contextual factors, and the impact of these difficulties, as well as giving a historical perspective. In addition to interviews, broadband rating scales completed by caretakers and teachers, such as the Parent Rating Scale or the Teacher Rating Scale of the Behavior Assessment System for Children (2nd ed.; Reynolds & Kamphaus, 2005) and the Child Behavior Checklist (Achenbach & Rescorla, 2001), provide a normative perspective of the child's functioning. Narrow-band ADHD rating scales, such as the Conners Global Index (Conners et al., 1997), the Home Situations Questionnaire (Barkley & Murphy, 2006), and the School Situations Questionnaire (Barkley & Murphy, 2006), may also provide more specific normative information. Finally, a brief index of impairment, such as the Children's Impairment Rating Scale (Fabiano et al., 2006), can be used to assess how these difficulties affect the child's functioning. Research has suggested that the severity of impact may be moderated by the subtype of ADHD (Gadow et al., 2006), with children with PDD exhibiting symptoms of predominantly inattentive subtype or combined subtype of ADHD demonstrating greater impairment than participants who were diagnosed with the predominantly hyperactive/impulsive subtype.

Direct observation of behaviors in contrived or naturalistic settings should supplement parent and teacher measures. Important information about the behavior in real time, the level of impairment caused by the symptoms, and contextual variants that may influence these behaviors may be gleaned through observations. For example, measures of off-task behavior across contexts may provide evidence of the stability or setting specificity of the problems. Corollary measures of task completion may provide evidence of impairment related to these symptoms. Finally, a functional assessment of the behaviors is recommended to further inform treatment.

Once a thorough assessment has been completed, professionals can tailor treatments to the specific symptom picture, adapting EBTs for ADHD to the unique autism characteristics of the child. Although a full review of EBTs for ADHD is beyond the scope of this chapter (see Hoza, Kaiser, & Hurt, 2008, for a review), comprehensive treatment should include behavioral strategies, social skills intervention, and consultation with a developmental pediatrician for medication management. Autism-specific adaptations to increase the likelihood that intervention will be helpful include the use of (a) visual strategies in teaching and maintenance of new behaviors; (b) multiple opportunities for practice with feedback for new behaviors; (c) salient, frequent reinforcement; and (d) natural environments to teach new skills to increase the chance of generalization (e.g., social skills taught in the school with peers).

Assessing and Treating Autism Spectrum Disorder and Co-Occurring Disruptive Behavior Disorder Symptoms

Current research reflects a high prevalence of disruptive behavior disorders in children with ASD (Lecavalier, 2006). Disruptive behavior disorders constitute a broad spectrum of acting-out behaviors ranging from yelling and throwing tantrums to physical aggressiveness and stealing. Conduct problems such as temper tantrums, aggression, noncompliance, and self-injurious behaviors are frequently part of the clinical descriptions of ASD.

For example, aggression, a common symptom of ODD and conduct disorder, is also regarded as being a common behavior among children with ASD (Antonacci, Manuel, & Davis, 2008; Mattila et al., 2010), with rates as high as 68% (Mazurek et al., 2012). However, in contrast to the risk factors for disruptive behavior disorders in the normative population, aggression in children with ASD has not been associated with impulsiveness, poor parental supervision, punitive or erratic parental discipline, cold parental attitude, child physical abuse, parental conflict, disrupted families, antisocial parents, large family size, low family income, antisocial peers, high delinquency rate schools, or high crime neighborhoods (Murray & Farrington, 2010). In addition, aggression has not been associated with the observed severity of ASD symptoms. Rather, individuals who are younger, come from a higher income families, have more parent reported social-communication problems, and/or who engage in repetitive behaviors are more likely to demonstrate aggression.

Similar to research with other populations of children with disruptive behavior symptoms, children with ASD exhibit lower nonverbal cognitive functioning, poor expressive language, and lower adaptive skills (Mazurek et al., 2012).

Research has suggested that deficits in social interactions and communication central to the diagnosis of ASD may present a unique symptom characterization of disruptive behavior when compared with the non-ASD population with disruptive behavior symptoms (Guttmann-Steinmetz et al., 2009). From a *DSM* perspective, these children do not engage in behaviors described as "spiteful or vindictive" or behaviors that are done to "deliberately annoy others" (*DSM–5*). The contextual determinants of disruptive behaviors may also be unique in the ASD population. For example, unlike their typically developing counterparts, children with ASD may engage in disruptive behaviors to avoid aversive sensory stimuli or to escape demands that interfere with repetitive behaviors (Mazurek et al., 2012). When aggression occurs in children with ASD, it is more likely to be reactive (i.e., impulsive and in response to a threat) rather than proactive (i.e., planned and premeditated; Mazurek et al., 2012), a pattern distinct from their purely aggressive counterparts.

Assessment of conduct problems in the ASD population is complex. A significant barrier in adequate assessment of conduct problems in individuals with ASD is the heterogeneity of symptoms presented by those with both disorders. Further, individuals may differ significantly in cognitive and adaptive functioning levels, and the impact of these individual differences on the occurrence and presentation of conduct problems beyond the core symptoms that define ASD is not well understood (Lecavalier, 2006). In addition, the symptoms of ODD and other disruptive behavior disorders may actually be a manifestation of the resistance and noncompliance that are often typical in children with ASD (Mattila et al., 2010). For these reasons, the assessment of disruptive behaviors in children with ASD should be multimodal, with a focus on direct observations of behaviors that are function based.

Because of the large number of co-occurring conditions that often present in youth with conduct problems, assessment must also be comprehensive. It is beneficial to begin with broadband behavior rating scales that screen for other difficulties as well as conduct problem behaviors; these scales include the Child Symptom Inventory—Fourth Edition and the Child Behavior Checklist (Achenbach, 2001). These broadband rating scales, for use with parents and teachers, screen for externalizing problems (including aggression) and demonstrate good psychometric properties in both clinic, community, and ASD population samples (Guttman-Steinmetz et al., 2009; Mazurek et al., 2012). In addition, both structured and semistructured interviews provide additional information regarding the stability and contextual factors of disruptive behaviors. The Autism Diagnostic Interview—Revised, a semistructured 93-item interview, focuses on both the child's developmental history and current presentation of symptoms (Rutter, Le Couteur, & Lord, 2003). It includes individual items that assess both current and historical instances of disruptive and aggressive behaviors directed toward both caregivers and noncaregivers (Mazurek et al., 2012).

Once targeted behaviors are identified through interviews and checklists, assessment continues with functionally based direct observations, both in natural and contrived settings. In natural settings, the behaviors can be observed in real time, identifying potential antecedents and consequences. Using contrived situations, as in a formal functional analysis of behaviors (Iwata, Vollmer, Zarcone, & Rodgers, 1993), specific purposes of maladaptive behaviors can be identified, and treatment can focus on teaching adaptive behaviors that serve the same purpose or function.

EBTs for individuals with disruptive behavior usually focus on two areas: teaching children problem-solving skills (Kazdin, Esveldt-Dawson, French, & Unis, 1987) and parent management training (Kazdin, 2003). It is recommended that the focus of intervention be on one or two behavioral symptoms instead of on broad diagnostic classifications (e.g., treat the aggression, not the ODD). To that effect, intervention research has shown that when child noncompliance is targeted, there is often concomitant improvement in other disruptive behaviors as well (McMahon & Frick, 2005).

However, children with ASD may also exhibit disruptive behaviors more frequently in response to increasing contextual stressors (e.g., academic demands, social situations). Because many interventions for children with ASD involve identifying antecedents for problematic behaviors, these same strategies could be applied to factors that precipitate disruptive or oppositional behaviors toward adults. Research that examines specific aspects of behavioral interventions in children both with and without ASD could help to determine whether similar strategies are useful in these cases, even though the antecedents and manifestations of noncompliance differ among these children (Gadow, DeVincent, & Drabick, 2008).

Assessing and Treating Autism Spectrum Disorder and Co-Occurring Internalizing Symptoms

Symptoms of depression and anxiety commonly occur in individuals with ASD and are particularly evident in individuals at the higher end of the ASD continuum who can describe their difficulties (Kim et al., 2000; Lainhart & Folstein, 1994; Muris, Steerneman, Merckelbach, Hodrinet, & Meesters, 1998). However, assessing self-reported internalizing concerns can be challenging, especially in a population defined by deficits in communication. Unlike externalizing disorders, in which most behaviors of concern are observable and can be reliably reported by others, the diagnosis of internalizing disorders is primarily based on reports of the individual who experiences these internal states in conjunction with behavioral correlates. Moreover, the presentation of mood and anxiety disorders in children with ASD differs from the symptoms observed in non-ASD children.

For example, symptoms of anxiety and depression in children with ASD often present as externalizing concerns that are directly observable (e.g., tantrums) due to the nature of behavior problems. Despite these potential difficulties, there is strong evidence that symptoms of comorbid internalizing conditions exist across the autism spectrum (Butzer & Konstantareas, 2003; Ghaziuddin et al., 1998; Kim et al., 2000).

The presentation of internalizing symptoms can be moderated by the severity of the disorder and the child's level of intellectual functioning. For example, depressive symptoms have been reported in 2% of children with classic autism (Ghaziuddin et al., 1992) but at a much higher rate of 30% of children with Asperger's syndrome (Ghaziuddin et al., 1998). Similar patterns are found for anxiety symptoms (Kim et al., 2000). Intellectual functioning moderates symptom presentation such that children who have mild intellectual difficulties coupled with ASD present symptoms that are similar to those seen in non-ASD populations (e.g., changes in sleep and eating habits, disturbance of mood, change in overall adaptive functioning), whereas children with more deficient intellectual abilities present a unique symptom picture (McBrien, 2003; White et al., 2009). Rather than classic internalizing symptoms, these disorders often present as externalizing concerns such as aggression, tantrum behavior, and agitation. Thus, children with ASD who present with mood and anxiety disorders may display behavioral concerns that are elevated from baseline levels. Even when symptoms overlap (e.g., self-injury), the qualitative differences in intentionality must be noted (with those at the higher end of the autism spectrum planning self-harm, whereas those at the lower end show little evidence of planning; Lainhart & Folstein, 1994).

There is a great deal of overlap between the associated characteristics of ASD and certain anxiety disorders complicating the assessment process and subsequent treatment choice. For example, children with ASD often require that strict routines be followed, display repetitive behaviors or stereotypical behaviors (e.g., echolalia, rocking, flicking, hand flapping), are overly attached to significant others, display communication deficits, and are awkward in social situations, which may lead to a fear of interacting with peers. These characteristics are also included as symptoms in obsessive–compulsive disorder, social phobia, separation anxiety disorder, and selective mutism.

Little is known about the presence of manic symptoms, also considered in the realm of internalizing disorders in children with ASD. Some have argued that the manic symptoms in children with ASD may be confused with the developmental features of ASD that are already present (e.g., irritability, overactivity, social disinhibition, sleep problems; Lainhart, 1999). For example, even older and higher functioning children with ASD may present with social skills deficits (e.g., inappropriate laughter, excessive talking, extreme degree of emotion, talking excitedly about grandiose imaginary ideas or preoccupations) that are similar to those of a manic disorder (Lainhart, 1999).

Reliable assessment of internalizing disorders in children with ASD is challenging, because no specific tools have been developed for children on the autism spectrum. Self-report scales, such as the Children's Depression Inventory–2 (Kovacs, 2010), the Multidimensional Anxiety Scale for Children (March, 1997), and the Revised Manifest Anxiety Scale–Second Edition (Reynolds & Richmond, 2008), are hallmark assessments of internalizing disorders, but they have questionable utility for children with ASD. In the typical population, these measures provide useful information concerning the child's perception of his or her mood and behavior. However, because of difficulties with language and perspective taking, children with ASD may struggle to accurately complete these measures. However, these self-report measures may be useful for children on the higher end of the spectrum (Ozonoff, Goodlin-Jones, & Solomon, 2007), with the following caveats.

First, professionals should be aware of the child's cognitive functioning and language abilities, take a developmental perspective on assessment, and consider the following questions. Will the child be able to read and understand the questions independently? Will the child provide reliable data that are not skewed by his or her attempt to please the professional or other relevant adults? Does the child have a general understanding of mood that can be reflected in the answers provided on a self-rating? Does the child have an understanding of time and sequence of events to accurately report on changes in symptoms? Children with ASD are at risk of denying existing problems, often due to their limited insight.

Because gathering information from children with ASD can be difficult, administering interviews and rating scales to parents and teachers is imperative, since these parties will supply information that the child may not be able to provide. Parents and teachers will have information regarding the child's usual mood and behavior at home and at school. In addition, because a change in functioning is the clearest indicator that depressive symptoms may have emerged, this parental perspective will provide a picture of current and past behavior. In addition to structured and semistructured interviews, broadband scales such as the Child Behavior Checklist (Achenbach, 2001), Aberrant Behavior Checklist (Aman, Singh, Stewart, & Field, 1985), and the Developmental Behavior Checklist (Clarke, Tonge, Einfeld, & Mackinnon, 2003), whose normative samples included children with ASD, and narrow-band scales such as the Anxiety, Depression, and Mood Scale

(Esbensen, Rojahn, Aman, & Ruedrich, 2003) are recommended. Finally, valuable information may be gleaned from having parents and teachers complete a child self-report scale from their impression of the child's perspective (Ozonoff et al., 2007).

Direct observation of symptoms of concern may also provide useful information when used in concert with information from interviews and rating scales. The most notable behavioral correlates of internalizing disorders in the ASD population include increased acting-out behaviors (e.g., crying, self-injury), social withdrawal, and compulsive behaviors (Lainhart, 1999), all of which notably overlap with classic symptoms of autism. In the case of individuals with limited language and cognitive functioning, a functional assessment of behaviors may be indicated, and rather than following classic treatments for depression and anxiety, more structured behavioral interventions can be implemented to alleviate symptoms.

Assessment for treatment planning may indicate several targets of intervention, especially in higher functioning individuals with ASD (Chalfant, Rapee, & Carroll, 2007; Rieske, Matson, May, & Kozlowski, 2012). Professionals can then peruse the evidence-based literature on depression and anxiety to determine a treatment course (see Curry & Becker, 2008, for a review of EBTs for depression, and Kendall, Furr, & Podell, 2010, for a review of EBTs for anxiety). The most commonly cited interventions with anxiety and depressive symptoms involve cognitive–behavioral strategies. Research supporting modified cognitive behavior therapy (CBT) approaches for the ASD population is emerging (Ooi et al., 2008; Sze & Wood, 2008). When using CBT with children with ASD, the general strategies of CBT should be used but should be modified to address the child's cognitive deficits due to ASD. This may include the use of visual strategies and behavioral strategies to improve the outcomes for children on the spectrum (Sze & Wood, 2008). Further, clinical work has highlighted the value of directly teaching coping strategies with these children using structured opportunities, practice with feedback, visual supports, and direct reinforcement for use in the natural environment. The efficacy of these interventions, however, will be dependent on the child's linguistic and cognitive abilities.

CONCLUSION

The purpose of this chapter was to highlight the co-occurring emotional and behavioral problems among children on the autism spectrum. Instead of taking a psychiatric, taxonomic perspective, we advocate focusing on symptoms and their effect on functioning. We recommend that psychologists and other professionals not struggle with issues of dual diagnosis from a taxonomic perspective but instead focus assessment on determining the areas of impairment and design autism-friendly interventions that may positively affect the child's quality of life.

REFERENCES

Achenbach, T. M. (2001). *Child behavior checklist for ages 6 to 18*. Burlington: University of Vermont, Research Center for Children, Youth, and Families.

Achenbach, T. M. & Rescorla, L. A. (2001). *Manual for the AESEBA school-age forms and profiles*. Burlington: University of Vermont, Research Center for Children, Youth, and Families.

Aman, M. G., Singh, N. N., Stewart, A. W., & Field C. J. (1985). The aberrant behavior checklist: A behavior rating scale for the assessment of treatment effects. *American Journal of Mental Deficiency, 485–491*.

Ambrosini, P. J. (2000). Historical development and present status of the Schedule for Affective Disorders and Schizophrenia for School-Age Children (K–SADS). *Journal of the American Academy of Child & Adolescent Psychiatry, 39,* 49–58. doi:10.1097/00004583-200001000-00016

American Psychiatric Association. (2000). *Diagnostic and statistical manual of mental disorders* (4th ed., text rev.). Washington, DC: Author.

American Psychiatric Association. (2013). *Diagnostic and statistical manual of mental disorders* (5th ed.). Washington, DC: Author.

Antonacci, D. J., Manuel, C., & Davis, E. (2008). Diagnosis and treatment of aggression in individuals with developmental disabilities. *Psychiatric Quarterly, 79,* 225–247. doi:10.1007/s11126-008-9080-4

Barkley, R. A., & Murphy, K. R. (2006). *Attention-deficit hyperactivity disorder: A clinical workbook*. New York, NY: Guilford Press.

Berkson, J. (1946). Limitations of the application of fourfold table analysis to hospital data. *Biometrics, 2,* 47–53. doi:10.2307/3002000

Butzer, B., & Konstantareas, M. M. (2003). Depression, temperament and their relationship to other characteristics in children with Asperger's disorder. *Journal on Developmental Disabilities, 10,* 67–72.

Caron, C., & Rutter, M. (1991). Comorbidity in child psychopathology: Concepts, issues, and research strategies. *The Journal of Child Psychology and Psychiatry,* 1063–1080. doi:10.1111/j.1469-7610.1991.tb00350.x

Carr, E. G., & Durand, V. M. (1985). Reducing behavior problems through functional communication training. *Journal of Applied Behavior Analysis, 18,* 111–126. doi:10.1901/jaba.1985.18-111

Chalfant, A. M., Rapee, R., & Carroll, L. (2007). Treating anxiety disorders in children with high-functioning autism spectrum disorders: A controlled trial. *Journal of Autism and Developmental Disorders,* 1842–1857. doi:10.1007/s10803-006-0318-4

Chambers, W. J., Puig-Antich, J., Hirsch, M., Paez, P., Ambrosini, P. J., Tabrizi, M. A., & Davies, M. (1985). The assessment of affective disorders in children and adolescents by semistructured interview. Test–retest reliability of the schedule for affective disorders and schizophrenia for school-age children, present episode version. *Archives of General Psychiatry, 42,* 696–702. doi:10.1001/archpsyc.1985.01790300064008

Clark, T., Feehan, C., Tinline, C., & Vostanis, P. (1999). Autistic symptoms in children with attention deficit-hyperactivity disorder. *European Child & Adolescent Psychiatry, 8,* 50–55. doi:10.1007/s007870050083

Clarke, A. R., Tonge, B. J., & Einfeld, S. L., & Mackinnon, A. (2003). Assessment of change with the developmental behaviour checklist. *Journal of Intellectual Disability Research, 47,* 210–212. doi:10.1046/j.1365-2788.2003.00470.x

Conners, C. K., Wells, K. C., Parker, J. D. A., Sitarenios, G., Diamond, J. M., & Powell, J. W. (1997). A new self-report scale for the assessment of adolescent psychopathology: Factor structure, reliability, validity and diagnostic sensitivity. *Journal of Abnormal Child Psychology, 25,* 487–497.

Curry, J. F., & Becker, S. A. (2008). Empirically supported psychotherapies for adolescent depression and mood disorders. In R. G. Steele, T. D. Elkin, & M. C. Roberts (Eds.), *Handbook of evidence-based therapies for children and adolescents* (pp. 161–176). New York, NY: Springer. doi:10.1007/978-0-387-73691-4_10

Davis, E., Saeed, S. A., & Antonacci, D. J. (2008). Anxiety disorders in persons with developmental disabilities: Empirically informed diagnosis and treatment. *Psychiatric Quarterly, 79,* 249–263. doi:10.1007/s11126-008-9081-3

Dominick, K. C., Davis, N. O., Lainhart, J., Tager-Flusberg, H., & Folstein, S. (2007). Atypical behaviors in children with autism and children with a history of language impairment. *Research in Developmental Disabilities, 28,* 145–162. doi:10.1016/j.ridd.2006.02.003

Esbensen A. J., Rojahn J., Aman M. G., & Ruedrich S. (2003). Reliability and validity of an assessment instrument for anxiety, depression, and mood among individuals with mental retardation. *Journal of Autism and Developmental Disorders, 33,* 617–629. doi:10.1023/B:JADD.0000005999.27178.55

Fabiano, G. A., Pelham, W. E., Waschbusch, D. A., Gnagy, E. M., Lahey, B. B., Chronis, A. M., . . . Burrows-MacLean, L. (2006). A practical measure of impairment: Psychometric properties of the impairment rating scale in samples of children with attention deficit hyperactivity disorder and two school-based samples. *Journal of Clinical Child and Adolescent Psychology, 35,* 369–385. doi:10.1207/s15374424jccp3503_3

Frazier, J. A., Biederman, J., Bellordre, C. A., Garfield, S. B., Geller, D. A., Coffey, B. J., & Faraone, S. V. (2001). Should the diagnosis of attention-deficit/hyperactivity disorder be considered in children with pervasive developmental disorders? *Journal of Attention Disorders, 4,* 203–211. doi:10.1177/108705470100400402

Frith, U., & Happé, F. (1994). Autism: Beyond theory of mind. *Cognition, 50,* 115–132. doi:10.1016/0010-0277(94)90024-8

Gadow, K. D., DeVincent, C. J., & Drabick, D. A. G. (2008). Oppositional defiant disorder as a clinical phenotype in children with autism spectrum disorder. *Journal of Autism and Developmental Disorders*, 1302–1310. doi:10.1007/s10803-007-0516-8

Gadow, K. D., DeVincent, C. J., & Pomeroy, J. (2006). ADHD symptom subtypes in children with pervasive developmental disorder. *Journal of Autism and Developmental Disorders*, 36, 271–283. doi:10.1007/s10803-005-0060-3

Gadow, K. D., & Sprafkin, J. (1994). *Manual for the Child Symptom Inventory— 4th Edition*. Stony Brook, NY: Checkmate Plus.

Garretson, H. B., Fein, S., & Waterhouse, L. (1990). Sustained attention in children with autism. *Journal of Autism and Developmental Disorders*, 20, 101–114. doi:10.1007/BF02206860

Ghaziuddin, M., Tsai, L., & Ghaziuddin, N. (1992). Comorbidity of autistic disorder in children and adolescents. *European Child & Adolescent Psychiatry*, 1, 209–213. doi:10.1007/BF02094180

Ghaziuddin, M., Weidmer-Mikhail, E., & Ghaziuddin, N. (1998). Comorbidity of Asperger syndrome: A preliminary report. *Journal of Intellectual Disability Research*, 42, 279–283. doi:10.1111/j.1365-2788.1998.tb01647.x

Goldstein, S., & Schwebach, A. J. (2004). The comorbidity of pervasive developmental disorder and attention deficit hyperactivity disorder: Results of a retrospective chart review. *Journal of Autism and Developmental Disorders*, 34, 329–339. doi:10.1023/B:JADD.0000029554.46570.68

Guttmann-Steinmetz, S., Gadow, K., & DeVincent, C. (2009). Oppositional defiant and conduct disorder behaviors in boys with autism spectrum disorder with and without attention-deficit hyperactivity disorder versus several comparison samples. *Journal of Autism and Developmental Disorders*, 976–985. doi:10.1007/s10803-009-0706-7

Happé, F., Ronald, A., & Plomin, R. (2006). Time to give up on a single explanation for autism. *Nature Neuroscience*, 1218–1220. doi:10.1038/nn1770

Hartley, S. L., & Sikora, D. M. (2009). Sex differences in autism spectrum disorder: An examination of developmental functioning, autistic symptoms, and coexisting behavior problems in toddlers. *Journal of Autism and Developmental Disorders*, 39, 1715–1722. doi:10.1007/s10803-009-0810-8

Hartley, S. L., Sikora, D. M., & McCoy, R. (2008). Prevalence and risk factors of maladaptive behaviour in young children with autistic disorder. *Journal of Intellectual Disability Research*, 52, 819–829. doi:10.1111/j.1365-2788.2008.01065.x

Hoza, B., Kaiser, N., & Hurt, E. (2008). Evidence-based treatment for attention-deficit hyperactivity disorder. In R. G. Steele, T. D. Elkin, & M. C. Roberts (Eds.). *Handbook of evidence-based therapies for children and adolescents* (pp. 197–220). New York, NY: Springer.

Iwata, B. A., Vollmer, T. R., Zarcone, J. R., & Rodgers, T. A. (1993). Treatment classification and selection based on behavioral function. In R. Van Houten & S. Axelrod (Eds.), *Behavior analysis and treatment* (pp. 101–125). New York, NY: Plenum Press. doi:10.1007/978-1-4757-9374-1_5

Kaufman, J., Birmaher, B., Brent, D., Rao, U., Flynn, C., Moreci, P., . . . Ryan, N. (1997). Schedule for Affective Disorders and Schizophrenia for School-Age Children—Present and Lifetime version (K–SADS–PL): Initial reliability and validity data. *Journal of the American Academy of Child & Adolescent Psychiatry, 36*, 980–988. doi:10.1097/00004583-199707000-00021

Kazdin, A. E. (Ed.). (2003). *Evidence-based psychotherapies for children and adolescents.* New York, NY: Guilford Press.

Kazdin, A. E., Esveldt-Dawson, K., French, N., & Unis, A. (1987). Problem-solving skills training and relationship therapy in the treatment of antisocial child behavior. *Journal of Consulting and Clinical Psychology, 55*, 76–85. doi:10.1037/0022-006X.55.1.76

Kazdin, A. E., & Whitley, K. (2006). Comorbidity, case complexity, and effects of evidence-based treatment for children referred for disruptive behavior. *Journal of Consulting and Clinical Psychology, 74*, 455–467. doi:10.1037/0022-006X.74.3.455

Kendall, P. C., Furr, J. M., & Podell, J. L. (2010). Child-focused treatment of anxiety. In J. R. Weisz & A. E. Kazdin (Eds.), *Evidence-based psychotherapies for children and adolescents* (2nd ed., pp. 45–60). New York, NY: Guilford Press.

Kim, J. A., Szatmari, P., Bryson, S. E., Streiner, D. L., & Wilson, F. J. (2000). The prevalence of anxiety and mood problems among children with autism and Asperger syndrome. *Autism, 4*, 117–132. doi:10.1177/1362361300004002002

Klin, A., Sparrow, S. S., Marans, W. D., Carter, A., & Volkmar, F. R. (2000). Assessment issues in children and adolescents with Asperger syndrome. In A. Klin, F. R. Volkmar, & S. S. Sparrow (Eds.), *Asperger syndrome* (pp. 309–339). New York, NY: Guilford Press.

Kovacs, M. (2010). *Children's Depression Inventory—2.* New York, NY: Multi-Health Systems.

Lainhart, J. E. (1999). Psychiatric problems in individuals with autism, their parents and siblings. *International Review of Psychiatry, 11*, 278–298. doi:10.1080/09540269974177

Lainhart, J. E. & Folstein, S. E. (1994). Affective disorders in people with autism: A review of published cases. *Journal of Autism and Developmental Disorders, 24*, 587–601. doi:10.1007/BF02172140

Lecavalier, L. (2006). Behavior and emotional problems in young people with pervasive developmental disorders: Relative prevalence, effects of subject characteristics, and empirical classification. *Journal of Autism and Developmental Disorders, 36*, 1101–1114. doi:10.1007/s10803-006-0147-5

Leyfer, O. T., Folstein, S. E., Bacalman, S., Davis, N. O., Dinh, E., Morgan, J., . . . Lainhart, J. E. (2006). Comorbid psychiatric disorders in children with autism: Interview development and rates of disorders. *Journal of Autism and Developmental Disorders, 36*, 849–861. doi:10.1007/s10803-006-0123-0

March, J. S. (1997). *MASC: Multidimensional Anxiety Scale for Children.* Toronto, Ontario, Canada: MHS.

Matson, J. L., & Nebel-Schwalm, M. S. (2007). Comorbid psychopathology with autism spectrum disorder in children: An overview. *Research in Developmental Disabilities, 28*, 341–352. doi:10.1016/j.ridd.2005.12.004

Mattila, M. L., Hurtig, T., Haapsamo, H., Jussila, K., Kuusikko-Gauffin, S., Kielinen, M., . . . Moilanen, I. (2010). Comorbid psychiatric disorders associated with Asperger syndrome/high-functioning autism: A community and clinic-based study. *Journal of Autism and Developmental Disorders, 40*, 1080–1093. doi:10.1007/s10803-010-0958-2

Mazurek, M. O., Kanne, S. M., & Miles, J. H. (2012). Predicting improvement in social–communication symptoms of autism spectrum disorders using retrospective treatment data. *Research in Autism Spectrum Disorders, 6*, 535–545. doi:10.1016/j.rasd.2011.07.014

McBrien, J. A. (2003). Assessment and diagnosis of depression in people with intellectual disability. *Journal of Intellectual Disability Research, 47*, 1–13. doi:10.1046/j.1365-2788.2003.00455.x

McMahon, R. J., & Frick, P. J. (2005). Evidence-based assessment of conduct problems in children and adolescents. *Journal of Clinical Child and Adolescent Psychology, 34*, 477–505. doi:10.1207/s15374424jccp3403_6

Muris, P., Steerneman, P., Merckelbach, H., Holdrinet, I., & Meesters, C. (1998). Comorbid anxiety symptoms in children with pervasive developmental disorders. *Journal of Anxiety Disorders, 12*, 387–393. doi:10.1016/S0887-6185(98)00022-X

Murray J., & Farrington, D. P. (2010). Risk factors for conduct disorder and delinquency: Key findings from longitudinal studies. *The Canadian Journal of Psychiatry / La Revue Canadienne de Psychiatrie, 55*, 633–642.

National Autism Center (2009). *National Standards Project*. Randolph, MA: Author.

National Professional Development Center on Autism Spectrum Disorders (2009). *Evidence-based practices*. Retrieved from http://autismpdc.fpg.unc.edu

Noterdaeme, M., Amorosa, H., Mildenberger, K., Sitter, S., & Monnow, F. (2001). Evaluation of attention problems in children with autism and children with a specific language disorder. *European Child & Adolescent Psychiatry, 10*, 58–66. doi:10.1007/s007870170048

Ooi, Y. P., Lam, C. M., Sung, M., Tan, W. T., Goh, T. J., Fung, D. S., . . . Chua, A. (2008). Effects of cognitive–behavioural therapy on anxiety for children with high-functioning autistic spectrum disorders. *Singapore Medical Journal, 49*, 215–220.

Ozonoff, S., Goodlin-Jones, B. L., & Solomon, M. (2007). Autism spectrum disorders. In E. J. Mash & R. A. Barkley (Eds.), *Assessment of childhood disorders* (4th ed., 487–525). New York, NY: Guilford Press.

Perry, R. (1998). Misdiagnosed ADD/ADHD; rediagnosed PDD. *Journal of the American Academy of Child & Adolescent Psychiatry, 37*, 113–114. doi:10.1097/00004583-199801000-00024

Reynolds, C. R., & Kamphaus, R. W. (2005). *Behavioral Assessment System for Children* (2nd ed.). Bloomington, MN: Pearson Assessments.

Reynolds, C. R., & Richmond, B. O. (2008). *Revised Children's Manifest Anxiety Scale manual* (2nd ed.). Los Angeles, CA: Western Psychological Services.

Rieske, R. D., Matson, J. L., May, A. C., & Kozlowski, A. M. (2012). Anxiety in children with high-functioning autism spectrum disorders: Significant differences and the moderating effects of social impairments. *Journal of Developmental and Physical Disabilities, 24*, 167–180. doi:10.1007/s10882-011-9264-y

Rutter, M., Le Couteur, A., & Lord, C. (2003). *Autism Diagnostic Interview—Revised manual*. Los Angeles, CA: Western Psychological Services.

Shaffer, D., Fisher, P., Lucas, C. P., Dulcan, M. K., & Schwab-Stone, M. E. (2000). NIMH Diagnostic Interview Schedule for Children Version IV (NIMH DISC–IV): Description, differences from previous versions, and reliability of some common diagnoses. *Journal of the American Academy of Child & Adolescent Psychiatry, 39*, 28–38. doi:10.1097/00004583-200001000-00014

Sikora, D. M., Hartley, S. L., McCoy, R., Gerrard-Morris, A. E., & Dill, K. (2008). The performance of children with mental health disorders on the ADOS-G: A question of diagnostic utility. *Research in Autism Spectrum Disorders, 2*, 188–197. doi:10.1016/j.rasd.2007.05.003

Simonoff, E., Pickles, A., Charman, T., Chandler, S., Loucas, T., & Baird, G. (2008). Psychiatric disorders in children with autism spectrum disorders: Prevalence, comorbidity, and associated factors in a population-derived sample. *Journal of the American Academy of Child & Adolescent Psychiatry, 47*, 921–929. doi:10.1097/CHI.0b013e318179964f

Sze, K. M., & Wood, J. J. (2008). Enhancing CBT for the treatment of autism spectrum disorders and concurrent anxiety. *Behavioural and Cognitive Psychotherapy, 36*, 403–409. doi:10.1017/S1352465808004384

Tsai, L. (2000). Children with autism spectrum disorder: Medicine today and in the new millennium. *Focus on Autism and Other Developmental Disabilities, 15*, 138–145. doi:10.1177/108835760001500302

Werner, E., Dawson, G., Munson, J., & Osterling J. (2005). Variation in early developmental course in autism and its relation with behavioral outcome at 3–4 years of age. *Journal of Autism and Developmental Disorders, 35*, 337–350. doi:10.1007/s10803-005-3301-6

White, S. W., Oswald, D., Ollendick, T., & Scahill, L. (2009). Anxiety in children and adolescents with autism spectrum disorders. *Clinical Psychology Review, 29*, 216–229. doi:10.1016/j.cpr.2009.01.003

II

EVIDENCE-BASED INTERVENTION FOR AUTISM SPECTRUM DISORDER

7

EVIDENCE-BASED INTERVENTIONS IN THE CLASSROOM

JESSICA SUHRHEINRICH, LAURA J. HALL, SARAH R. REED,
AUBYN C. STAHMER, AND LAURA SCHREIBMAN

In 1997, the Individuals With Disabilities Education Act (IDEA) designated autism as a separate special education category. Since then, the number of children served in this category has increased sharply each year and has become a greater proportion of the total number of children in special education. Enrollment in the autism category has quadrupled nationwide since 2000 (Data Accountability Center, 2012). Schools are now the primary intervention providers for children with autism spectrum disorder (ASD).

This increase in the number of students, combined with the high cost of care for children with ASD, has placed a significant financial burden on the education system. In 1999, the national average annual expenditure per pupil was $7,000 for children in regular education, $12,000 for children in special education, and $18,000 for children with ASD (United States Government Accountability Office, 2005). Only children in the multiple disabilities category of special education had higher expenditures. Based on these numbers,

http://dx.doi.org/10.1037/14338-008

Autism Spectrum Disorder in Children and Adolescents: Evidence-Based Assessment and Intervention in Schools, L. A. Wilkinson (Editor)

ASD-related education funding in the United States has increased from less than 0.1% of the total special education budget in 1995 to 6.1% in 2005. Increasingly, families use due process and grievance procedures to obtain services for their children (Turnbull, Wilcox, & Stowe, 2002). When districts do not use interventions with proven efficacy, the courts can require them to provide costly alternatives, such as increased one-to-one intervention or placement in a private school, paid for by the district (Lester & Kelman, 1997; Lord & McGee, 2001). The dramatic rise in the number of children with ASD, combined with the high cost of their care and families' increased advocacy for services, makes it critical to identify cost-effective, evidence-based interventions (EBIs) that are acceptable to families, effective for students and feasible to implement in most school districts. Finding methods of enhancing effective implementation of EBIs for ASD in school districts is imperative to improve child outcomes and reduce the cost and burden to schools of serving this growing population.

In recent years, there has been growing demand that decision making at all levels of the education system be based on the best available scientific evidence. This expectation is commonplace in more mature fields such as medicine, engineering, and pharmacology, and given the societal importance of education, it is reasonable to hold our field to the same standard (Boardman, Arguelles, Vaughn, Hughes, & Klingner, 2005; Carnine, 2000). The federal legislation known as No Child Left Behind, passed in 2002, clearly specifies that the practices used in schools must be those supported by scientifically based evidence and professional wisdom (No Child Left Behind Act, 2008). Yet, how do psychologists determine whether a practice qualifies as evidence based? The following section reviews how EBIs for children with ASD have been identified.

REVIEW OF EVIDENCE-BASED INTERVENTIONS FOR ASD

The use of the term *evidence-based practice* began in medicine (Reichow, Volkmar, & Cicchetti, 2008), where randomized group designs that compare a treatment with a placebo-control condition are commonly used to determine effectiveness. Randomized controlled treatment methods are considered the gold standard for addressing research questions (Odom et al., 2005). It can be a challenge, however, to use randomized controlled trials in educational settings. School districts often do not allow random assignment of learners to a classroom or to a control condition with no intervention (Gersten et al., 2005). Therefore, the use of single-subject or single-case designs replicated across participants may be a better fit when evaluating some educational interventions (Horner et al., 2005; Odom et al., 2005). They have been used extensively to evaluate specific procedures, strategies or interventions with individuals with ASD.

A hallmark of scientifically based evidence is whether or not it is replicable. A strategy or intervention should be defined well enough so that demonstrations of effectiveness can be repeated over time, with multiple individuals with ASD, and by multiple interventionists. A strategy that is shown to be effective only when used by the developer would have limited usefulness. Ideally, demonstrations of implementing the strategy or approach effectively for individuals with ASD could be repeated when used by experts, school personnel, parents, and paraprofessionals.

Several reviews of the published research literature have focused on individuals with ASD in order to determine which strategies (National Standards Project, 2009; Odom, Collet-Klingenberg, Rogers, & Hatton, 2010) or program models (Odom, Boyd, Hall, & Hume, 2010; Rogers & Vismara, 2008) have sufficient evidence to be identified as scientifically based. Recent reviews by the National Professional Development Center (NPDC) and National Standards Project (NSP) have identified specific evidence-based practices and established treatments that are key for school psychologists and special educators (NSP, 2009; Odom, Collet-Klingenberg, et al., 2010). They include antecedent based and self-management strategies to prevent problem behavior, behavioral packages including functional behavior analysis (FBA), educational strategies such as video modeling, visual schedules, peer mediated interventions and naturalistic interventions such as pivotal response training (PRT). Table 7.1 provides a matrix illustrating the strategies each of these two reviews identified as an EBI, as well as the overlap between the results of the reviews. When summarizing these findings, the authors stated that approximately two thirds of these strategies are based solely on the behavioral literature and 75% of the remaining third are also based in part on behavioral principles (NSP, 2009). In other words, over 90% of the published studies reviewed focused on the implementation of strategies or comprehensive models based on behavioral principles. Therefore, practitioners will need to have a good understanding of behavioral principles and applied behavioral analysis in order to implement interventions effectively and with fidelity.

The website of the NPDC on ASD (http://autismpdc.fpg.unc.edu) contains additional information valuable for practitioners working in schools. For each of the 24 interventions the center identified as an EBI, there is a list of the relevant references organized by age group or school level (e.g., preschool, elementary, middle, and high school). There is also a brief description of the practice, a checklist for measuring the fidelity of implementation that can be used to guide skill acquisition for educators, and sample data collection forms. Some of the practices are also connected to video modules (autism Internet modules) with examples of practices.

TABLE 7.1

Overlap Between Evidence-Based Practices Identified by the National Professional Development Center (NPDC) on ASD and the National Standards Project (NSP)

Evidence-based practices identified by the National Professional Development Center (NPDC) on ASD	Established treatments identified by the National Standards Project (NSP)										
	Antecedent package	Behavioral package	Story-based intervention package	Modeling	Naturalistic teaching strategies	Peer training package	Pivotal response treatment	Schedules	Self-management	Comprehensive behavioral treatment for young children	Joint attention intervention
Prompting	X			X							The NPDC on ASD did not review comprehensive treatment models. Components of The Comprehensive Behavioral Treatment of Young Children overlap with many NPDC-identified practices.
Antecedent-based intervention	X										
Time delay	X										The NPDC on ASD considers joint attention to be an outcome rather than an intervention. Components of joint attention interventions overlap with many NPDC-identified practices.
Reinforcement		X									
Task analysis		X									
Discrete trial training		X									
Functional behavior analysis		X									
Functional communication training		X									
Response interruption/redirection		X									
Differential reinforcement		X									

Intervention	
Social narratives	X
Video modeling	X
Naturalistic interventions	X
Peer mediated intervention	X
Pivotal response training	X
Visual supports	X
Structured work systems	X
Self-management	X
Parent implemented intervention	The NSP did not consider parent-implemented intervention as a category of evidence-based practice. However, 24 of the studies reviewed by the NSP under other intervention categories involve parents implementing the intervention.
Social skills training groups	Social Skills Training Groups (Social Skills Package) was identified as an emerging practice by the NSP.
Speech generating devices	Speech Generating Devices (Augmentative and Alternative Communication Device) was identified as an emerging practice by the NSP.
Computer aided instruction	Computer Aided Instruction (Technology-based Treatment) was identified as an emerging practice by the NSP.
Picture exchange communication	Picture Exchange Communication System was identified as an emerging practice by the NSP.
Extinction	Extinction (Reductive Package) was identified as an emerging practice by the NSP.

In addition to specific practices or strategies used to address the defining characteristics of ASD, comprehensive treatment models have also been evaluated in two recent reviews. These comprehensive treatments were evaluated with participants across the life span, with a focus on those used in early intervention (Rogers & Vismara, 2008) and those with detailed descriptions in published book chapters and journal articles (Odom, Boyd, et al., 2010). Using the treatment classification criteria established by Chambless and Hollon (1998) that categorized comprehensive treatment models, Rogers and Vismara (2008) found that only the Lovaas treatment approach met criteria for the category of "probably efficacious," having two or more strong group designs or three or more strong single-subject designs published prior to 2007.

Odom, Boyd, et al. (2010) evaluated 30 comprehensive treatment models across six dimensions (operationalization, fidelity of implementation measures, replication, empirical evidence for the model, quality of the research evidence, and published focused intervention studies by model developers) using a 5-point rating scale. The dimension that was scored highest overall for these models was operationalization, with many models having clear manuals of procedures and curriculum. The dimension that was the weakest overall was in the measurement of fidelity of implementation. Many models incorporated staff training procedures in which one supervisor evaluated a trainee until he or she met criteria, but few had interrater agreement between supervisors on staff performance, and only one program validated their staff training checklist. Eikeseth (2009) evaluated the quality of the research for 25 outcomes studies of comprehensive treatment programs for young children with ASD. Only the study by Smith, Groen, and Wynn (2000) met their highest criteria that included a randomized controlled design. This model was based on applied behavior analysis and was classified under the Lovaas approach in the study by Odom, Boyd, et al. (2010). Four studies, all programs based on applied behavior analysis, were classified in the second level of scientific rating for studies that did not include random assignment (Eikeseth, 2009). Studies of the TEACCH approach received a rating on the third of fourth levels in this system for retrospective studies with a comparison group or those that measured outcomes by comparing pre- and posttest data using a single-case experimental design.

In summary, several recent reviews evaluated the evidence supporting interventions for children with ASD. Although there is some inconsistency in their conclusions, there is also variability in the methods of the different reviews and the definitions for specific levels of research support. In general, however, strategies and programs based on behavior analysis have the strongest evidence base for improving outcomes for children with ASD.

IMPLEMENTING EVIDENCE-BASED INTERVENTIONS

Knowing which strategies are evidence based is important, but implementing these strategies with fidelity (i.e., correctly and as they were designed to be used) is essential for effective outcomes. Although many educational practices have been identified as effective by experimental research, the dissemination and implementation of these practices in applied settings is limited (Cook, Landrum, Tankersley, & Kauffman, 2003). The method for translating research findings into practice is referred to as *implementation science* (McHugh & Barlow, 2010). A review of the literature in implementation science across diverse fields, including agriculture, business, child welfare, engineering, health, juvenile justice, manufacturing, medicine, mental health, nursing, and social services, by the National Implementation Research Network (NIRN) contains clear recommendations for moving research into practice (Fixsen, Naoom, Blase, Friedman, & Wallace, 2005). The authors stated that good outcomes for consumers (individuals with ASD and their families) occur when EBIs are implemented effectively. In other words, practitioners need to have the skills to implement EBIs, and they need the support to use these skills in their work environment. Successful training in the use of EBIs requires both providing didactic information and competency training, "defined as the process of acquiring skills necessary to administer a treatment skillfully and with fidelity" (McHugh & Barlow, 2010, p. 74).

Information alone, or workshop training, is not an effective implementation method (Fixsen et al., 2005). Lerman, Vorndran, Addison, and Kuhn (2004) found a lack of generalization of direct teaching strategies following a week-long workshop in strategies based on applied behavior analysis for public school teachers. Although skills obtained at the workshop for the implementation of preference assessments generalized to the classroom, teachers performed less than 80% of the steps for direct teaching correctly in the absence of feedback. The authors recommend ongoing consultation and support in the classroom to better facilitate the teachers' generalization of strategies learned in the workshop setting (Lerman et al., 2004). Similarly, other researchers identified additional training components necessary for the generalization of training to practice, including coaching on-site, performance evaluation, program evaluation, facilitative administrative practices, and methods for systems interventions (Fixsen et al., 2005). Vismara, Young, Stahmer, Griffith, and Rogers (2009) found that although there was no difference whether training was conducted live or through distance learning, both forms needed to include didactic information with video examples, as well as supervisor feedback from a trained and skilled therapist, in order to increase the skills of professionals and produce positive outcomes for the learners with ASD. Consequently, additional training beyond the traditional didactic workshop is necessary to promote implementation of EBI and should be incorporated into settings where practitioners are expected to use EBI consistently, including schools.

THE RESEARCH-TO-PRACTICE GAP IN SPECIAL EDUCATION

Despite the recent emphasis on the identification of implementation of EBIs in education, the research-to-practice gap in both regular and special education remains. Exploration of the breakdown between research and practice in special education has focused primarily on investigating teachers' perceptions of education research and their beliefs regarding what constitutes an effective practice. One theme that arises consistently is that teachers' major motivation for using any practice is because they feel "it works" for their students (Boardman et al., 2005; Landrum, Cook, Tankersley, & Fitzgerald, 2002; Slavin, 2002). Teachers' other primary considerations when selecting an intervention to use are: difficulty using the practice (Agran & Alper, 2000; Ayres, Meyer, Erevelles, & Park-Lee, 1994), the available professional support for the practice (Whitehurst, 2002), and the fit between the practice and their day-to-day classroom needs (Gersten, Woodward, & Morvant, 1992).

Very rarely is the empirical evidence for a particular practice one of teachers' criteria for selection (Boardman et al., 2005; Stahmer, Collings, & Palinkas, 2005). Practices that teachers report using most often are those with very limited research support (Burns & Ysseldyke, 2009). Some researchers have suggested that teachers prefer informal sources of information when selecting interventions (Landrum et al., 2002) or even that there is an inverse relationship between empirical support and teacher acceptability (Kauffman, 1996). Given the focus in research on statistical significance, average effects, and group comparisons, it is not surprising that teachers do not look to research journals for information on what to do with a particular student on a particular day.

The research-to-practice gap in special education is perhaps widest in the area of ASD. There is enormous heterogeneity in how students with ASD are served in the education system, both in the services or programs provided and the educators who are providing the services (Carlson et al., 2002). Additionally, there is little standardization in the type and amount of training that educators receive to address the complex needs of students with ASD. Very few states have a specific licensure in ASD, and thus specific guidelines or requirements on what it means to be prepared to teach students with ASD are virtually nonexistent (Muller, 2006). For example, a survey of nearly 200 higher education institutions offering personnel preparation in ASD found extreme variability in the type, content, and amount of training provided (Barnhill, Polloway, & Sumutka, 2010).

Teachers of all areas of focus (e.g., learning disabilities, intellectual disabilities, emotional disturbance) have children with ASD on their caseloads. Determining how to best serve these students within the context of the education system is an important goal for research and practice alike (Hendricks, 2011). To date, few studies have examined interventions for students with ASD being used in public educational settings, although it is a growing area of focus (Hendricks, 2011). The handful of studies that have been conducted rely on teacher report of interventions used in the classroom. For example, researchers in Georgia conducted an online survey of nearly 200 preschool to 12th grade teachers serving children with ASD in both general and special education settings and found that although interventions varied significantly by grade level and classroom type, the top five most frequently endorsed strategies lacked scientific support. Over 70% of the teachers surveyed did not report using even a single intervention with strong or promising support (criteria for support from Simpson, 2005) and less than 10% of the entire body of strategies teachers reported using were evidence based (Hess, Morrier, Heflin, & Ivey, 2008).

A similar study using focus group methodology with special education teachers in Southern California found that teachers were equally as likely to report using EBIs as non-EBIs for their students with ASD (Stahmer et al., 2005). Additionally, when specifically discussing the use of EBIs in the classroom, teachers unanimously reported that they made alterations and modifications to EBIs to fit the needs of their individual students and the constraints of their classrooms and resources. As they did in studies in other areas of special education, teachers reported selecting practices based on what they felt "worked" for their students or their personal preference (Stahmer et al., 2005).

A recent web-based survey in Virginia collected information on teachers' self-reported knowledge and implementation of interventions in domains that typically require attention for students with ASD (Hendricks, 2011). The areas included individualization of intervention, behavior management, communication skills, sensory motor support, and social skills. Survey results indicated that special education teachers reported low to intermediate levels of knowledge and implementation of effective instructional practices in all areas, indicating a need for additional attention to both teacher preparation and quality service provision in educational settings (Hendricks, 2011).

Studies assessing teachers' actual implementation of EBI in the classroom (vs. reported use) are also limited, but those that have been done reveal similarly worrisome findings. An observational investigation of teachers' use of one EBI for ASD, pivotal response training (PRT), indicated that teachers demonstrate specific strengths and weaknesses when using all the components of the intervention (Suhrheinrich et al., 2013). Although it has been demonstrated that teachers are able to successfully implement PRT in the classroom with proper support (Suhrheinrich, 2011), examination of teachers' continued use of the practice reveals that they do not choose to implement it regularly (Zandi et al., 2011). This highlights an area of concern for the implementation of EBI in schools. It is not sufficient that teachers are capable of utilizing an intervention as presented and tested in research studies. The practice must also fit within their classroom context and meets their varied needs such that they choose to implement that intervention on a regular basis, and to do so in its entirety and with fidelity. Chapter 9 describes techniques to ensure that interventions are implemented with fidelity.

TRANSLATION OF EVIDENCE-BASED INTERVENTION TO ENHANCE USABILITY IN SCHOOLS

The aforementioned studies indicate that although there has been substantial progress in the development of interventions for ASD over the past 20 years, even interventions with a strong evidence base have not been successfully translated to community school settings. One possible reason for this is that historically, interventions for children with ASD have been developed by researchers and evaluated in controlled settings such as clinics or laboratory schools. Although this process has been very useful for identifying effective programs that work under specific conditions or within clinical research programs, it has not been as successful in developing interventions that are both effective and easily used in real-world settings such as schools. Thus, it is important that researchers distinguish between *efficacy* and *effectiveness* when considering the usefulness of an intervention. Treatment efficacy generally refers to whether a particular intervention/treatment has been found to work by means of experimental procedures (e.g., random assignment, control groups), whereas effectiveness involves determining whether a particular intervention has been found to produce a positive outcome in settings and conditions in which the intervention is implemented (e.g., classroom, clinic; Mash & Hunsley, 2005).

In response to these issues and with the goal of creating more usable, effective intervention programs, the traditional model of translation is changing. There is clear evidence that "simply creating an inventory of evidence-based treatments will not result in their broad implementation in practice" (National Advisory Mental Health Council's Workgroup on Services and Clinical Epidemiology Research, 2006, p. 7). Rather, EBIs need to be adapted in collaboration with community teachers to fit the context of the classroom environment.

For example, PRT was originally developed in laboratory settings as a one-on-one intervention implemented by highly trained research personnel. Yet for this evidence-based teaching strategy to be used in community settings, such as classrooms, it needed to be adapted and tested in group settings where laboratory-level control of setting variables and one-to-one implementation were unrealistic. Thus, research was directed at adapting PRT for use by teachers in classroom settings and with multiple students at the same time. In this example, as in all efforts to implement EBI, the context and resources available in community settings were primary considerations.

COLLABORATIVE DEVELOPMENT OF CLASSROOM PIVOTAL RESPONSE TEACHING

One EBI for children with ASD is pivotal response training (PRT; Odom, Collet-Klingenberg, et al., 2010). While PRT clearly has a strong evidence base and has been shown to be efficacious, very little research to date has examined its effectiveness in the context of school systems (Stahmer et al., 2005). However, the limited evidence on how teachers implement PRT does indicate significant amounts of modification (Stahmer, 2005) and low fidelity (Suhrheinrich, Stahmer, & Schreibman, 2007). These findings suggest that a collaborative adaptation of PRT may be beneficial for students with ASD in school settings. Toward this end, we collaboratively conducted the following series of studies to examine ways to adapt PRT for classroom use while maintaining the integrity of the intervention:

1. First, we conducted focus groups of special education teachers (both those who did and did not use PRT) to gather information about components of PRT that were perceived as easy and/ or important to implement in their classrooms and components that were more difficult or less valued.
2. Next, we observed teachers using PRT to determine the extent to which they were implementing the intervention with fidelity.
3. We looked for convergence of results by examining the relationship between teachers' reported difficulty with PRT components in the qualitative data and observed difficulty in the quantitative results. We used this information to develop recommendations for adaptations. Adaptations were then subjected to confirmatory testing using controlled, single-subject design methodology.
4. Using an iterative approach in collaboration with a group of teachers and administrators, we developed an adapted PRT implementation manual and accompanying training materials based on these data.

5. Finally, we conducted a pilot study of the adapted intervention, classroom pivotal response teaching (CPRT; Stahmer, Suhrheinrich, Reed, Bolduc, & Schreibman, 2011) in community classrooms to examine program feasibility.

CPRT Components

Below is a brief practical description of the CPRT components. As an applied behavioral intervention, CPRT is based on antecedent strategies (components that the teacher uses to elicit behavior from the child) and consequence strategies (components that the teacher uses to respond to the child's behavior).

Antecedent Strategies

Each interaction begins with the teacher providing a cue to elicit a student response. A cue can be very specific, such as asking a question (e.g., "What color is this?"), or open-ended (e.g., placing a student's favorite snack in a difficult to open container to encourage asking for help). CPRT provides helpful guidelines for setting up the teaching opportunity. Our research indicated that many teachers found the antecedent strategies to be consistent with good teaching strategies, and most could implement them with relatively high levels of fidelity.

1. *Student attention.* Because students with ASD have difficulty shifting attention, which can effect contingency learning (Bush, 2001), it is important that a cue or instruction is presented only when the student is paying attention.
2. *Clear and appropriate instruction.* The cue needs to be clear, unambiguous (R. Koegel, Dunlap, Richman, & Dyer, 1981), and at the student's developmental level (Lifter, Sulzer-Azaroff, Anderson, & Cowdery, 1993).
3. *Easy and difficult tasks (maintenance/acquisition).* To enhance motivation by keeping the overall success and reinforcement level high, previously mastered (maintenance) tasks are interspersed among new (acquisition) tasks, which are more difficult (Dunlap, 1984; L. Koegel & Koegel, 1986; Neef, Iwata, & Page, 1980). Examples of this strategy include asking the child to use language at varying levels (e.g., "Block," "Green block," "I want that block please"); interspersing easier problems among harder ones (e.g., addition problems among multiplication problems on a worksheet); or mixing simple, concrete questions with more abstract, open-ended inquiries (e.g., alternating between "What

is the boy's name?" and "How did Sam feel when he lost his dog?" or "What happened in the story?"). This strategy ensures frequent success and reduces frustration during teaching interactions. Teachers reported that determining maintenance and acquisition tasks for each student was often difficult for paraprofessional staff. To assist with this, examples of how to determine whether a task was easy or difficult and how to know when to consider a task acquired were provided.

4. *Shared control.* To maximize the student's interest in the learning situation, she or he is given input in determining the specific stimuli and the nature of the learning interaction (R. Koegel, Dyer, & Bell, 1987; Moes, 1998). In the classroom, this may mean that a variety of activities (e.g., independent or buddy reading, listening to the teacher read aloud) are available (choice of activity), or that the student is allowed to select materials (e.g., a book about trains or animals) for a specific learning activity (choice of materials). A teacher may alter the curriculum to include a child's specific interest in the activity (e.g., during a U.S. geography lesson, the teacher discusses the types of cars made in Michigan because her student has a strong interest in cars). The teacher is alert to the child's changing interests and allows him or her to switch to another preferred activity, or embeds the child's interests into existing activities (e.g., using numbered SpongeBob stickers to complete addition problems). During the teaching interaction, the teacher and child (or several students) take turns with the materials, sharing control. This allows the child to become accustomed to the back-and-forth nature of verbal and social interaction and provides opportunities for modeling appropriate or more complex behavior with the materials. Shared control was one component of PRT teachers found difficult to implement in groups. Examination of this component individually led us to recommend that teachers use turns (including modeling and contingency) differentially based on child language level and the specific skills being taught. This allows teachers to modify the procedures to reduce the amount of turn taking needed and uses turn taking during interactions where the strategy provides the most benefit for students. Examples of how to use this strategy in groups were added to the manual to assist with implementation.

5. *Multiple cues/broadening attention.* Early research indicates that many individuals with ASD have *overselective* responding, meaning that they exhibit a tendency to respond to only

one component of a complex cue, limiting the generalization of new skills (R. Koegel & Wilhelm, 1973; Lovaas & Schreibman, 1971; Lovaas, Schreibman, Koegel, & Rehm, 1971; Schover & Newsom, 1976). Training on a series of successive conditional discriminations has been shown to help these individuals accurately respond to simultaneous multiple cues (R. Koegel & Schreibman, 1977; Schreibman, Charlop, & Koegel, 1982). A *conditional* discrimination is one that requires attention and response to more than one descriptive element of the item. For example, a student may be asked to find a red marker in a mixed box of crayons and markers. The student must attend to the descriptive element "red" (and not another color) and the element "marker" (and not a crayon) to respond correctly to this opportunity. Because responsivity to multiple cues is so important to learning, this procedure is a component of CPRT. However, additional strategies for broadening attention and increasing generalization have since been developed. Varying instructor, setting, cues and materials and contingently providing feedback have been shown to increase generalization by ensuring that students with ASD respond to multiple aspects of the environment (e.g., Jahr, 2001; Reeve, Reeve, Townsend, & Poulson, 2007; Whalen, Massaro, & Frank, 2009). We found that teachers typically omitted this particular component when using PRT in the classroom. Based on our confirmatory studies, we recommend that conditional discrimination training not be used for students with a cognitive level below 36 months (Reed, Stahmer, Schreibman, & Suhrheinrich, in press). For all students, the use of multiple exemplars is emphasized to broaden attention. Conditional discrimination training is recommended only for students who exhibit stimulus overselectivity.

Consequence Strategies

Once the student has responded to the cue provided by the teacher, the teacher provides feedback on the basis of the student's response (i.e., whether the student is correct, incorrect, or making a reasonable attempt).

6. *Direct reinforcement.* Direct, rather than indirect, reinforcement is used because it is effective and encourages generalization and maintenance of behavior change (e.g., Cowan & Allen, 2007; R. Koegel & Williams, 1980; Williams, Koegel, & Egel, 1981).

Direct reinforcement is naturally related to the response it follows (e.g., a direct reinforcer for the verbal response "car" might be access to a toy car, as opposed to a food or token reinforcer). Teachers reported difficulty using direct reinforcement strategies during group activities. Because this is an essential component of PRT, extensive examples and ideas of how to integrate students' preferred reinforcers naturally into typical classroom activities were provided.

7. *Contingent consequence.* A wealth of behavioral research illustrates that consequences should be presented immediately after a behavior occurs and dependent on the child's response because the strength and effectiveness of a consequence is directly related to its timing (Baer, Wolf, & Risley, 1968; Miltenberger, 2008; Neef, Bicard, & Endo, 2001). Therefore, teachers are taught to provide consequences immediately. Again, this can be difficult in a busy classroom with multiple students requiring the teacher's attention. The adapted manual provides examples of how to reinforce students immediately during both small- and large-group activities.

8. *Reinforcement of attempts.* To maximize reinforcement and enhance the student's motivation, teachers reinforce reasonable attempts made by the student (R. Koegel & Egel, 1979; R. Koegel, O'Dell, & Dunlap, 1988). Thus, reinforcers are contingent upon attempts that are within a broader range of correct responses, though they may not be completely accurate or represent the student's best performance. For example, a teacher may respond to a student's approximation of "buh" for bubbles by blowing bubbles, even if the student has previously said the entire word "bubble," because "buh" is a goal-directed attempt. Toward the goal of improving reading comprehension, a teacher may accept a student's attempt at writing a chapter summary even if the punctuation is not accurate. The teacher reinforces the good effort and focuses on punctuation during another lesson, which will motivate the student to complete future writing assignments. Teachers found this step to be intuitive and very helpful with increasing student motivation.

Exhibit 7.1 presents a brief vignette of how a teacher might target a student's learning goals using CPRT strategies. Specific components of CPRT are noted throughout the text in parentheses.

EXHIBIT 7.1
Classroom Pivotal Response Training (CPRT) Example Vignette

Student profile	Sample individualized education plan goal
Jordan is a 6-year-old boy with autism who attends a K-1 special day class. He can match uppercase letters but does not yet label them expressively. Jordan loves any instructional materials that include construction vehicles (e.g., books, figurines).	Jordan will name the uppercase letters when they are presented in random order, with 100% accuracy on four out of five opportunities.

Using CPRT during Language Arts—Jordan's teacher sets up a letter recognition activity with a small group of students, including Jordan. The students have varied abilities but all have a goal of letter identification. The teacher begins by playing the "ABC song" while pointing to each letter because the students enjoy the song (*Shared Control*). Next she holds up individual letter cards to each student, waits to ensure the student is looking at her, and asks them to "pick one" (*Student Attention; Clear and Appropriate Instruction*). Each letter card has a sticker on it of an object that starts with that letter. Some of the stickers are of construction vehicles (F-forklift, D-dump truck, S-semi) because they interest Jordan, but other stickers include ocean animals (W-whale, M-manatee) or popular characters (B-Bob the builder, C-Calliou) based on other students' interests (*Shared Control*). When the teacher holds up the card choices, she either waits for the student to name the letter or provides a verbal model such as "C or D?" (*Easy/Difficult task*). She waits for an attempt or a correct response from each student before handing them the letter card (*Direct Reinforcement, Contingent Consequence, Reinforcement of Attempts*). Then, she moves to the next student and presents another opportunity to respond. The teacher also takes a turn labeling a letter and uses this as an opportunity to model a more advanced skill, "M says mma, mma, manatee" (*Shared Control*). The students keep the cards they correctly label and after all the cards have been completed, they slowly sing the "ABC song" again (*Direct Reinforcement*). Each student is encouraged to hold up the letter card that corresponds with each letter in the song. After they complete the song, the teacher brings out a box of small figurines that correspond with the stickers on the cards. She holds up one figurine at a time and asks, "Who has the match?" When the student with the corresponding card, reaches for the figurine, she holds the letter card next to the figurine and again asks, "What letter?" When the student labels the letter she provides praise, "That's right F is for forklift!" and gives the student the forklift to play with (*Broadening Attention*).

CONCLUSION

The rising number of children receiving an ASD diagnosis presents a tremendous challenge to educators. We now have the task and opportunity of providing effective educational services to many children who in the past likely had minimal access to EBIs, since these are most often available in programs affiliated with universities or via expensive private providers. This opportunity is exciting, yet it must be met in a manner well founded in sound research.

A strong and comprehensive body of research has identified several EBIs that are associated with substantial improvement in the symptoms of children with ASD. However, since most of these interventions were developed in tightly controlled laboratory settings with one-on-one implementation, we now must transfer them to educational settings. Much like the support of the interventions themselves, this transfer must be guided by appropriate research. We have provided an example of how this can be accomplished with one EBI, PRT. However, this model of developing adaptations to existing strategies can be generalized to other interventions and should lead to effective teaching strategies that our front-line education practitioners—teachers, paraprofessional educators, and specialists—can successfully use in the classroom.

REFERENCES

Agran, M., & Alper, S. (2000). Curriculum and instruction in general education: Implications for service delivery and personnel preparation. *Journal of the Association for Persons With Severe Handicaps, 25*, 167–174. doi:10.2511/rpsd.25.3.167

Ayres, B., Meyer, L., Erevelles, N., & Park-Lee, S. (1994). Easy for you to say: Teacher perspectives on implementing most promising practices. *Journal of the Association for Persons With Severe Handicaps, 19*, 84–93.

Baer, D. M., Wolf, M. M., & Risley, T. R. (1968). Some current dimensions of applied behavior analysis. *Journal of Applied Behavior Analysis, 1*(1), 91–97. doi:10.1901/jaba.1968.1-91

Barnhill, G. P., Polloway, E. A., & Sumutka, B. M. (2011). A survey of personnel preparation practices in autism spectrum disorders. *Focus on Autism and Other Developmental Disabilities, 26*, 75–86. doi:10.1177/1088357610378292

Boardman, A. G., Arguelles, M. E., Vaughn, S., Hughes, M. T., & Klingner, J. (2005). Special education teachers' views of research-based practices. *The Journal of Special Education, 39*, 168–180. doi:10.1177/00224669050390030401

Burns, M. K., & Ysseldyke, J. E. (2009). Reported prevalence of evidence-based instructional practices in special education. *The Journal of Special Education, 43*, 3–11. doi:10.1177/0022466908315563

Bush, D. (2001). Shifting attention and contingency learning in autism. *Dissertation Abstracts International: Section B: The Sciences and Engineering, 62*(3-B), 1566.

Carlson, R. J., Navone, A., McConnell, J. P., Burritt, M., Castle, M. C., Grill, D., & Jaffe, A. S. (2002). Effect of myocardial ischemia on cardiac troponin I and T. *American Journal of Cardiology, 89*, 224–226.

Carnine, D. (2000). *Why education experts resist effective practices (and what it would take to make education more like medicine)*. Retrieved from Thomas B. Fordham Institute website: http://www.edexcellence.net/publications/edexpertsresist.html

Chambless, D. L., & Hollon, S. D. (1998). Defining empirically supported therapies. *Journal of Consulting and Clinical Psychology, 66*, 7–18. doi:10.1037/0022-006X.66.1.7

Cook, B. G., Landrum, T. J., Tamkersly, M., & Kauffman, J. M. (2003). Bringing research to bear on practice: Effecting evidence-based instruction for students with emotional or behavioral disorders. *Education & Treatment of Children, 26*, 345–361.

Cowan, R. J., & Allen, K. D. (2007). Using naturalistic procedures to enhance learning in individuals with autism: A focus on generalized teaching within the school setting. *Psychology in the Schools, 44*, 701–715. doi:10.1002/pits.20259

Data Accountability Center (2012). *Part B Child Count.* Retrieved from http://www.ideadata.org/PartBChildCount.asp

Dunlap, G. (1984). The influence of task variation and maintenance tasks on the learning and affect of autistic children. *Journal of Experimental Child Psychology, 37*, 41–64. doi:10.1016/0022-0965(84)90057-2

Eikeseth, S. (2009). Outcome of comprehensive psycho-educational interventions for young children with autism. *Research in Developmental Disabilities, 30*, 158–178. doi:10.1016/j.ridd.2008.02.003

Fixsen, D. L., Naoom, S. F., Blase, K. A., Friedman, R. M., & Wallace, F. (2005). *Implementation research: A synthesis of the literature.* Retrieved from http://cfs.cbcs.usf.edu/_docs/publications/NIRN_Monograph_Full.pdf

Gersten, R., Fuchs, L. S., Compton, D., Coyne, M., Greenwood, C., & Innocenti, M. S. (2005). Quality indicators for group experimental and quasi-experimental research in special education. *Exceptional Children, 71*(2), 149–164.

Gersten, R., Woodward, J., & Morvant, M. (1992). Refining the working knowledge of experienced teachers. *Educational Leadership, 49*(7), 34–39.

Hendricks, D. (2011). Special education teachers serving students with autism: A descriptive study of the characteristics and self-reported knowledge and practices employed. *Journal of Vocational Rehabilitation, 35*(1), 37–50.

Hess, K. L., Morrier, M. J., Heflin, L. J., & Ivey, M. L. (2008). Autism treatment survey: Services received by children with autism spectrum disorders in public school classrooms. *Journal of Autism and Developmental Disorders, 38*, 961–971. doi:10.1007/s10803-007-0470-5

Horner, R. H., Carr, E. G., Halle, J., McGee, G. G., Odom, S. L., & Wolery, M. (2005). The use of single-subject research to identify evidence-based practice in special education. *Exceptional Children, 71*, 165–179.

Individuals With Disabilities Education Act Amendments of 1997, Pub. L. No. 105-17, 20 U.S.C. Chapter 33 § 1400 *et seq.*

Jahr, E. (2001). Teaching children with autism to answer novel wh-questions by utilizing a multiple exemplar strategy. *Research in Developmental Disabilities, 22*, 407–423. doi:10.1016/S0891-4222(01)00081-6

Kauffman, J. M. (1996). Research to practice issues. *Behavioral Disorders*, 22, 55–60.

Koegel, L. K., & Koegel, R. L. (1986). The effects of interspersed maintenance tasks on academic performance in a severe childhood stroke victim. *Journal of Applied Behavior Analysis*, 19, 425–430. doi:10.1901/jaba.1986.19-425

Koegel, R. L., Dunlap, G., Richman, G. S., & Dyer, K. (1981). The use of specific orienting cues for teaching discrimination tasks. *Analysis & Intervention in Developmental Disabilities*, 1, 187–198. doi:10.1016/0270-4684(81)90031-8

Koegel, R. L., Dyer, K., & Bell, L. K. (1987). The influence of child-preferred activities on autistic children's social behavior. *Journal of Applied Behavior Analysis*, 20, 243–252. doi:10.1901/jaba.1987.20-243

Koegel, R. L., & Egel, A. L. (1979). Motivating autistic children. *Journal of Abnormal Psychology*, 88, 418–426. doi:10.1037/0021-843X.88.4.418

Koegel, R. L., O'Dell, M. C., & Dunlap, G. (1988). Producing speech use in nonverbal autistic children by reinforcing attempts. *Journal of Autism and Developmental Disorders*, 18, 525–538. doi:10.1007/BF02211871

Koegel, R. L., & Schreibman, L. (1977). Teaching autistic children to respond to simultaneous multiple cues. *Journal of Experimental Child Psychology*, 24, 299–311. doi:10.1016/0022-0965(77)90008-X

Koegel, R. L., & Wilhelm, H. (1973). Selective responding to the components of multiple visual cues by autistic children. *Journal of Experimental Child Psychology*, 15, 442–453. doi:10.1016/0022-0965(73)90094-5

Koegel, R. L., & Williams, J. A. (1980). Direct versus indirect response-reinforcer relationships in teaching autistic children. *Journal of Abnormal Child Psychology*, 8, 537–547. doi:10.1007/BF00916505

Landrum, T. J., Cook, B. G., Tankersley, M., & Fitzgerald, S. (2002). Teacher perceptions of the trustworthiness, usability, and accessibility of information from different sources. *Remedial and Special Education*, 23, 42–48. doi:10.1177/074193250202300106

Lerman, D. C., Vorndran, C. M., Addison, L., & Kuhn, S. C. (2004). Preparing teachers in evidence-based practices for young children with autism. *School Psychology Review*, 33, 510–526.

Lester, G., & Kelman, M. (1997). State disparities in the diagnosis and placement of pupils with learning disabilities. *Journal of Learning Disabilities*, 30, 599–607. doi:10.1177/002221949703000603

Lifter, K., Sulzer-Azaroff, B., Anderson, S. R., & Cowdery, G. E. (1993). Teaching play activities to preschool children with disabilities. *Journal of Early Intervention*, 17, 139–159. doi:10.1177/105381519301700206

Lord, C., & McGee, J. P. (2001). *Educating children with autism*. Washington, DC: National Academies Press.

Lovaas, O. I., & Schreibman, L. (1971). Stimulus overselectivity of autistic children in a two stimulus situation. *Behaviour Research and Therapy*, 9, 305–310. doi:10.1016/0005-7967(71)90042-8

Lovaas, O. I., Schreibman, L., Koegel, R. L., & Rehm, R. (1971). Selective responding by autistic children to multiple sensory input. *Journal of Abnormal Psychology, 77*, 211–222. doi:10.1037/h0031015

Mash, E. J., & Hunsley, J. (2005). Evidence-based assessment of child and adolescent disorders: Issues and challenges. *Journal of Clinical Child and Adolescent Psychology, 34*, 362–379. doi:10.1207/s15374424jccp3403_1

McHugh, R. K., & Barlow, D. H. (2010). Dissemination and implementation of evidence-based psychological interventions: A review of current efforts. *American Psychologist, 65*, 73–84. doi:10.1037/a0018121

Miltenberger, R. G. (2008). *Behavior Modification: Principles and Procedures* (4th ed.). Belmont, CA: Thomas Wadsworth.

Moes, D. R. (1998). Integrating choice-making opportunities within teacher-assigned academic tasks to facilitate the performance of children with autism. *Journal of the Association for Persons with Severe Handicaps, 23*, 319–328. doi:10.2511/rpsd.23.4.319

Muller, E. (2006). *State approaches to serving students with autism spectrum disorders*. Alexandria, VA: National Association of State Directors of Special Education. Retrieved from http://www.projectforum.org/docs/StateApproachestoServing StudentswithAutismSpectrumDisorders.pdf

National Advisory Mental Health Council's Workgroup on Services and Clinical Epidemiology Research (2006). *The road ahead: Research partnerships to transform services*. Retrieved from http://www.nimh.nih.gov/about/advisory-boards-and-groups/namhc/reports/road-ahead.pdf

National Standards Project. (2009). *National Standards Report*. Retrieved from http://www.nationalautismcenter.org/pdf/NAC%20Standards%20Report.pdf

Neef, N. A., Bicard, D. F., & Endo, S. (2001). Assessment of impulsivity and the development of self control in students with attention deficit hyperactivity disorder. *Journal of Applied Behavior Analysis, 34*, 397–408. doi:10.1901/jaba.2001.34-397

Neef, N. A., Iwata, B. A., & Page, T. J. (1980). The effects of interspersal training versus high-density reinforcement on spelling acquisition and retention. *Journal of Applied Behavior Analysis, 13*, 153–158. doi:10.1901/jaba.1980.13-153

No Child Left Behind (NCLB) Act of 2001, 20 U.S.C. § 6319 (2008).

Odom, S. L., Boyd, B. A., Hall, L. J., & Hume, K. (2010). Evaluation of comprehensive treatment models for individuals with autism spectrum disorders. *Journal of Autism and Developmental Disorders, 40*, 425–436. doi:10.1007/s10803-009-0825-1

Odom, S. L., Brantlinger, E., Gersten, R., Horner, R. H., Thompson, B., & Harris, K. R. (2005). Research in special education: Scientific methods and evidence-based practices. *Exceptional Children, 71*, 137–148.

Odom, S. L., Collet-Klingenberg, L., Rogers, S. J., & Hatton, D. D. (2010). Evidence-based practices in interventions for children and youth with autism spectrum disorders. *Preventing school failure: Alternative education for children and youth, 54*, 275–282.

Reed, S., Stahmer, A. C., Schreibman, L., & Suhrheinrich, J. (in press). Examining the use of multiple cues as a necessary component of pivotal response training. *Journal of Applied Behavior Analysis*.

Reeve, S. A., Reeve, K. F., Townsend, D. B., & Poulson, C. L. (2007). Establishing a generalized repertoire of helping behavior in children with autism. *Journal of Applied Behavior Analysis, 40*, 123–136. doi:10.1901/jaba.2007.11-05

Reichow, B., Volkmar, F. R., & Cicchetti, D. (2008). Development of the evaluative method for evaluating and determining evidence-based practice in autism. *Journal of Autism and Developmental Disorders, 38*, 1311–1319. doi:10.1007/s10803-007-0517-7

Rogers, S. J., & Vismara, L. A. (2008). Evidence-based comprehensive treatments for early autism. *Journal of Clinical Child and Adolescent Psychology, 37*, 8–38. doi:10.1080/15374410701817808

Schover, L. R., & Newsom, C. D. (1976). Overselectivity, developmental level, and overtraining in autistic and normal children. *Journal of Abnormal Child Psychology, 4*, 289–298. doi:10.1007/BF00917765

Schreibman, L., Charlop, M. H., & Koegel, R. L. (1982). Teaching autistic children to use extra-stimulus prompts. *Journal of Experimental Child Psychology, 33*, 475–491. doi:10.1016/0022-0965(82)90060-1

Simpson, R. L. (with de Boer-Ott, S. R., Griswold, D. E., Myles, B. S., Byrd, S. E., Ganz, J. B., Cook, K. T., . . . Adams, L. G.) (2005). *Autism spectrum disorders: Interventions and treatments for children and youth*. Thousand Oaks, CA: Corwin Press.

Slavin, R. E. (2002). Evidence-based education policies: Transforming educational practice and research. *Educational Researcher, 31*, 15–21. doi:10.3102/0013189X031007015

Smith, T., Groen, A. D., & Wynn, J. W. (2000). Randomized trial of intensive early intervention for children with pervasive developmental disorder. *American Journal on Mental Retardation, 105*, 269–285. doi:10.1352/0895-8017(2000)105<0269:RTOIEI>2.0.CO;2

Stahmer, A. (2005, February). *Teaching professionals and paraprofessionals to use pivotal response training: Differences in training methods*. Paper presented at the Annual Meeting of the California Association for Behavior Analysis, Dana Point, CA.

Stahmer, A., Suhrheinrich, J., Reed, S., Bolduc, C., & Schreibman, L. (2011). *Classroom pivotal response teaching: A guide to effective implementation*. New York, NY: Guilford Press.

Stahmer, A. C., Collings, N. M., & Palinkas, L. A. (2005). Early intervention practices for children with autism: Descriptions from community providers. *Focus on Autism and Other Developmental Disabilities, 20*, 66–79. doi:10.1177/10883576050200020301

Suhrheinrich, J. (2011). Training teachers to use pivotal response training with children with autism: Coaching as a critical component. *Teacher Education and Special Education, 34*, 339–349. doi:10.1177/0888406411406553

Suhrheinrich, J., Stahmer, A. C., Reed, S., Schreibman, L., Reisinger, E., & Mandell, D. (2013). Implementation challenges in translating pivotal response training into community settings. *Journal of Autism and Developmental Disorders.* doi:10.1007/s10803-013-1826-7

Suhrheinrich, J., Stahmer, A. C., & Schreibman, L. (2007). A preliminary assessment of teachers' implementation of pivotal response training. *Journal of Speech–Language Pathology, and Applied Behavior Analysis, 2*, 8–20.

Turnbull, H. R. I., Wilcox, B. L., & Stowe, M. J. (2002). A brief overview of special education law with focus on autism. *Journal of Autism and Developmental Disorders, 32*, 479–493. doi:10.1023/A:1020550107880

United States Government Accountability Office (2005). *Special education: Children with autism.* Washington, DC: Author.

Vismara, L. A., Young, G. S., Stahmer, A. C., Griffith, E. M., & Rogers, S. J. (2009). Dissemination of evidence-based practice: Can we train therapists from a distance? *Journal of Autism and Developmental Disorders, 39*, 1636–1651. doi:10.1007/s10803-009-0796-2

Whalen, C., Massaro, D. W., & Frank, L. (2009). Generalization in computer-assisted intervention for children with autism spectrum disorders. In C. Whalen (Ed.), *Generalization in computer-assisted intervention for children with autism spectrum disorders: Autism life lessons: Generalization of treatment for children with autism spectrum disorders wearable computing (Technical insights)* (pp. 105–146). Baltimore, MD: Brookes.

Whitehurst, G. J. (2002, March). *Scientifically based research on teacher quality: Research on teacher preparation and professional development.* Paper presented at the White House Conference on Preparing Tomorrow's Teachers. Retrieved from http://www.stcloudstate.edu/tpi/initiative/documents/assessment/Scientifically%20Based%20Research%20on%20Teacher%20Quality.pdf

Williams, J. A., Koegel, R. L., & Egel, A. L. (1981). Response-reinforcer relationships and improved learning in autistic children. *Journal of Applied Behavior Analysis, 14*, 53–60. doi:10.1901/jaba.1981.14-53

Zandi, V., Stahmer, A., Reed, S., Lee, E. L., Shin, S., & Mandell, D. S. (2011, May). *Fidelity of implementation of evidence-based practices by paraprofessionals in community classrooms.* Paper presented at the 10th Annual International Meeting for Autism Research, San Diego, CA.

8

CONTINUUM OF SERVICES AND INDIVIDUALIZED EDUCATION PLAN PROCESS

SHEILA J. WAGNER

Parents of children with autism spectrum disorder (ASD) expect public school systems to partner with them in tackling the challenges of this condition by using qualified personnel and providing appropriate services to educate their child. At the same time, school systems face difficulties in educating students with ASD because of wide variations within the disability, unclear legal regulations, and budget shortfalls. Relationships between family and school can quickly become adversarial when services are undisclosed or not provided, terminology is not explained, and parental perspective is not respected. This can often result in parental confusion and anger added to the fear of the unknown that comes with parenting a child with ASD.

To develop an appropriate individualized education plan (IEP) under the regulations of the Individuals With Disabilities Education Act (IDEA; 2004), all members of the IEP team must fully understand the procedures that guide their decisions (Giangreco, 2001). This chapter details IDEA's

http://dx.doi.org/10.1037/14338-009
Autism Spectrum Disorder in Children and Adolescents: Evidence-Based Assessment and Intervention in Schools, L. A. Wilkinson (Editor)

IEP process for a child with ASD, identifies appropriate public school special education services, and outlines the major requirements of IDEA. Although a comprehensive discussion of the entire law and procedural regulations are beyond the scope of this chapter, it addresses those provisions that have particular significance for the student with ASD. For more detail on legal issues related to special education eligibility and program placement under IDEA, see Chapter 11.

SPECIAL EDUCATION CLASSIFICATIONS

Students with ASD may present with ASD alone, or the disorder may occur in combination with other medical conditions (Gadow, Guttmann-Steinmetz, Rieffe, & DeVincent, 2011), which makes the eligibility process for special education services complex and lengthy. When considering eligibility for the student with ASD, all special education classifications relevant to the individual student's needs must be examined. A student with ASD may have dual or even triple special education service eligibilities. For example, a special education student may have autism, specific learning disability, and other health impaired eligibilities listed on their IEP, resulting in three separate categories requiring education intervention. Many students with ASD are placed under autism eligibility alone. Others may be included under the emotional and behavior disorders category of eligibility. Some only receive speech eligibility or an occupational eligibility and are not recognized as having ASD at all. Conversely, some students with a medical or clinical diagnosis of ASD may be denied the autism eligibility because they do not meet the educational criteria set forth by their state for this category. Psychiatric versus educational classification systems are discussed in Chapter 3.

To further complicate the issue, some students with ASD go unidentified, receiving no specialized support at school to assist in ameliorating their atypical characteristics. For example, MacFarlane and Kanaya's (2009) report on the Office of Special Educational Programs' data for 2007 found that approximately one third of students clinically diagnosed with autism were not receiving special education services under the autism category. Presumably, this surprising statistic may be explained by the school's lack of identification of the condition or by the school providing placement under other categories.

The range of special education eligibilities that students with ASD may be classified under include (a) intellectual impairment, (b) hearing impairment, (c) vision impairment, (d) speech or language impairment, (e) emotional or behavior disorders, (f) orthopedic impairment, (g) traumatic brain injury, (h) other health impairment, (i) learning disability, (j) deaf-blindness, or (k) multiple disabilities. If they are under the age of 9, they are likely to be found under such labels as *significantly developmentally delayed* eligibility for special education services. Obviously, autism services can have many identities.

It is also important to note that autism eligibility criteria vary widely from state to state (MacFarlane & Kanaya, 2009) and that states have the flexibility to develop their own definitions, which may be changed at any time. If a child meets criteria for autism eligibility in one state, there is no guarantee that he or she will be eligible if the family moves to another state or even to another district in the same state. Obviously, this variability affects the overall number of identified students with ASD in any given district, so whereas some students will be appropriately placed in the autism category, other students with ASD may be left unidentified and still others placed under nonautism eligibilities. Unfortunately, it can also lead to parental frustration and confusion if their child has a medical diagnosis of ASD, but the student does not meet local educational criteria for autism eligibility. A medical diagnosis does not assure special education eligibility.

When a student is suspected of having ASD, the student support team (which includes the parents) should request a comprehensive evaluation. This will involve the school system's psychologist and other therapists relevant to the child's condition (e.g., speech and/or occupational therapist, physical therapist, other school personnel). Once the parents request or consent to the evaluation, an in-depth assessment of all ability areas must be completed within the 60-day limit outlined by IDEA (2004), unless the state has another designated timeline or the team agrees on an alternate timeline. This comprehensive evaluation should produce valuable information on the student's intellectual functioning, academic performance, adaptive behaviors, language ability, and motor development, as well as identify strengths and challenges to guide the team in decision making. Chapter 3 provides a description of the comprehensive developmental approach to assessment of ASD.

If ASD is suspected, it is particularly important that the evaluators conduct an in-depth assessment of all the student's disability areas, including communication, behavior, and especially their social skills development, because deficits in this domain are associated with poor outcomes for students with ASD (Eaves & Ho, 2008; Weiss & Harris, 2001). Parent, teacher, and if possible, student reports on social skills functioning can provide data to compare across settings and give insight into the student's view of his own generalized social behaviors. Gresham and Elliott's (2008) Social Skills Improvement System measures social skills sufficient to build IEP objectives. Other instruments exist that may also serve this purpose.

Autism eligibility, of course, has its pros and cons. Autism eligibility on an IEP allows school personnel to select effective, research-based strategies for intervention specific for this disability. However, from the parent's perspective, the long-term effects of having the label of *autism* on their child's records, and the possibility that it may limit opportunities in the future, can take precedence over the decision to accept this designation. Refusing or eliminating the autism eligibility for the student heightens the chance that underlying social deficits will be neither recognized nor addressed, thereby limiting a critical opportunity for intervention.

The advantages and disadvantages of conducting student-led IEPs is an additional area to discuss with parents. In student-led IEPs, the student can volunteer valuable information for decision making (Danneker & Bottge, 2009). Although the student often learns of his or her own diagnosis, he or she may not be ready to accept this disability classification. Foden and Anderson (2011) discussed the difficulties adults with autism have with self-identifying. Yet self-advocacy is important (Lee, Simpson, & Shogren, 2007); it is essential that the student ultimately learn of his or her own diagnosis to become a self-advocate, because it takes time to become comfortable and knowledgeable about his or her own condition. The advantages and disadvantages associated with the autism eligibility should be discussed with the parent prior to the student's entry into the IEP to prevent uncomfortable situations or emotional stress for either the parent or the student.

CONTINUUM OF SERVICES

IDEA (2004) allows for a wide range of school-supported services for students with disabilities, and the following sections discuss these in the case of the student with ASD. IDEA clearly states that when recommending placement and services, every effort should be made to have the student learn alongside typically developing students in general education classes. First and foremost, the student should be viewed as a typical student who has special needs, rather than as a special education student who might "visit" the general education class. This philosophical change is necessary to find the most appropriate services to maintain the student in the general school population. Creativity and flexibility are key when recommending the most appropriate placement for the student with ASD, whether in general education classes, special education classes, or a combination of both. Individual students with autism will respond differently to the methods and placements because of the diversity of profiles. This makes having a wide variety of options available within the school district critical to the success of the student (Simpson, Mundschenk, & Heflin, 2011). Inappropriate or inadequate placement options are the most frequently cited reason for litigation (Yell, Katsiyannis, Drasgow,

& Herbst, 2003), often resulting in lengthy and expensive due process procedures. Coordination, cooperation, and patience are called for when conducting IEP meetings because the alternative is costly to both families and school systems. Case vignettes are presented in Chapter 9 to illustrate service delivery options.

INDIVIDUAL PROCESS

IDEA (2004) mandates that a child with a disability has the right to a free appropriate public education and a special education program specifically designed for their individual needs. The IEP is the process in which parents are introduced to IDEA and parents and school personnel initially identify the difficulties and special factors that influence the child's learning and then develop a plan to meet the child's unique educational needs. An IEP is designed for 1 year. In subsequent years, team members review the student's progress (or lack thereof) and establish the next year's goals and objectives. Although the IEP is intended to last for 1 year, additional IEP meetings can be called within that year by the parents or the school to develop amendments and make adjustments to the program. Amendments do not necessarily require that the entire team reassemble. Once completed by the parent and the appropriate school personnel, the amendment is attached to the IEP document. Schools are required to provide the parents with a copy of the completed IEP and any amendments, signed by all team members.

IEP meetings can be a calm and positive means of relating information and plans about the student; however, they can become emotionally charged and antagonistic and can result in hours-long marathons. Parents and educational systems can become adversarial if regulations established by IDEA (2004) are not followed, if controversy surrounds the student's abilities or needs, or if parents are overwhelmed by dispassionate comments regarding the challenges their child faces. Although IDEA mandates what must be included in the student's IEP, each state interprets the process differently, producing variability in forms and procedures.

According to IDEA (2004), the IEP is to be implemented for 1 year. However, a multiyear option is permissible as a pilot project in 15 states with the consent of the parent. Even if this option is taken, the IEP can be no longer than 3 years unless the parent agrees. For students with ASD, who often require frequent adjustments to programming, multiyear IEPs would most likely be problematic, difficult to measure, and ill advised. The following case study illustrates the major provisions of IDEA related to the development and implementation of the IEP.

Case Study: Gina

Gina[1] is 13 years old and a sixth-grade student in a public school in Georgia. She received a diagnosis of attention-deficit/hyperactivity disorder prior to a medical diagnosis of autistic disorder. She was diagnosed with autism at age 7 years, 6 months through a comprehensive evaluation that included the Autism Diagnostic Interview—Revised (Le Couteur, Lord, & Rutter, 2003) and the Autism Diagnostic Observation Schedule (Lord, Rutter, DiLavore, & Risi, 2002). She is receiving special education support through the autism, speech impairment, and other health impaired disability categories. Gina has been included in general education classrooms since kindergarten, when her parents requested an inclusive program. She has shown dramatic progress in language development over the years, eliminating her echolalia in favor of conversational speech. Her repetitive self-stimulatory behaviors have decreased, and she displays functional play with age mates. Although she continues to struggle with academics and in securing a best friend, socially she enjoys ongoing relationships with all her classmates, is well liked, and has a large support group of typical peers who accept her and include her in all their school activities. Gina's academics are modified, and she receives resource support for reading and mathematics. She transitioned to middle school in the fall of 2012.

Parent Rights

Under the regulations of IDEA (2004), school systems are required to provide a list of parental rights at the beginning of each IEP meeting in the language best understood by the parents (written in English, Spanish, Japanese, etc., or verbally, through a translator). The school administrator or member leading the meeting must be assured that the parents understand this document and must answer any questions they may have in regard to their legal rights. The parent rights document given to the family can vary in length from state to state and district to district, being as short as one page to possibly 18 pages or more. Parents have specific rights mandated by IDEA; most important, they are to be considered equal partners in developing the IEP for their child. For an initial IEP, the parent may be confused over the technical wording and should be given sufficient time to understand the document and how it affects their child's rights under federal law.

If the parents do not realize that the school has identified behavioral characteristics of ASD in their child and first learn of the school's intentions to discuss the autism eligibility at the IEP meeting, they may well be frustrated,

---

[1]The details of the case study have been changed to preserve the anonymity of the individuals involved.

confused, or surprised, all of which can interfere with their understanding of their parental rights. Care and patience are required at this time, and the parents should be given time to express their concerns and fully understand the parent rights document and the scope and benefits of the IDEA (2004) legislation. Resources should be provided for the parents to learn more about IDEA and ASD, along with the explanation that schools do not "diagnose" children's conditions but only describe observable behaviors that match eligibilities for special education services.

Although it was not the first IEP for their child, Gina's parents asked that the parent rights portion of IDEA (2004) outlining least restrictive environment (LRE) be read aloud and documented for the minutes of the meeting. Once this was done, the parents provided all team members with, and then read aloud, a typed sheet of their concerns, stating that they felt Gina's IEP had not been followed as directed in the previous IEP, specifically in relation to computer programs that were purchased for Gina and a perceived lack of ongoing information and collaboration. A timeline of the events causing parental distress over the course of the year was furnished to the teachers and administrators. School personnel assured the parents that these concerns were taken seriously and would be remedied in the coming year's program.

Individualized Education Plan Participants

IDEA (2004) regulations specify that the IEP team must include at least one parent or legal guardian, one special education teacher (usually the case manager), at least one general education teacher (if the student is or will be participating in general education), a specialist who can explain test results from any evaluation they conducted (usually the school psychologist), an administrator with the authority to explain and commit to services and resources, and related specialists if relevant to the student (e.g., speech–language therapist, occupational therapist, physical therapist, nurse). If the student is at the age of transition (age 16, or younger, if needed), an individual who specializes in preparation for postsecondary options as well as individuals from those agencies who can explain their services should also be present.

When possible, the student should be invited to the IEP meeting. Student-led IEPs are becoming more prevalent and add a unique perspective to the IEP document (Martin et al., 2006). The team may also invite other individuals (e.g., autism specialists, family members, physicians, advocates) to attend, but the parent can dismiss any member if their input is not necessary to decision making. When scheduling the meeting, the school must make every effort to notify the parent sufficiently early so that he or she will be able to attend. However, a school can hold the IEP meeting without the parent if the parent refuses to or cannot attend. If this occurs, all alternatives should be considered, including conference calls, electronic means, or other options in order to complete an IEP for the student. Parents also have a mechanism within IDEA (2004) to pursue their right of a due process complaint if they do not agree with the decisions of the IEP team. Timelines and procedures for accessing mediation or filing a complaint are also defined in the parent rights document.

Gina's IEP team meeting was attended by both parents; the speech, occupational, and physical therapists; her resource teacher; and two general education teachers (science and social studies). In addition, the principal and an administrator from the school system's special education department attended the meeting, as did an autism specialist contracted through the school system (at the request of the parents) and a private clinical psychologist contracted by the parents.

Present Levels of Performance

Before developing the next year's goals and objectives, it is necessary to evaluate present levels of performance in relation to the instruction received from the prior year and to review the most recent testing from psychological evaluations and end-of-course tests along with developmental, achievement, or any other testing data or data designed to document performance over time. Progress (or lack thereof) should be explained by the student's teachers from the previous year and compared with the benchmarks defined in the expiring IEP.

The discussion of Gina's present level of performance included the most recent state and district assessments (for sixth grade, Georgia's [2011] Criterion-Referenced Competency Test [CRCT]). On the CRCT, a score of 800 indicates that a student has met the standard for that subject. Gina did not meet the standards for any subject (science, social studies, language arts, reading, or math). The selected computer reading program and the data from the previous year were discussed. Gina performs at the second-grade reading level. She has had difficulty with comprehension of text but retains information well if text is read aloud. She continues to be inconsistent with money skills and one-to-one correspondence. Gina has remained on the CRCT track and has taken the CRCT tests over the years, though she has not met standards to date in any subject area tested. Data graphs produced by the computer reading program did not provide sufficient information on mastery levels of vocabulary words and comprehension. Test scores of three assessment instruments used to document Gina's progress were discussed. Because this was a special concern for the parents, there was a discussion of teacher support, supplementary reading materials, and instruction methods used in Gina's reading program during the year.

On a positive note, both the science and social studies teachers reported that Gina's social skills and peer interactions increased over the year. She sits next to a typical peer buddy who assists with prompting during class. She now raises her hand to answer questions (she receives preteaching) and is following group cues, decreasing the number of individual prompts needed. Gina is now more frequently looking to peers for help when needed, though she also has a paraprofessional who delivers direct and indirect prompts to her to increase participation in her general education classes.

Gina's occupational therapist gave her update, stating that Gina is now able to independently open her locker with a key. Although her handwriting has improved, her proficiency goes down when speed is required. She is currently learning to sign her name in cursive. Gina is also learning to use assistive technology to write sentences. Gina's physical therapist stated that she is functioning at the 18th percentile on the Bruinicks–Oseretsky Test of Motor Proficiency, Second Edition (Bruininks & Bruininks, 2005). In speech, Gina continues to struggle with inclusion and exclusion concepts, location, temporal, and sequencing.

Objectives to Measure Progress

The IEP team is charged with developing a method of documenting progress over the course of the year toward measurable annual goals for academics and functional skills. IDEA (2004) has removed the requirement for short-term objectives in favor of measurable annual goals. However, for students participating in alternate assessments, short-term objectives or benchmarks are required to monitor progress. Huefner (2000) commented that for students who are not taking alternate assessments and who receive instruction in the core academic areas, "the emphasis on accessing the general curriculum is not meant to negate other educational needs that result from the child's disability" (p. 198). Unfortunately, the No Child Left Behind Act (2001) placed an emphasis on academic test scores that take "the teacher's focus away from the functional, developmental, and social skills students with autism need" (Kalaei, 2008, p. 75). IDEA clearly emphasizes the need for addressing not only academics but also the student's developmental and functional needs, and an IEP team may elect to place short-term objectives into the student's educational plan for those not on the alternate assessment track.

The numbers of goals and short-term objectives vary among students depending on individual needs, but goals should be observable, measurable, reasonable, and able to be accomplished between IEP meetings. For students with ASD, team members should ensure goals and objectives also address their area of disability, including communication, age-appropriate behaviors, and especially social skills. Extensive research (L. Koegel, Koegel,

Frea, & Smith, 1995; Tonge, Brereton, Gray, & Einfeld, 1999) has documented that poor social skills can lead to increased interference with the ability for the student with ASD to interact and sustain social activities with peers. Academic and functional skills are important for all students requiring IEPs, but social skills development is an area of critical need for those with ASD; establishing those skills requires years of close attention and intervention.

Although it may not be the usual practice, Gina's IEP meetings tend to be lengthy. As a result, her meeting was conducted in segments held over several days. Gina's team developed a total of 14 goals, with short-term objectives for each. These were developed both at the main meeting and through e-mail discussions between teachers and parents. The resulting annual goals and objectives address sight words and comprehension, spelling, functional math, writing, grammar, independent work, motor skills, articulation, and pragmatic language. Social skills objectives were added in the final meeting prior to the discussion of extended school year (ESY), for which she qualified.

Interpretation of Assessment

If the student has received a psychological evaluation through the school system prior to the IEP meeting, the results are reported and explained sufficiently for the parents to understand. The school psychologist usually does this every 3 years (though it can be more often if the parent requests it and the team agrees), or it can be considered unnecessary if the parents consent. This evaluation may also be conducted at the behest of the parent or the system by an independent evaluator who is not associated with the school system. This may be done for a number of reasons (e.g., parents disagree with the system's test results, the system does not currently have the appropriate evaluation specialist on staff, contradictory test results). Students with ASD pose unique challenges to test score reliability due to difficulties with unfamiliar testers and test settings, interruption of their daily routines, and lack of motivation (R. Koegel, Koegel, & Smith, 1997).

Hence, test results for students with ASD must always be interpreted with caution because their performance may differ widely from that predicted by test scores (Estes, Rivera, Bryan, Cali, & Dawson, 2011). The test battery for students with ASD should include more than the routine cognitive and achievement measures. A comprehensive assessment should include an evaluation of the student's adaptive, social, and behavior functioning, as well as autism-specific rating scales. If the student is in the transition years, vocational and interest inventories and any instrument that would assist the student in meeting postsecondary goals should be included. Many states require the reporting of exact scores in the written documentation to assist in the determination of eligibility for special education services, though this varies from state to state.

Gina's eligibility evaluations were completed in November 2011. She is not due for another at this time. However, Gina's parents enlisted a private clinical psychologist to conduct the same reading tests that her teacher administered during the year. Discrepancies between the results were discussed at this time. Limitations of the reading program were identified, and decisions were made to more closely monitor her reading program and pursue options that may prove more effective.

Related Services

IDEA (2004) allows for a wide range of related services to support a student's learning. When considering the wide variety of profiles in students with ASD, any number of related services may be required, including (a) audiology services, (b) physical therapy, (c) speech–language support, (d) counseling, (e) medical services, (f) occupational therapy, (g) orientation or mobility services, (h) parent counseling and training, (i) psychological services, (j) recreation, (k) rehabilitation counseling services, (l) school health services, (m) school-based social work services, and (n) transportation. Related services typically provided to students with ASD are speech, occupational, and physical therapies and special education transportation. If the student with ASD has additional conditions, they may require access to the wider range of these options and to other services as necessary. Related services are determined by their impact on the student's learning and the disability, but they do not include certain medical practices (e.g., medical implant devices).

Gina's speech, occupational, and physical therapy services were discussed at the meeting. For speech therapy, she will continue with 1 hour per week. As have many other states, Georgia has adopted an evaluation method for determining the amount of occupational and physical therapy relevant for the student's education (Consideration for Educationally Relevant Therapy; Georgia Board of Education, 2011). Gina's parents were quite distressed because her score allowed for fewer related services than she had previously received. The IEP team discussed this concern and assured the parents that the IEP was to be developed with their daughter's individual needs as the determining factor. Given Gina's low level of adaptive behavior and limited academic progress, the team recommended that she receive the same level of occupational and physical therapy that was provided in previous years.

Accommodations and Modifications

Many students with ASD require some level of accommodations or modifications to instruction to meet their annual goals and objectives and for their involvement in the general curriculum. This varies according to the severity of the ASD and any accompanying intellectual impairment (which can vary widely) and includes, but is not limited to, extra time on tests, larger text, reduced work load, supplemental materials, specialized curricula, preferential seating, use of a computer, visual supports, one-to-one instruction, oral reading of materials, short work sessions, peer note takers, and preteaching, to name just a few. *Accommodations* make the existing work more accessible to the learner; *modifications* change the level of difficulty to match the student's level of developmental ability. Students with ASD often require both.

Gina's accommodations and modifications determined by the IEP team include one-to-one and small group instruction combined with repetition and overlearning (including preteaching). Conceptual level of material will be adjusted to her instructional level, additional time will be allowed for tests or quizzes, and homework and classwork assignments will be shortened or reduced. She will be given short and specific directions and paraprofessional support during inclusion time. Peer programs and direct instruction of social skills in an integrated, small-group setting (once weekly) were also recommended.

Placement Options

IDEA (2004) clearly states that the student must be educated alongside children without disabilities to the maximum extent appropriate. Because the characteristics of students with ASD vary widely, educational placements can range from full inclusion in general education classrooms without additional support, to cotaught classes (both a special and general education teacher in class), to supportive classes (general education teacher and a paraprofessional), to pullout resource classes (assistance for selected core academic subjects), to self-contained classrooms (either full or partial day), to specialized school placements outside of the public school setting (homebound or hospital environment, specialized residential-behavioral treatment programs, a college campus or other appropriate settings).

Given the impact of LRE, students with ASD are most often placed in general education classrooms for at least a portion of the school day (Simpson, de Boer-Ott, & Smith-Myles, 2003). As a result, the support staff necessary to the success of the placement must also be considered during the IEP meeting. Once trained, these support personnel can assist the student with ASD (or with any disability) with a wide range of activities, including both academics and social skills, and can record data to assess progress and help determine future action (Boomer, 2004; Scheuermann, Webber, Boutot, & Goodwin, 2003). Although placement and inclusion in the general education classroom is more prevalent, Zirkel (2011) related that the National Research Council report published in 2001 stated that no outcome studies to date have been published that recommend one model or approach as being superior to another. Determining placement for students with ASD will always be dependent on individual needs.

During the IEP meeting, the team decided that Gina's diploma track should be changed from the standard core curriculum to the alternative assessment method of measuring progress and focusing on the development of her adaptive skills. She will continue to receive supportive instruction in two general education classes (for the purposes of generalization of social skills), as well as homeroom, electives (connections classes), and lunch. As a result, she will receive 10 segments of one-to-one instruction and 20 segments outside of the special education classroom per week. Gina will also be supported by a paraprofessional during her times in the general education classes.

Transition Services

IDEA (2004) requires that the first IEP in effect when the student turns 16 must address transitioning from the educational system to postsecondary options. This is a crucial issue requiring close attention because outcomes for students with ASD have not been promising (Shattuck et al., 2012). The IEP team should take into consideration the student's life goals, the remaining coursework necessary to achieve those goals, legal guardianship (if turning 18), vocational rehabilitation evaluations and predictions for opportunities in the work or postsecondary world, and parental concerns once the student exits the educational system (students can remain through age 21). If the student with ASD plans to enter postsecondary institutions (e.g., colleges, universities, community coursework), qualifying tests should be discussed. If the Scholastic Achievement Test and the ACT Assessment are taken early in the high school years, they may be repeated if the student's initial scores are lower than acceptable college entry limits.

Too often, students with ASD and their IEP team fail to establish goals higher than remaining at home with few job and social opportunities. Shattuck et al. (2012) found that youth with ASD had the lowest rates of employment and participation in postsecondary education compared with youth with other disabilities. Taylor and Seltzer (2011) reported that young adults with ASD without accompanying intellectual disability were 3 times more likely to have no activities during the day compared with those who had ASD and intellectual disability. One might assume that resources such as sheltered workshops, supported employment, and group homes are more appropriate for individuals with a profile of ASD and intellectual disability than for those with mild characteristics of ASD and higher levels of independence. However, many who have milder presentations of ASD may also be in need of long-term assistance and require behavioral support into the adult years. In the educational transition years, there should be an intense focus on all areas of the student's profile to improve outcomes for students with ASD, both with and without intellectual disability. Unfortunately, time is of the essence; these final educational years slip away all too quickly.

At 13, Gina has not yet reached the "formal" transition year of 16, though a transition plan was discussed at her IEP meeting concerning the move to middle school. Gina will be making several visits to the new school to become familiar with the environment. She will meet her new middle school teachers prior to the end of the present school term and during the summer months. Gina will be attending ESY because of her difficulties with retention of learning over breaks. This will assist with the transition to middle school. Because she has not improved in her reading levels, Gina will receive intensive instruction in reading during the summer extended school year, as well as speech, occupational therapy, and physical therapy classes.

EVALUATING INDIVIDUALIZED EDUCATION PLAN QUALITY

Although IDEA (2004) provides the legal requirements and groundwork for the development of an IEP, each state is permitted to adopt its own forms and set additional requirements for the development of educational programs for students with disabilities. Unfortunately, there is little research available to guide parents and school districts in developing quality IEPs (Wilczynski, Menousek, Hunter, & Mudgal, 2007). Although some research has been given to various sections of the IEP (Jung, 2007; Jung, Baird, Gomez, & Galyon-Keramidas, 2008; Smith, Slattery, & Knopp, 1993), there is no uniform standard for evaluating the quality of this important document. A recently developed IEP evaluation tool (Ruble, McGrew, Dalrymple, & Jung, 2010) shows promise, but there is a need for further studies in this area. Because litigation resulting from IEP disputes appears to be the "fastest growing and most expensive area of educational litigation" (Etscheidt, 2003, p. 51), all students with ASD would benefit from a means to better evaluate IEPs.

Schools often receive parent requests at IEPs for other, autism-specific services that are used in the ASD population. The idiosyncrasies of ASD have led to demands for a wide range of treatment options. Some of these are supported by empirical research; others have little to no supporting research but are promoted by advertisers and given media attention (Herbert, Sharp, & Gaudiano, 2002; Simpson, 2005) and may be supported through anecdotal reports from other parents. Although IDEA (2004) requires that schools provide services based on peer-reviewed research "to the extent practicable" (34 C.F.R. § 300.320(a)(4) 2011), it is possible that some districts might agree to provide nonresearch-based therapies to avoid lengthy due process court cases and expensive litigation.

An additional resource often requested by the parent (or provided by the system) is an individual highly trained in ASD (i.e., an autism specialist) who can consult on the student's education program and monitor progress. This consultant, once established in the system, may become an important resource for all students in the school with ASD; he or she may analyze the system's overall programming and serve as a source of information to increase the organization's expertise in ASD. Safran and Safran (2001) commented that to assure that students receive the full benefit of the consultation, the consultant must provide a wide range of services and ensure coordination between those and other services available to the students. Coordination between teachers, home, and community therapists will increase effectiveness of programming and provide benefits to the system and students. Although IDEA (2004) requires schools to consider the full continuum of programs and services, budget shortfalls and lack of resources can affect the availability of services provided in the neighborhood school. In the recent economic downturn, at least 34 states cut kindergarten to 12th grade aid to schools and defunded various programs (Johnson, Oliff, & Williams, 2011). Likewise, reduced tax revenues will be an ongoing challenge for all schools (Reschovsky, 2004).

Although schools receive federal monies for special education students, IDEA (2004) has never been fully funded, and schools must make up the difference to provide the most appropriate programs for students with disabilities. With reduced federal funding, some states are facing shortened school days or weeks and extensive job losses (Johnson, Williams, & Oliff, 2010). This further jeopardizes education reforms, quality of instruction, and availability of resources. With the incidence of ASD on the rise, and given the intensity of intervention required for this disorder, this issue will become more and more of a challenge for school budgets.

PARENT ADVOCACY

IDEA (2004) mandates that parents have a legal right to be a part of all aspects of their child's programming. Unfortunately, an unawareness of this statute may prohibit parents from becoming partners in the educational process. Throughout their school careers, students are instructed by numerous teachers and support personnel, making ongoing and knowledgeable parent advocacy imperative to maintain consistency. Regardless of the postsecondary plans for the student, parent advocacy throughout the student's educational years is critical to the development of independent life skills for adulthood and to ensure the greatest educational benefit (Trainor, 2010).

Parent involvement and advocacy has many levels of intensity, from a complete absence to continual on-site visits and demands for minute-by-minute information on the student's daily activities. Parent stress and anxiety due to the demands of parenting a child with ASD and apprehension regarding the child's future outcome drive the need for information. However, close, continual, and overly intensive involvement with teachers and school can exacerbate negative attitudes toward the parent and the student's program, undermining the willingness to collaborate. Conversely, if teachers and the school refuse to reassure the parent through regular and routine delivery of information about the student's behaviors and performance, parent confusion and resentment might result (Stoner et al., 2005), sometimes extending to litigation. A balance between the two extremes is ideal.

The Georgia Parent Mentor Partnership (2013) is an example of a parent advocacy program. This statewide initiative is based on Ohio's Department of Education Parent Mentor Project (n.d.). The program provides a bridge between the home and school by pairing an experienced individual who has a child with a disability with other parents who require help and support when trying to understand special education procedures or school policies that affect their child. These unique programs assist parents of students with ASD by providing disability information, explaining parental rights under IDEA (2004; unofficially, because a parent mentor is not a legal advocate), and defusing tense situations between school and home. Parent mentor programs provide an opportunity to build positive parent advocacy through the enhancement of parent training in IDEA and should be considered by all states.

Many parents can seek knowledge and training on IDEA (2004) and can advocate for their child without school assistance. In contrast, other parents often struggle with the confusing and complex regulations that afford certain educational rights for their child. They may invoke their right to bring a parent advocate or legal representative with them to the meeting. Unfortunately, once legal representatives are included at the meeting or the team is involved in the legal process, traditional barriers to collaboration between parent and school can become more pronounced, making it difficult to regain the trust needed between the two parties. Clearly, parent advocacy and knowledge of rights afforded under IDEA are necessary to ensure the development of the most appropriate program for the student. Knowledge is power; when the key players have equal status, the results of collaborative decision making can achieve the desired results outlined in the IEP (Biklen, 1976).

Intentional trust building between school and home will continue to be an area of great need, especially in light of shrinking school system budgets and increasing resistance to providing necessary services. The challenging and complex nature of ASD makes it even more critical that the parents are invested and involved in their child's educational program. For many students with ASD, the only stable individuals in their lives will be their parent(s), family members, or primary caregivers. Furthermore, many adults with ASD face ongoing dependency issues and will remain with their families for their entire lives (Krauss, Seltzer, & Jacobson, 2005). Therefore, much depends on parents and schools working together to decrease the symptoms of ASD and plan for the best possible outcome. The development of an effective IEP for the student with ASD requires advocacy and partnership from both parent and school system. Chapter 10 describes how professionals and families can work collaboratively to advocate for expanded services.

CONCLUSION

Students with ASD are entitled to a free appropriate public education (FAPE) under IDEA (2004). Although there is no known "cure" for ASD, symptom severity can be reduced by a program of intensive educational and behavioral intervention. However, IDEA does not define "most appropriate." The resulting ambiguity and the fact that parents of children with ASD have become more knowledgeable and vocal about their rights under IDEA have led to increasing demands for services (Nussbaum, 2004). Currently, FAPE and LRE court cases are over 10 times more likely to concern a child with autism than one would expect given the proportion of children with this disability in the special education population (Zirkel, 2011).

Parent–professional communication and collaboration are key to making educational and treatment decisions. Ongoing training and education in ASD is also important for both parents and professionals. Educators and support professionals who are trained in specific methodology and techniques will be most effective in providing the appropriate services and in modifying the curriculum on the basis of the unique needs of the individual child with ASD.

REFERENCES

Biklen, D. (1976). Advocacy comes of age. *Exceptional Children, 42,* 308–313.

Boomer, L. (1994). The utilization of paraprofessionals in programs for students with autism. *Focus on Autistic Behavior, 9*(2), 1–9.

Bruininks, R. H., & Bruininks, B. D. (2005). *Bruininks–Oseretsky Test of Motor Proficiency, Second Edition (BOT–2).* San Antonio, TX: Pearson.

Danneker, J. E., & Bottge, B. A. 2009). Benefits of and barriers to elementary student-led individualized education programs. *Remedial and Special Education, 30,* 225–233. doi:10.1177/0741932508315650

Eaves, L. C., & Ho, H. H. (2008). Young adult outcome of autism spectrum disorders. *Journal of Autism and Developmental Disorders, 38,* 739–747. doi:10.1007/s10803-007-0441-x

Estes, A., Rivera, V., Bryan, M., Cali, P., & Dawson, G. (2011). Discrepancies between academic achievement and intellectual ability in higher-functioning school-aged children with autism spectrum disorder. *Journal of Autism and Developmental Disorders, 41,* 1044–1052. doi:10.1007/s10803-010-1127-3

Etscheidt, S. (2003). An analysis of legal hearings and cases related to individualized educational programs for children with autism. *Research and Practice for Persons with Severe Disabilities, 28,* 51–69. doi:10.2511/rpsd.28.2.51

Foden, T., & Anderson, C. (2011). *Adults with ASD: Deciding when to disclose.* Retrieved from http://www.iancommunity.org/cs/adults/deciding_when_to_disclose

Gadow, K. D., Guttmann-Steinmetz, S., Rieffe, C., & DeVincent, C. J. (2011). Depression symptoms in boys with autism spectrum disorder and comparison samples. *Journal of Autism and Developmental Disorders, 42,* 1353–1363. doi:10.1007/s10803-011-1367-x

Georgia Department of Education, Division for Special Education Services and Supports. (2011). *Considerations for educationally relevant therapy.* Retrieved from http://archives.gadoe.org/DMGetDocument.aspx/GaCERT_8_2011.pdf?p=6CC6799F8C1371F6D6231D4427F169FD2D4299ACF21AC08C46E0D008356DFD50&Type=D

Georgia Parent Mentor Partnership. (2013). *About us.* Retrieved from http://www.parentmentors.org/about-us/

Giangreco, M. F. (2001). Interactions among program, placement, and services in educational planning for students with disabilities. *Mental Retardation, 39,* 341–350. doi:10.1352/0047-6765(2001)039<0341:IAPPAS>2.0.CO;2

Gresham, F. M., & Elliott, S. N. (2008). *Social Skills Improvement System (SSIS).* San Antonio, TX: Pearson.

Herbert, J. D., & Sharp, I. R., & Gaudiano, B. A. (2002). Separating fact from fiction in the etiology and treatment of autism. *The Scientific Review of Mental Health Practices, 1*(1), 1–35.

Huefner, D. S. (2000). The risks and opportunities of the IEP requirements under IDEA '97. *The Journal of Special Education, 33,* 195–204. doi:10.1177/002246690003300402

Individuals With Disabilities Education Act, 20 U.S.C. § 1400 (2004).

Johnson, N., Oliff, P., & Williams, E. (2011). *An update on budget state budget cuts: At least 46 states have imposed cuts that hurt vulnerable residents and cause job loss.* Retrieved from http://www.cbpp.org/cms/?fa=view&id=1214

Johnson, N., Williams, E., & Oliff, P. (2010). *Governors' new budgets indicate loss of many jobs if federal aid expires*. Washington, DC: Center on Budget and Policy Priorities. Retrieved from http://www.cbpp.org/files/2-5-10stim.pdf

Jung, L. A. (2007). Writing SMART objectives and strategies that fit the ROUTINE. *Teaching Exceptional Children, 39*(4), 54–58.

Jung, L. A., Baird, S. M., Gomez, C., & Galyon-Keramidas, C. (2008). Family-centered intervention: Bridging the gap between IEPs and implementation. *Teaching Exceptional Children, 41*(1), 26–33.

Kalaei, S. (2008). Students with autism left behind: No Child Left Behind and the Individuals With Disabilities Education Act. *Thomas Jefferson Law Review, 30*, 723–750.

Koegel, L. K., Koegel, R. L., & Smith, A. (1997). Variables related to differences in standardized test outcomes for children with autism. *Journal of Autism and Developmental Disorders, 27*, 233–243. doi:10.1023/A:1025894213424

Koegel, R. L., Koegel, L. K., Frea, W. D., & Smith, A. E. (1995). Emerging interventions for children with autism: Longitudinal and lifestyle implications. In R. L. Koegel & L. K. Koegel (Eds.), *Teaching children with autism: Strategies for initiating positive interactions and improving learning opportunities* (pp. 1–15). Baltimore, MD: Brookes.

Krauss, M. W., Seltzer, M. M., & Jacobson, H. T. (2005). Adults with autism living at home or in non-family settings: Positive and negative aspects of residential status. *Journal of Intellectual Disability Research, 49*, 111–124. doi:10.1111/j.1365-2788.2004.00599.x

Le Couteur, A. L., Lord, C., & Rutter, M. (2003). *Autism Diagnostic Interview—Revised*. Torrance, CA: Western Psychological Services.

Lee, S.-H., Simpson, R. L., & Shogren, K. A. (2007). Effects and implications of self-management or students with autism: A meta-analysis. *Focus on Autism and Other Developmental Disabilities, 22*, 2–13. doi:10.1177/10883576070220010101

Lord, C., Rutter, M., DiLavore, P. C., & Risi, S. (2002). *Autism Diagnostic Observation Schedule*. Torrance, CA: Western Psychological Services.

MacFarlane, J. R., & Kanaya, T. (2009). What does it mean to be autistic? Inter-state variation in special education criteria for autism services. *Journal of Child and Family Studies, 18*, 662–669. doi:10.1007/s10826-009-9268-8

Martin, J. E., Van Dycke, J. L., Christensen, W. R., Green, B. A., Gardner, J. E., & Lovett, D. L. (2006). Increasing student participation in IEP meetings: Establishing the self-directed IEP as an evidenced-based practice. *Exceptional Children, 72*, 299–316.

National Research Council. (2001). *Educating children with autism*. Washington, DC: National Academy Press.

No Child Left Behind Act of 2001, 20 U.S.C. § 6319 (2002).

Nussbaum, D. (2004, February 8). A surge in autism, but why? *The New York Times*, p. NJ-6.

Ohio Department of Education. (n.d.). *For mentors*. Retrieved from http://education.ohio.gov/Topics/Teaching/Resident-Educator-Program/Resident-Educator-Mentor-Resources

Reschovsky, A. (2004). The impact of state government fiscal crises on local governments and schools. *State and Local Government Review*, 36(2), 86–102. doi:10.1177/0160323X0403600201

Ruble, L. A., McGrew, J., Dalrymple, N., & Jung, L. A. (2010). Examining the quality of IEPs for young children with autism. *Journal of Autism and Developmental Disorders*, 40, 1459–1470. doi:10.1007/s10803-010-1003-1

Safran, J. S., & Safran, S. P. (2001). School-based consultation for Asperger syndrome. *Journal of Educational & Psychological Consultation*, 12, 385–395. doi:10.1207/S1532768XJEPC1204_05

Scheuermann, B., Webber, J., Boutot, E. A., & Goodwin, M. (2003). Problems with personnel preparation in autism spectrum disorders. *Focus on Autism and Other Developmental Disabilities*, 19, 197–206. doi:10.1177/10883576030180030801

Shattuck, P. T., Narendorf, S. C., Cooper, B., Sterzing, P. R., Wagner, M., & Taylor, J. L. (2012). Postsecondary education and employment among youth with an autism spectrum disorder. *Pediatrics*, 29, 1042–1049. doi:10.1542/peds.2011-2864

Simpson, R. L. (2005). Evidence-based practices and students with autism spectrum disorders. *Focus on Autism and Other Developmental Disabilities*, 20, 140–149.

Simpson, R. L., de-Boer-Ott, S., & Smith-Myles, B. (2003). Inclusion of learners with autism spectrum disorders in general education settings. *Topics in Language Disorders*, 23, 116–133. doi:10.1097/00011363-200304000-00005

Simpson, R. L., Mundschenk, N. A., & Heflin, L. J. (2011). Issues, policies, and recommendations for improving the education of learners with autism spectrum disorders. *Journal of Disability Policy Studies*, 22(1), 3–17. doi:10.1177/1044207310394850

Smith, S. W., Slattery, W. J., & Knopp, Y. T. (1993). Beyond the mandate: Developing individualized education programs that work for students with autism. *Focus on Autistic Behavior*, 8(3), 1–15. doi:10.1177/108835769300800301

Stoner, J. B., Bock, S. J., Thompson, J. R., Angell, M. E., Heyl, B. S., & Crowley, E. P. (2005). Welcome to our world: Parent perceptions of interactions between parents of young children with ASD and education professionals. *Focus on Autism and Other Developmental Disabilities*, 20, 39–51. doi:10.1177/10883576050200010401

Taylor, J. L., & Seltzer, M. M. (2011). Employment and post-secondary activities for young adults with autism spectrum disorders during the transition to adulthood. *Journal of Autism and Developmental Disorders*, 41, 566–574. doi:10.1007/s10803-010-1070-3

Tonge, B. J., Brereton, A. V., Gray, K. M., & Einfeld, S., L. (1999). Behavioural and emotional disturbance in high-functioning autism and Asperger syndrome. *Autism*, 3, 117–130. doi:10.1177/1362361399003002003

Trainor, A. A. (2010). Diverse approaches to parent advocacy during special education home-school interactions. *Remedial and Special Education, 31,* 34–47. doi:10.1177/0741932508324401

Weiss, M. J., & Harris, S. L. (2001). Teaching social skills to people with autism. *Behavior Modification, 25,* 785–802. doi:10.1177/0145445501255007

Wilczynski, S. M., Menousek, K., Hunter, M., & Mudgal, D. (2007). Individualized education programs for youth with autism spectrum disorders. *Psychology in the Schools, 44,* 653–666. doi:10.1002/pits.20255

Yell, M. L., Katsiyannis, A., Drasgow, E., & Herbst, M. (2003). Developing legally correct and educationally appropriate programs for students with autism spectrum disorders. *Focus on Autism and Other Developmental Disabilities, 18,* 182–191. doi:10.1177/10883576030180030601

Zirkel, P. A. (2011). Autism litigation under the IDEA: A new meaning of "disproportionality"? *Journal of Special Education Leadership, 24,* 92–103.

9

CURRICULUM AND PROGRAM STRUCTURE

SUSAN KABOT AND CHRISTINE REEVE

Lily[1] is an 8-year-old second grader who is included most of the day in Ms. Harris's classroom. She receives some pullout services for small group instruction in reading and writing in the resource room and is supported by Ms. Morris as her case manager and special educator. Lily has a diagnosis of autism and is functioning in the average range cognitively. She participates well in the general education classroom but sometimes needs prompting to stay on task. She occasionally throws materials when she is frustrated with a task, and this behavior occurs in both the resource and general education classrooms. In addition, Lily perseverates on whether her pencil is sharp enough and will become upset if she is not allowed to sharpen the pencil.

Michael is an 8-year-old second-grade student with autism who is served primarily in a self-contained classroom environment for students with autism

---

[1]The details of the case studies have been changed to preserve the anonymity of the individuals involved.

http://dx.doi.org/10.1037/14338-010

Autism Spectrum Disorder in Children and Adolescents: Evidence-Based Assessment and Intervention in Schools, L. A. Wilkinson (Editor)

spectrum disorder (ASD) and low-incidence disabilities. Recent evaluations indicated his cognitive functioning is in the moderate range of intellectual disability and his autism is severe. Michael has a history of significant challenging behaviors, including self-injury and aggression. A functional behavior assessment indicated that his behaviors serve to gain attention from adults and to escape from difficult situations. A behavior support plan has been written by the education team and is reviewed on a monthly basis for effectiveness and implementation integrity.

Both of these students, who will be referenced throughout the chapter, have a diagnosis of ASD but are educated in much different types of settings. ASD is a particularly challenging disorder to address in educational settings. In addition to the legal obligation to provide a free and appropriate public education to eligible students from 3 to 21 years old, the learning characteristics and behaviors related to ASD are unique in their impact on individual students. Also, the students present with the full range of academic and functional abilities (National Research Council, 2001). As a result, educators working with individuals with ASD must be proficient at providing highly individualized programming in the context of diverse educational settings. This chapter describes a process for developing effective educational environments for these learners in the setting that can best serve their needs, and it discusses how to plan educational programming for effective intervention.

Students with ASD are found in every service delivery option along the continuum of services discussed in the Individuals With Disabilities Education Improvement Act (2004). In school settings, programs may include self-contained, specialized autism programs, self-contained special education programs that are not disability specific, resource rooms, and general education classrooms that are supported through a variety of teaching models, including coteaching. Each of these environments should provide certain elements to be effective in the education of students with ASD. These elements include (a) highly structured physical environments; (b) consistent and predictable classroom schedules and routines for engaging both students and staff; (c) visual supports to facilitate independence, receptive language, self-regulation, academic achievement, and to enhance participation in classroom and learning activities; (d) integration of the curriculum with individual needs; (e) specialized instructional strategies that address the learning style of students with ASD; (f) systematic review of each student's progress through periodic curriculum-based assessment and regular data collection and data analysis to inform instruction; and (g) specialized training and support to all school staff involved in educating students with ASD (Iovannone, Dunlap, Huber, & Kincaid, 2003; National Research Council, 2001). The continuum of special education services is discussed in Chapter 8 of this volume.

This chapter describes a systematic process that is used for designing structured educational environments through examination of the following steps: (a) learning about the student through collaboration with other professionals and parents, review of records, and development of a comprehensive plan for supporting the student; (b) developing a program that provides structure and routines through the organization of the physical environment, materials, classroom schedule, visual supports, and staff; (c) understanding and choosing appropriate curriculum elements and adapting them through accommodations and modifications to meet the needs of the individual learner; and (d) ensuring the successful implementation of the curriculum through staff training, evaluating fidelity of intervention, and evaluating individual and program outcomes.

COLLABORATION AND STUDENT-CENTERED PLANNING

The systematic planning of educational intervention for any student involves knowing about the student's learning style, strengths and weaknesses, and behavioral presentation (Myles, Grossman, Aspy, Henry, & Bixler Coffin, 2007). Learning about the student begins with a review of the student's current records, individualized education plan (IEP), and previous learning history. It continues with the discussion of the student's needs and strengths through a case conference that includes the teachers, paraprofessionals, related service providers (e.g., speech pathologists, occupational therapists), and other relevant professionals (e.g., psychologists, behavior specialists, administrators). This meeting could also include families, but if families are absent, the discussion could include their input. If a student is receiving services from outside agencies or individual service providers, their information should be requested and considered in the planning process. The case conference serves as the opportunity for all team members to become familiar with the strengths and needs of each student. The information discussed at this meeting becomes more crucial at transition points in the student's school career, such as changing schools or changing classrooms.

Lily's Case Conference

In the case conference, Lily's team discussed the need to ensure that prompts are used in a systematic way and adult support is faded throughout the day. As indicated in Exhibit 9.1, Lily requires mostly visual and gestural prompting for tasks. Her toileting is independent, and she has a behavior plan in place to address throwing items and becoming overly focused on sharpening her pencil frequently throughout the day to escape from a frustrating task.

EXHIBIT 9.1
Excerpt of Case Conference Information for Lily

Present Level of Skills

Overall Independence
- ☐ Mostly independent ☒ Mostly visual/gestural prompting
- ☐ Primarily verbal prompting ☐ Dependent on physical prompts

Toileting ☒ Independent ☐ Scheduled ☐ Diapers
- ☐ Emerging schedule trained ☐ Initiates to go

Behavior plan attached? ☒ Yes ☐ No

Behavior student may exhibit: throwing items as a way to escape from an undesired task; sharpening her pencil to a specific point before beginning work

Peer interaction: greets teachers with a prompt but typically not peers; limited peer interaction; more likely to interact with adults, but still needs prompts

Fine/gross motor skills: gross motor is fine; writing is sometimes difficult for her, and she uses an adapted pencil

Michael's Case Conference

An excerpt from Michael's case conference notes can be seen in Exhibit 9.2. Michael has been using the Strategies for Teaching Based on Autism Research (STAR) curriculum (Arick, Loos, Falco, & Krug, 2003) and is currently on Level 2. A copy of the protocol being used for curriculum-based assessment was passed from last year's teacher to this year's teacher. In addition, his class is using the Unique Learning System (2012) as an overall curriculum based on the common core standards, with additional curricula as noted.

EXHIBIT 9.2
Michael's Case Conference Form

Curriculum assessment
- ☐ Help ☐ Brigance ☐ Carolina
- ☐ Functional Skills Assessment ☒ STAR Level: 2
- ☐ State core curriculum ☒ Unique Learning System ☐ Other _____

Functional curriculum tools: N/A
- ☐ Murdoch programs (listed on back) ☐ LCCE ☐ PASS-D
- ☐ Other _____

Academic curriculum tools: ☒ Edmark Level: 1 Lesson: 20
- ☐ Reading milestones Book____ Level____ ☒ TouchMath Level: Pre-K
- ☐ Sensible pencil ☒ Handwriting without tears ☐ Other _____

Once the team has completed the case conference process, the teacher should use the Comprehensive Autism Planning System (CAPS; Henry & Myles, 2007) to assemble all of the information discussed into a single document that will guide the implementation of the student's educational program, including the IEP goals and objectives; accommodations; data collection procedures; and communication, social, and sensory supports. The CAPS serves as a useful presentation of the way the teacher and other staff will ensure that the IEP is implemented, thereby increasing a parent's confidence in the teacher and school.

Lily's Comprehensive Autism Planning System

As can be seen in Exhibit 9.3, Lily's IEP goals focus on academics that require explicit instruction (e.g., reading), social skills with peers, and communication skills. She also has a goal for working independently because she currently relies heavily on prompting from staff to stay on task. As can be seen in the excerpt from her CAPS, Lily participates in Ms. Harris's reading class with the second grade with support from Ms. Morris. She also receives pullout assistance in a small group at other times of the day to reinforce and preteach her reading skills. Because there are a number of skills that are either part of the routine or the overall curriculum (and therefore not reflected in Lily's IEP), the team chose to include those skills in the targeted skills area and to highlight the skill that reflected an objective from her IEP.

Michael's Comprehensive Autism Planning System

Michael's IEP goals include academic, social, independent functioning, self-care, language and communication, and basic learning readiness skills (see Exhibit 9.4). His teacher, Ms. Hilliard, chose to use the CAPS–Teaching Plan for him because she was designing the schedule for the whole classroom and had to base that schedule on the needs of all the students. This model allowed her to map out the type of instruction needed on the basis of the goals and objectives of each student.

For many students with ASD, the lack of effective reinforcers prevents them from mastering skills and prevents behavioral interventions from being effective (Koegel & Egel, 1979; Koegel & Mentis, 1985). To address this need, it is important that a preference assessment be completed. There are several ways to gather this information for an individual student: (a) ask the parent what the student likes, (b) give the parent a list of items and activities to rate, (c) conduct a preference assessment by presenting a number of items and activities to the student and observing interest in each in comparison with the others in order to rank them, (d) watch the student in the classroom

EXHIBIT 9.3
Comprehensive Autism Planning System (CAPS)

Child/student: Lily Standifer

Date: 8/25/11

Teacher: Ms. Morris

Time	Activity	Targeted skills to teach	Structure/ modifications	Reinforcement	Sensory strategies	Communication social skills	Data collection	Generalization plan
7:55–8:45	Reading with Ms. Harris	• Following directions • Making deductions, inferences • Getting information from the story • Parts of speech • Subject–verb agreement • Vocabulary • Drawing conclusions • Relating character traits	• One-to-one instruction assistance with staying on task • More assistance with reading comprehension • Assessments can be read aloud • Checklists for independence • Picture cues for vocabulary • Reread directions • Break assignments into smaller components with breaks provided • Use a marker to keep track of place in reading • fewer questions	• High fives and token system	• Fidget with toy at desk • Velcro under desk for tactile stimulation	• Asking for assistance	• Work product	• Fade proximity of adult as a prompt for being on task

Note. From *The Comprehensive Autism Planning System (CAPS) for Individuals With Asperger Syndrome, Autism and Related Disabilities: Integrating Best Practices Throughout the Student's Day,* by S. A. Henry and B. S. Myles, 2007, p. 184, Shawnee Mission, KS: Autism Asperger Publishing Company. Copyright 2007 by the Autism Asperger Publishing Company. Adapted with permission.

EXHIBIT 9.4
Comprehensive Autism Planning System (CAPS)/Teaching Plan

Student: Michael Angel

Communication system:
Michael is verbal but sometimes needs visual prompts

Date completed: 2/1/11

Grade: 2nd grade

Common reinforcers (embedded throughout the day):
Soda, tops, pop toobs

Sensory strategies (embedded throughout the day):
Weighted vest, fidget toys

Case manager/teacher: Susie Everly

School year: 2010–2011

For students served primarily in self-contained classrooms or as part of the process for designing a self-contained classroom, begin completing the following grid with the student's IEP and curriculum objectives to build the schedule. For students who are primarily participating in a general education classroom, you might start with the schedule column and target the goals/skills from that, completing the rest of the grid as needed.

Goal/objective/ targeted skill	Primary teaching activity/ scheduled activity	Teaching strategy	Structure/ modifications/ accommodations	Reinforcers	Communication/ social supports	Data collection	Generalization plan
By January 2011, Michael will establish eye contact with minimal prompts and cues when greeting peers and teachers 4 out of 5 trials.	Morning meeting; arrival	Pivotal Response Training (PRT)	Visual cues as needed	Token system	Availability of pictures to use as needed	Embedded data sheet twice weekly	Throughout the day

Note. From The Comprehensive Autism Planning System (CAPS) for Individuals With Asperger Syndrome, Autism and Related Disabilities: Integrating Best Practices Throughout the Student's Day, by S. A. Henry and B. S. Myles, 2007, p. 184, Shawnee Mission, KS: Autism Asperger Publishing Company. Copyright 2007 by the Autism Asperger Publishing Company. Adapted with permission.

and see what he or she is drawn to, or (e) ask the student if he or she is able to provide that information.

It is also critical that a discussion regarding curriculum take place for all students. Higher functioning students with ASD who are in general education settings and are meeting academic standards may still need to have an articulation of the accommodations, assistive technology, and autism-specific teaching strategies necessary to master the curriculum content. For those students who are working toward alternate standards, specific curricula that are designed to cover the content at a modified level or to build skills through specialized instructional strategies should be discussed and selected for use.

PROGRAM STRUCTURE

The next step, developing the program structure, includes the design of the physical environment, effective organization of materials for the staff, presentation of the learning materials for students, and development of effective visual supports. A daily schedule of activities must be developed and take into account the needs and schedules of other students served in the same environment. Finally, the team must organize staff time and supports for students to effectively meet the needs across the learning community. This includes development of the staff schedule or zoning plan, the use of one-to-one support for students, and the development of mechanisms for staff collaboration and communication across the day.

The arrangement of the physical environment of a classroom has an effect on student learning, social interactions, and behavior (Dunlap, Strain, & Fox, 2006; Nordquist & Twardosz, 1990; Nordquist, Twardosz, & McEvoy, 1991; Sasso, Peck, & Garrison-Harrell, 1998). Care must be taken in the way the furniture of the classroom is arranged to support the type of learning activities taking place (Kabot & Reeve, 2010). In the general education classroom, thought must be given to whether the teacher delivers the majority of his or her instruction to the whole class simultaneously or to smaller groups of students and whether space is needed to support both types of instruction. The placement of the student with autism should also receive consideration if he or she is supported by a one-to-one paraprofessional, needs to be near the teacher's point of instruction for proximity control, or is supported by an assigned peer.

In the self-contained classroom, oftentimes there is more than one adult who provides instruction to small groups of children or even to one child at a time. There must be several work areas that can be used simultaneously, with furniture or dividers used as barriers to separate the different areas. Materials should be organized and stored in the area in which they will be used or should be in close proximity to it. The amount of visual stimulation in the classroom should be considered as well. The type of furniture selected for the classroom may also contribute to the student's ability to attend to and participate in learning activities (e.g., chairs with arms).

For any classroom to operate efficiently, the teaching materials that are used throughout the day must be well-organized and efficiently stored. In a general education classroom, there should be a routine for receiving assigned seatwork and a place for delivering work once it has been completed. In the special education classroom, where student programs are likely to be individualized and concrete materials used instead of paper-and-pencil tasks, each student may have a shoebox with materials needed for the teaching activity at each of the teaching tables. Storage for materials used in particular activities (e.g., art, snack) should be in close proximity to the area where the instruction takes place. Shelving units can serve a dual purpose by storing materials and dividing instructional areas.

Visual supports are designed to promote independence, receptive language, self-regulation, and academic success and to increase meaningful participation and engagement in classroom activities (Dettmer, Simpson, Myles, & Ganz, 2000; Heflin & Alberto, 2001; Hume & Reynolds, 2010; Krantz & McClannahan, 1993; MacDuff, Krantz, & McClannahan, 1993). For example, in the general education classroom, there may be a group schedule posted for the class or a story map to facilitate comprehension of a story. In the self-contained classroom, examples would include individual picture schedules that are manipulated as the student moves through the classroom or a visual cueing belt worn by the classroom staff, with pictures to accompany verbal directions. Tasks may also be set up with specific visual supports to help students to complete the task independently though the use of structured work systems (Hume & Odom, 2007; Hume, Plavnick, & Odom, 2012; Reeve & Kabot, 2012).

Schedules

Effective schedule development has been shown to significantly reduce problem behavior and increase engagement for students with cognitive impairments (O'Reilly, Sigafoos, Lancioni, Edrisinha, & Andrews, 2005). For students with ASD, routines and understanding the planned activities of the day can make the difference between success in an environment and needing a more restrictive one (Dettmer et al., 2000; Heflin & Alberto, 2001). In a general education setting, the schedule for a student with ASD must be developed to meet the student's individual needs while keeping him or her in step with the context of the classroom. Lily's schedule follows the general education classroom schedule except for times when she is pulled out for more explicit instruction in the resource room.

In a self-contained classroom, the schedule would be made to address the individual needs of each student by prioritizing the needs on the basis of the type of instruction (e.g., large group, one-to-one) that is required by the students in the class. For Michael, Ms. Hilliard used the CAPS to construct the classroom schedule (see Exhibit 9.5) to meet the curricular and IEP needs of each individual student. She used a grid that allowed her to write out each student's activities by time of day.

Within the classroom schedule, it is important to have a consistent manner of making transitions within the classroom and between environments in the school. This predictability can reduce anxiety during the day and help the student learn to make the transitions as independently as possible (Dettmer et al., 2000; Goodman & Williams, 2007; MacDuff et al., 1993). For younger students, this type of transition might involve being dismissed one at a time by name from a large group activity to check their schedules. For older students, it might involve checking a visual checklist that gives them information (e.g., the next class, materials needed).

Staff Organization

In most situations there is more than one staff member working with each student throughout the day (Jewell, Grippi, & Hupp, 2007). Therefore, to maintain engagement with the students and limit the need for directions to be given among the staff, the class should have a staff schedule or zoning plan (Lelaurin & Risley, 1972). A *zoning plan* outlines the duties of each staff member for every activity of the day and the responsibilities within the activity (e.g., data collection) and assigns who is responsible for itinerant duties (e.g., cleaning up activities). Over time, staff should be rotated through duties in the classroom (e.g., on a monthly basis) to ensure that the teacher observes the students in different situations. Staff zoning plans should be developed as a team, with a sharing of duties to promote teamwork and collaboration. Time should be set aside to facilitate collaboration among the staff and plan the schedule to ensure that the teacher, as the class leader, has information from all the members of the staff and can make decisions appropriately.

For Lily, the zoning plan includes all the students from Ms. Morris's class who are served by Ms. Morris and the paraprofessionals she supervises (see Exhibit 9.6). The zoning plan created by Michael's teacher is shown in Exhibit 9.7.

In a self-contained setting, one-to-one aides are often assigned because of behavioral concerns, whereas in inclusion settings the reason may be both behavioral and instructional (Suter & Giangreco, 2009). It is critical to remember that the use of an aide in no way replaces a sound functional behavior assessment and behavior support plan. An alternative to a

EXHIBIT 9.5
Michael's Class Schedule

Names	Jim	Ray	AJ	Michael	Sarah	Vince	Missy	Dillon	Laura	Trey
8:00–8:15	Table tasks[a]									
8:15–8:30	Breakfast									
8:30–9:00	Group	Speech M/W	Group	Group	Group	Speech T/Th	Group	Group	Group	Group
9:00–9:20	Read	Math	DI[b]	Read	Read	DI	IW[c]	Math	IW	Math
9:20–9:40	Math	DI	IW	Math	Math	IW	Read	DI	Read	DI
9:40–10:00		IW	Read	DI	DI	Read	Math	IW	Math	

Note. Shaded areas indicate time out of class.
[a]Table tasks can be visual–motor tasks at the table or journals. [b]DI = direct instruction or some form of systematic instruction for specific skills. [c]IW = independent work based on structured teaching with a visually cued work system.

EXHIBIT 9.6
Zoning Plan for Lily's Staff

Time	Ms. Morris	Paraprofessional 1	Paraprofessional 2	Paraprofessional 3
7:55–8:15	Planning with 3rd-grade teachers	Arrival with Lily and Tim in Ms. Harris's room	Arrival and bell work with Jim, Sally, Dontel, and Missy in Ms. Singh's class	Arrival and table tasks with Ashley, Mike, and Brian
8:15–8:45	Reading with Lily and Tim in Ms. Harris's room	Support physical education	Physical education with Jim, Sally, Dontel, and Missy	Physical education with Ashley, Mike, and Brian
8:45–9:00	Calendar time in resource room	Reading with Lily and Tim in Ms. Harris's room, then transition to physical education at 8:55	Calendar in resource room with Jim, Sally, Dontel, and Missy	Calendar with Ashley, Mike, and Brian
9:00–9:30	Reading group with Jim and Sally	Support Lily and Tim in physical education	Independent work with Dontel and Missy	Math group with Ashley, Mike, and Brian
9:30–10:00	Reading group with Tim and Lily in resource room	Edmark/ computer with Dontel and Missy	Independent work with Ashley, Mike, and Brian	Math with Jim and Sally
10:00–10:30	Reading group with Ashley, Mike, and Brian	Edmark/ computer with Jim and Sally	Independent work with Tim and Lily	Math group with Dontel and Missy

one-to-one aide is to consider setting up a schedule so that the student has supervision and support throughout the day though the support comes from a variety of assigned paraprofessionals and/or professionals. This strategy avoids many of the pitfalls of using one-to-one aides, such as difficulty generalizing skills and behavioral control to different staff members, and it minimizes the impact of the absence of one staff member on the student's behavior (Giangreco & Suter, 2010). It continues to be important with either situation to have a structured plan that fades the individual support to the student to increase independence.

EXHIBIT 9.7
Classroom Zoning Plan for Michael's Classroom

Time/activity	Teacher	Paraprofessional 1	Paraprofessional 2	Comments/contingency plans
8:00–8:15 Table tasks	• Set up group time • Take responsibility for timer	• Supervise table tasks take data on two students per day	• Transition students into the room, help them check their schedule, and transition to table tasks	Ensure that someone is responsible for the timer throughout the day
8:15–8:30 Breakfast	• Run table tasks with students who enter room	• Accompany children to breakfast • Take data as needed	• Accompany children to breakfast • Take data as needed	Establish who is responsible for transitioning which children regularly from group activities
8:30–9:00 Group time	• Run group time	• Facilitate and prompt students (AJ) • Take data on one student per day	• Facilitate and prompt students (Jim)	The person with Michael takes responsibility for his schedule
9:00–9:20 Center 1	• Direct instruction with AJ, Vince; data daily supervise independent work with Missy, Laura	• Math center with Ray, Dillon, Trey • Take data on one student per day	• Reading with Jim, Michael, Sarah • Take data on one designated student's targeted goals per day	Take your children to the schedule, transition them to next person there; take new kids back to center
9:20–9:40 Center 2	• Direct instruction with Ray, Dillon, Trey; data daily supervise independent work with AJ, Vince	• Math center with Jim, Michael, Sarah supervise independent work with AJ, Vince take data on one designated student's targeted goals per day	• Reading with Missy, Laura take data on one designated student's targeted goals per day	Give students something to do while waiting for others to transition to center
9:40–10:00 Center 3	• Direct instruction with Michael, Sarah; data daily	• Math center with Missy, Laura supervise independent work with Ray, Dillon take data on one designated student's targeted goals per day	• Reading with AJ, Vince—functional Edmark work product, daily data on Edmark sheet	

CURRICULUM

The No Child Left Behind Act (2008) requires that all students be educated with reference to the general education standards of their state. Students who have severe or significant intellectual disabilities should have the standard curriculum significantly modified to meet their needs and will typically be evaluated through alternate assessments. Students who are able to master and complete the general education curriculum typically will need accommodations, and possibly modifications, to assist them with learning the material, because of difficulties with language, attention, and behavior that affect their ability to comprehend and process information from the classroom.

Many states have adopted the *common core*, a set of standards that are available for math and English/language arts that raises the achievement bar for all students (Common Core Standards Initiative, 2012). Many students with ASD are expected to master the same standards as other students. These standards form the basis for the scope and sequence of skills presented in the classroom curricula. For students who are exempt from these standards, states often have designated alternate or access standards for them.

There is general confusion about the terms *accommodation* and *modification* (Florida Department of Education, 2010). *Accommodations* are changes to how something is taught. Students being exposed to the standard curriculum are often provided a variety of accommodations to support their ability to be successful by helping them compensate for their unique learning styles (e.g., graphic organizers to support written compositions). *Modifications* are changes to what is taught. For example, most students working toward a standard diploma are mastering state or common core standards and would not be allowed to complete assignments that contain less curricular content than others were expected to master. This would be a modification, and without mastery of the complete assignment, the student would not learn all that was expected for that grade level. Generally, students who require extensive modifications to the curriculum are educated in more specialized settings.

Curriculum-based assessments (CBAs) are useful when working with students with ASD to assist with data collection. CBAs are often packaged as part of the curriculum used to teach subjects in general education settings such as reading, mathematics, science, and social studies. For students who are being educated using more specialized curricula, it is more important to use these CBAs because there is often a paucity of student work, unit tests, or standardized measures being collected at the end of the year. Alternative curricula such as the Unique Learning System (2012) offer pretests and posttests for each monthly content unit provided. Developmental curricula such as the STAR (Arick et al., 2003) or the Brigance (Curriculum Associates,

Inc., 1991, 1999) family of curricula can be used several times during the year to monitor progress toward mastery of skills across domains.

INSTRUCTIONAL DESIGN

Instructional design principles must be used by teachers to ensure that students benefit from the instruction provided them. These principles include the creation of learning experiences that make acquisition of knowledge and development of skills effective and efficient for the student. Instructional design principles encourage teachers to make these learning experiences meaningful and motivating to the students to increase the engagement necessary for active learning.

Planning Instruction

It is critical that teachers emphasize certain elements of instructional design when planning instruction for students with ASD. Most students with ASD need explicit instruction (Heflin & Alberto, 2001; Iovannone et al., 2003). Archer and Hughes (2010) defined 16 elements of explicit instruction. The use of these elements will meet the learning style and characteristics of students with ASD. Differentiating instruction is necessary so that unique goals and objectives can be embedded into classroom lessons. This requires extensive planning and organizing on the part of the teacher to insure that lessons are targeted. It is also important to provide opportunities for practice of previously learned skills to assure maintenance of those skills (Myles et al., 2007).

It is critical to collect data on student performance on a frequent basis and use those data to inform instruction. For students who are being educated in inclusive settings, work products with documentation of support provided for the student's performance, unit tests, and standardized assessments all serve to document student mastery. This information should be reviewed frequently to ensure that the student is meeting instructional targets with the accommodations provided. For those students being educated in more specialized settings with modifications to the curricula or specialized curricula, other types of data will provide the indicators of progress.

Although the importance of frequent data collection cannot be overstated, it is equally as important to take the time to analyze the data (Farlow & Snell, 1994; Hojnoski, Gischlar, & Missall, 2009). If the data do not show progress toward the instructional targets for an individual student with ASD, a problem-solving session will allow the team to consider the appropriateness of the target, the reliability of the data collected, the choice and use of the accommodations provided, and the fidelity of the intervention. Each of these may contribute to the success of the student in mastering instructional targets.

It is not enough for students with ASD to be successful in performing a skill. *Fluency*, or the automatic performance of a skill, is a critical component of proficient academic achievement (Weiss, 2001). Practice through timed assignments with motivation to work faster allows students with ASD to reach a point of fluent performance.

Difficulties with the maintenance and generalization of learned skills to materials, environments, and people are two aspects of the unique learning style of individuals with ASD that must be considered when planning instruction (Heflin & Alberto, 2001; Iovannone et al., 2003). Skills that have been mastered must be reviewed on a periodic basis to ensure that the skill is maintained over time. Students must be taught with a variety of materials and perform the skill with a number of teaching staff and peers in an array of school environments. As students with ASD get older, attention must be paid to using skills learned in home and community environments. The application of school and academic skills to meet the demands of independent living, such as making purchases, budgeting, and organizing unscheduled time, creates challenges due to a lack of generalization of skills.

The selection of appropriate curricula to meet the learning needs of a student with ASD must be made carefully with an eye to the targeted outcomes. For students who are academically capable and are being successful in general education settings with and without support, the curriculum choice is not difficult. The student should be working toward the state standards or common core using the same curricular materials as other students. The challenge for these higher functioning students is ensuring that the skills and knowledge they acquire are consistently applied to everyday living and across environments. The demands of the general education setting may make it difficult to include extra classes in the student's schedule. Consequently, it may be advisable to increase the time needed to complete high school to include some functional skills courses.

For students who are not able to meet the challenge of the state standards, access standards or alternate curricula are used to guide instruction and set instructional targets. The challenge for these students is to find functional curricula that build skills and encourage students to master academic work on an appropriate level while ensuring the focus on becoming independent to the extent possible. The use of skills in home and community settings should be a strong component of programs and curricula for these students. Another consideration in programs for students who are unable to benefit from the general education curricula is to make certain that the programs offered are appropriate in terms of both age level and skill level.

Assistive technology must also be considered. In general education settings, software that helps organize narrative writing and has word prediction capabilities may allow the student to have more success with written composition. Hardware such as portable keyboards, laptop computers, and tablets may lessen the physical demands of writing for students with weak fine motor skills or difficulty coordinating ideas with writing. Students who have difficulty with expressive communication may be more successful in social interaction and expressing their wants and needs with a low technology augmentative communication system such as the Picture Exchange Communication System (Bondy & Frost, 1996; Flippin, Reszka, & Watson, 2010). A speech-generating device may meet the needs of a child who has more vocabulary but limited expressive language, by making the child more acceptable to peers because he "has a voice." A referral to an assistive technology specialist or speech–language pathologist for an evaluation would be appropriate for a student who has assistive technology and/or augmentative communication needs.

Delivering Instruction

There are a number of factors that should provide the foundation for how instruction is delivered to students with ASD, whether they are being educated in general education or special education settings. It is important that students with ASD remain engaged in the lessons and activities occurring in the classroom. The higher the level of engagement in a classroom, the less likely there will be challenging behaviors and the more likely the student will be to perform academically (Dunlap & Kern, 1996). Students with ASD require high rates of reinforcement and a variety of motivators. As discussed in relation to CAPS, preference assessments are critical to help teachers know how to effectively reinforce students for both behavior and skill acquisition.

Allowing students with ASD to make choices (e.g., writing with a pen or a pencil, order of activities) whenever possible is another variable that increases engagement, increases compliance with task demands, and reduces challenging behavior (Munk & Repp, 1994). Choices that are offered must be honored when made, so classroom staff should use caution when selecting choices.

The pace of instruction is another variable that must be considered when delivering a lesson (Archer & Hughes, 2010; Munk & Repp, 1994). Waiting between activities and opportunities to respond reduces engagement and provides time when students with ASD may begin to exhibit behavior problems. The less time available between the presentation of a direction or task will result in higher engagement, less self-stimulatory behaviors, and higher rates of correct responding. Behavior problems can also be reduced when novel tasks are interspersed with familiar ones, difficult tasks interspersed with easier ones, and preferred tasks interspersed with less preferred ones (Munk & Repp, 1994; O'Reilly et al., 2005). The reinforcing properties of familiar, easy, and preferred tasks should be used to encourage students with ASD to work when other tasks are presented to them.

There are a variety of procedures to deliver instruction that either increase engagement or increase the likelihood that the student with ASD is able to provide the correct answer (Goodman & Williams, 2007). Strategies that allow the entire group to respond in unison increase the engagement and decrease waiting for an opportunity to respond. Students are more likely to pay attention because they know that they have to respond to each question instead of waiting to be called on after other classmates have had a turn. *Choral responding,* where everyone in the class responds in unison, is one of those strategies. *Response cards*, where each student writes a response on a small white board and holds it up for teacher review, or moves a clothespin to mark whether the answer is true or false, increases engagement because each student provides an answer to each question (Christle & Schuster, 2003; Lambert, Cartledge, Heward, & Lo, 2006; Narayan, Heward, Gardner, Courson, & Omness, 1990). The use of a *cloze procedure*, which involves filling in the blank, or completing a work or sentence when given a verbal cue, can increase the likelihood that a student with ASD will respond with the right answer.

IMPLEMENTATION FIDELITY AND REPORTING PROGRESS

There is an increasing emphasis on using evidence-based practices when teaching all children, including those on the autism spectrum. Implementing these programs the way they were designed—with fidelity—increases the likelihood of getting the results that the curricula and teaching methods promote. Teachers must collect and use data to verify that students are making adequate progress. Techniques to ensure fidelity and collect data are described next.

Implementation Fidelity

All strategies used in the classroom should be scientifically based. But strategies can only be considered evidence-based when they are implemented in a way consistent with the research. Although treatment fidelity is receiving increased attention in the research literature (Hume et al., 2011), there is significant debate over the use of strategies (e.g., discrete trial training) in ways that are not identical to their use in the general research literature (e.g., outside 40-hour per week programs; see Odom, Hume, Boyd, & Stabel, 2012).

Methods for improving treatment fidelity include (a) ensuring that staff is trained in the application of the intervention; (b) using treatments that have corresponding research-based manuals for implementation, documentation, and data collection; and (c) sensitizing professionals to the issues involved with treatment implementation (Kaderavek & Justice, 2010). In the field of ASD, there are some interventions that have manuals that are tied to research conducted on the outcomes of comprehensive programs (e.g., Randolph, Stichter, Schmidt, & O'Connor, 2011). Few, however, have included treatment fidelity in the research supporting them (Wheeler, Baggett, Fox, & Blevins, 2006), and few tools, beyond teacher-made assessments, have been developed for teachers' use in the classroom (Odom et al., 2012).

Direct fidelity assessment involves someone from outside the environment using a competency-based checklist to determine whether the steps and components of the intervention are being implemented as planned. The checklist may be a research-based tool or a task analysis of the steps involved (e.g., the steps involved in implementing an individual's behavior plan). Examples of *indirect assessment* are a practitioner using a self-report measure or completing an interview with an administrator about the implementation of a practice in the classroom (Kaderavek & Justice, 2010).

At present, the most commonly used method for assessing fidelity is to have an experienced observer use a checklist of steps, such as a competency checklist, to determine whether the steps of intervention are being implemented appropriately; for example, a teacher might observe a paraprofessional implementing a structured work system in the classroom (Wheeler et al., 2006). It is important to understand that agreement between professionals does not always imply objectivity because both the observer and person implementing the intervention might have similar training and implement the intervention in a way that is different than was intended in the research. For more information regarding the implications of data reliability and treatment integrity, the reader is referred to Vollmer, Sloman, and St. Peter Pipkin (2008) and Wilkinson (2006, 2010).

A number of resources have been developed for assessing intervention fidelity through the National Professional Development Center on Autism Spectrum Disorders (http://autismpdc.fpg.unc.edu/). These include checklists that can be used to assess fidelity of specific evidence-based practices. Some recently published research studies have provided competency-based checklists or fidelity assessment tools that could be adopted for use in the classroom (Bennett, Reichow, & Wolery, 2011; Randolph et al., 2011). Professionals in the classroom are encouraged to develop and use checklists and maintain documentation of reviews of intervention and training with the students' records or in their own portfolio.

Data Collection and Analysis

Research has indicated that students make more progress when teachers collect and analyze educational data on a regular basis (Farlow & Snell, 1994; Hojnoski et al., 2009). Data can take a variety of forms, including permanent products (i.e., work products), frequency counts of behavior, trial-by-trial data in skill acquisition instruction, periodic probes or sample data of embedded skills, portfolios, and tests. Teachers should be trained to make decisions about the type of data needed specific to the student, the behavior or skill being assessed, and the context of the data collection. Although trial-by-trial data may be needed if the student is having difficulty acquiring a skill, students making good progress toward their goals might require only periodic data collection (Farlow & Snell, 1994).

In addition, professionals should consider whether taking data too frequently would interfere with instruction, and they should decide which is more critical in the situation. In the authors' experiences, teachers frequently attempt to collect too much data, often producing inaccurate results because it was not possible to record every behavior or skill and maintain instruction with the class. Without using data to inform instruction, data serves only to document teaching and progress but contributes little to problem solving if the student is having difficulties. Teachers should be trained to graph the data and review it on a weekly basis and adjust their instruction accordingly on the basis of the student's performance (Farlow & Snell, 1994). Browder, Liberty, Heller, and D'Huyvetters (1986) suggested strategies for regular review of data and how best to use it to make decisions and instructional changes. Finally, data collection and analysis serves as a method for documenting intervention delivery and implementation, evaluating student progress, and making instructional decisions to ensure positive outcomes in instruction for students with ASD.

CONCLUSION

School psychologists and other support personnel play an important role in the education of students with ASD. In addition to providing assessment information that informs the team about program planning, these professionals also can assist in planning appropriate interventions in the classroom and assessing the effectiveness of the programming. This chapter provided information for school psychologists on making decisions about curriculum and organization strategies for the classroom.

REFERENCES

Archer, A. L., & Hughes, C. A. (2010). *Explicit instruction: Effective and efficient teaching.* New York, NY: Guilford Press.

Arick, J., Loos, L., Falco, R., & Krug, D. (2003). *The STAR program: Strategies for teaching based on autism research.* Austin, TX: PRO-ED.

Bennett, K., Reichow, B., & Wolery, M. (2011). Effects of structured teaching on the behavior of young children with disabilities. *Focus on Autism and Other Developmental Disabilities, 26,* 143–152. doi:10.1177/1088357611405040

Bondy, A. S., & Frost, L. (1996). *PECS—The Picture Exchange Communication System.* Newark, DE: Pyramid Educational Consultants.

Browder, D. M., Liberty, K., Heller, M., & D'Huyvetters, K. K. (1986). Self-management by teachers: Improving instructional decision making. *Professional School Psychology, 1,* 165–175. doi:10.1037/h0090506

Christle, C. A., & Schuster, J. W. (2003). The effects of using response cards on student participation, academic achievement, and on-task behavior during whole-class, math instruction. *Journal of Behavioral Education, 12,* 147–165. doi:10.1023/A:1025577410113

Common Core Standards Initiative. (2012). *Implementing the common core standards.* Retrieved from http://www.corestandards.org

Curriculum Associates, Inc. (1991). *Brigance Diagnostic Inventory of Early Development II.* Woburn, MA: Author.

Curriculum Associates, Inc. (1999). *Brigance Comprehensive Inventory of Basic Skills—Revised.* Woburn, MA: Author.

Dettmer, S., Simpson, R. L., Myles, B. S., & Ganz, J. B. (2000). The use of visual supports to facilitate transitions of students with autism. *Focus on Autism and Other Developmental Disabilities, 15,* 163–169. doi:10.1177/108835760001500307

Dunlap, G., & Kern, L. (1996). Modifying instructional activities to promote desirable behavior: A conceptual and practical framework. *School Psychology Quarterly, 11,* 297–312. doi:10.1037/h0088936

Dunlap, G., Strain, P. S., & Fox, L. (2006). Prevention and intervention with young children's challenging behavior: Perspectives regarding current knowledge. *Behavioral Disorders, 32,* 29–45. doi:10.1177/0013916506293987

Farlow, L. J., & Snell, M. E. (1994). *Making the most of student performance data.* Washington, DC: American Association on Mental Retardation.

Flippin, M., Reszka, S., & Watson, L. R. (2010). Effectiveness of the Picture Exchange Communication System (PECS) on communication and speech for children with autism spectrum disorders: A meta-analysis. *American Journal of Speech–Language Pathology, 19,* 178–195. doi:10.1044/1058-0360(2010/09-0022)

Florida Department of Education. (2010). *Accommodations: Assisting students with disabilities* (3rd ed.). Tallahassee, FL: Author.

Giangreco, M. F., & Suter, J. C. (2010). Paraprofessionals in inclusive schools: A review of recent research. *Journal of Educational & Psychological Consultation, 20,* 41–57. doi:10.1080/10474410903535356

Goodman, G., & Williams, C. M. (2007). Interventions for increasing the academic engagement of students with autism spectrum disorders in inclusive classrooms. *Teaching Exceptional Children, 39*(6), 53–61.

Heflin, L. J., & Alberto, P. A. (2001). Establishing a behavioral context for learning for students with autism. *Focus on Autism and Other Developmental Disabilities, 16,* 93–101. doi:10.1177/108835760101600205

Henry, S. A., & Myles, B. S. (2007). *The Comprehensive Autism Planning System (CAPS) for individuals with Asperger syndrome, autism, and related disabilities: Integrating best practices throughout the student's day.* Shawnee Mission, KS: Autism Asperger Publishing Company.

Hojnoski, R. L., Gischlar, K. L., & Missall, K. N. (2009). Improving child outcomes with data-based decision making graphing data. *Young Exceptional Children, 12*(4), 15–30. doi:10.1177/1096250609337696

Hume, K., Boyd, B., McBee, M., Coman, D., Gutierrez, A., Shaw, E., . . . Odom, S. (2011). Assessing implementation of comprehensive treatment models for young children with ASD: Reliability and validity of two measures. *Research in Autism Spectrum Disorders, 5,* 1430–1440. doi:10.1016/j.rasd.2011.02.002

Hume, K., & Odom, S. (2007). Effects of an individual work system on the independent functioning of students with autism. *Journal of Autism and Developmental Disorders, 37,* 1166–1180. doi:10.1007/s10803-006-0260-5

Hume, K., Plavnick, J., & Odom, S. L. (2012). Promoting task accuracy and independence in students with autism across educational setting through the use of individual work systems. *Journal of Autism and Developmental Disorders, 42,* 2084–2099. doi:10.1007/s10803-012-1457-4

Hume, K., & Reynolds, B. (2010). Implementing work systems across the school day: Increasing engagement in students with autism spectrum disorders. *Preventing School Failure: Alternative Education for Children and Youth, 54,* 228–237. doi:10.1080/10459881003744701

Individuals With Disabilities Education Act, 20 U.S.C. § 1401 *et seq.* (2004).

Iovannone, R., Dunlap, G., Huber, H., & Kincaid, D. (2003). Effective educational practices for students with autism spectrum disorders. *Focus on Autism and Other Developmental Disabilities, 18,* 150–165. doi:10.1177/10883576030180030301

Jewell, J. D., Grippi, A., & Hupp, S. D. (2007). The effects of a rotating classroom schedule on classroom crisis events in a school for autism. *North American Journal of Psychology, 9,* 37–52.

Kabot, S., & Reeve, C. (2010). *Setting up classroom spaces that support students with autism spectrum disorders.* Shawnee Mission, KS: Autism Asperger Publishing Company.

Kaderavek, J. N., & Justice, L. M. (2010). Fidelity: An essential component of evidence-based practice in speech-language pathology. *American Journal of Speech-Language Pathology, 19,* 369–379. doi:10.1044/1058-0360(2010/09-0097)

Koegel, R. L., & Egel, A. L. (1979). Motivating autistic children. *Journal of Abnormal Psychology, 88*, 418–426. doi:10.1037/0021-843X.88.4.418

Koegel, R. L., & Mentis, M. (1985). Motivation in childhood autism: Can they or won't they? *The Journal of Child Psychology and Psychiatry, 26*, 185–191. doi:10.1111/j.1469-7610.1985.tb02259.x

Krantz, P. J., & McClannahan, L. E. (1993). Teaching children with autism to initiate to peers: Effects of a script-fading procedure. *Journal of Applied Behavior Analysis, 26*, 121–132. doi:10.1901/jaba.1993.26-121

Lambert, M. C., Cartledge, G., Heward, W. L., & Lo, Y. Y. (2006). Effects of response cards on disruptive behavior and academic responding during math lessons by fourth-grade urban students. *Journal of Positive Behavior Interventions, 8*, 88–99. doi:10.1177/10983007060080020701

Lelaurin, K., & Risley, T. R. (1972). The organization of day-care environments: "Zone" versus "man-to-man" staff assignments. *Journal of Applied Behavior Analysis, 5*, 225–232. doi:10.1901/jaba.1972.5-225

MacDuff, G. S., Krantz, P. J., & McClannahan, L. E. (1993). Teaching children with autism to use photographic activity schedules: Maintenance and generalization of complex response chains. *Journal of Applied Behavior Analysis, 26*, 89–97. doi:10.1901/jaba.1993.26-89

Munk, D. D., & Repp, A. C. (1994). The relationship between instructional variables and problem behavior: A review. *Exceptional Children, 60*, 390–401.

Myles, B. S., Grossman, B. G., Aspy, R., Henry, S. A., & Bixler Coffin, A. (2007). Planning a comprehensive program for students with autism spectrum disorders using evidence-based practices. *Education and Training in Developmental Disabilities, 42*, 398–409.

Narayan, J. S., Heward, W. L., Gardner, R., Courson, F. H., & Omness, C. K. (1990). Using response cards to increase student participation in an elementary classroom. *Journal of Applied Behavior Analysis, 23*, 483–490. doi:10.1901/jaba.1990.23-483

National Research Council. (2001). *Educating children with autism*. Washington, DC: National Academies Press.

No Child Left Behind Act of 2001, 20 U.S.C. § 6319 (2008).

Nordquist, V. M., & Twardosz, S. (1990). Preventing behavior problems in early childhood special education classrooms through environmental organization. *Education & Treatment of Children, 13*, 274–287.

Nordquist, V. M., Twardosz, S., & McEvoy, M. A. (1991). Effects of environmental reorganization in classrooms for children with autism. *Journal of Early Intervention, 15*, 135–152. doi:10.1177/105381519101500203

Odom, S., Hume, K., Boyd, B., & Stabel, (2012). Moving beyond the intensive behavior treatment versus eclectic dichotomy: Evidence-based and individualized programs for learners with ASD. *Behavior Modification, 36*, 270–297. doi:10.1177/0145445512444595

O'Reilly, M., Sigafoos, J., Lancioni, G., Edrisinha, C., & Andrews, A. (2005). An examination of the effects of a classroom activity schedule on levels of self-injury and engagement for a child with severe autism. *Journal of Autism and Developmental Disorders, 35*, 305–311. doi:10.1007/s10803-005-3294-1

Randolph, J. K., Stichter, J. P., Schmidt, C. T., & O'Connor, K. V. (2011). Fidelity and effectiveness of PRT implemented by caregivers without college degrees. *Focus on Autism and Other Developmental Disabilities, 26*, 230–238. doi:10.1177/1088357611421503

Reeve, C. E., & Kabot, S. (2012). *Building independence: How to create and use independent work systems.* Shawnee Mission, KS: Autism Asperger Publishing Company.

Sasso, G. M., Peck, J., & Garrison-Harrell, L. (1998). Social interaction setting events: Experimental analysis of contextual variables. *Behavioral Disorders, 24*, 34–43.

Suter, J. C., & Giangreco, M. F. (2009). Numbers that count: Exploring special education and paraprofessional service delivery in inclusion-oriented schools. *The Journal of Special Education, 43*, 81–93. doi:10.1177/0022466907313353

Unique Learning System. (2012). *Elementary level.* Retrieved from http://unique.n2y.com

Vollmer, T. R., Sloman, K. N., & St Peter Pipkin, C. (2008). Practical implications of data reliability and treatment integrity monitoring. *Behavior Analysis in Practice, 1*, 4–11.

Weiss, M. J. (2001). Expanding ABA intervention in intensive programs for children with autism: The inclusion of natural environment training and fluency based instruction. *Behavior Analyst Today, 2*, 182–186.

Wheeler, J. J., Baggett, B. A., Fox, J., & Blevins, L. (2006). Treatment integrity: A review of intervention studies conducted with children with autism. *Focus on Autism and Other Developmental Disabilities, 21*, 45–54. doi:10.1177/10883576060210010601

Wilkinson, L. A. (2006). Monitoring treatment integrity: An alternative to the 'consult and hope' strategy in school-based behavioural consultation. *School Psychology International, 27*, 426–438. doi:10.1177/0143034306070428

Wilkinson, L. A. (2010). *A best practice guide to assessment and intervention for autism and Asperger syndrome in schools.* London, England: Kingsley.

10

COLLABORATION BETWEEN FAMILIES AND SCHOOLS

GENA P. BARNHILL

Because of the unique challenges and the complexity of autism spectrum disorder (ASD; Ellis, Lutz, Schaefer, & Woods, 2007), it is essential that all stakeholders, including parents, teachers, and related educational and medical personnel, collaborate to develop an individual and comprehensive plan for students with ASD. Developing respectful family–professional partnerships that honor the strengths, cultures, customs, and expertise of all team members (Family Voices, 2008) requires a system-wide effort that is intentional and requires a commitment of time, effort, and leadership (Esler, Godber, & Christenson, 2008). Turnbull and Turnbull (2001) described collaboration that results in empowerment as a "dynamic process of families and professionals equally sharing their resources (motivation and knowledge/skills) in order to make decisions jointly" (p. 50). This partnering is more than an activity to be put into practice; it is an attitude that should permeate the collaboration process and recognize the significance of the family as the primary stakeholder

http://dx.doi.org/10.1037/14338-011
Autism Spectrum Disorder in Children and Adolescents: Evidence-Based Assessment and Intervention in Schools, L. A. Wilkinson (Editor)

for their children and as a constant in the child's life (Christenson, 2004; Christenson & Sheridan, 2001).

An essential belief is that this preventive, problem-solving approach between the home and school can accomplish more together than each entity can accomplish alone (Esler et al., 2008). To begin this process, professionals should be self-aware; possess knowledge of the characteristics of families, family life cycles, and family functions; and also honor diversity. This includes the ability to "'stand in the shoes' (sand and all)" of the families they serve (Turnbull & Turnbull, 2001, p. 60). The research literature provides examples of several collaborative and consultative approaches, including conjoint behavioral consultation (Sheridan, Eagle, Cowan, & Mickelson, 2001; Wilkinson, 2005) and family-centered care (Gabovitch & Curtin, 2009). This chapter focuses on how school professionals can support families of children with ASD.

SUPPORTING FAMILIES OF CHILDREN WITH AUTISM SPECTRUM DISORDER

It was not too long ago that parents, especially mothers, were thought to be the cause of their child's autism. We now know that ASD has a neurological basis and is not the result of poor parenting. However, parents still struggle to cope with autism, with blame often placed on family members and within families in an attempt to make sense of this complex spectrum of conditions. Koegel and LaZebnik (2004) stated that autism is one of the most frightening disabilities because the diagnosis does not predict the child's prognosis. No one can truthfully say, "We know exactly what your child will be like when he is twenty" (p. xiii). O'Brien and Daggett (2006) reported, "Hearing the news that a child has an autism spectrum disorder is a life-changing event" (p. 115).

Parents may experience emotions and stages similar to the stages associated with bereavement (Altiere & von Kluge, 2009; Koegel & LaZebnik, 2004). Webber and Scheuermann (2008) suggested that the following stages may occur for families learning to accept their child's diagnosis and who come to the realization that this is a lifelong disability: (a) discovery of the diagnosis, (b) denial, (c) guilt or bargaining, (d) anger, (e) depression, and (f) acceptance or coping. Not every parent goes through all of these stages, and those who do may not progress in the same order or with the same intensity. It is critical that professionals be aware of these possible stages; however, it is not their role to diagnose the stage or label the parents (Webber & Scheuermann, 2008).

Parents worldwide often experience a range of emotions when their child is first diagnosed with autism. For example, parents in China were reported to react to the initial diagnosis of autism in their child with shock, devastation, and confusion. The stigma associated with having a child with a disability and rejection from others is further complicated by the Chinese family planning policy that limits most couples to one child (McCabe, 2008). Moh and Magiati (2012) found that parents in Singapore were more likely to feel satisfied with the diagnostic process when they experienced it as a starting point toward appropriate interventions instead of as an endpoint.

Sansosti, Lavik, and Sansosti (2012) studied parents in the United States and found that there was a 2-year delay from the time parents first spoke to professionals (frequently the pediatrician) about their child to the time the diagnosis of ASD was given. Moreover, children from minority families received the ASD diagnosis 6 months later than children who were not from minority families. All of the parents expressed dissatisfaction with the diagnostic process, with more significant dissatisfaction being expressed by families who received the diagnosis later. Interestingly, many of the parents had an adequate understanding regarding evidence-based treatments for ASD through self-education; however, they also believed that interventions that did not have empirical support were just as effective.

Because of the severe and pervasive features of ASD, parents face substantial emotional demands raising their children (McCabe, 2008). Parents of children with high functioning autism (HFA) and Asperger's syndrome (AS) experience challenges because their children are frequently diagnosed later than children with classic autism. Moreover, children with higher functioning ASD often have abilities that mask their significant social challenges (Epstein, Saltzman-Benaiah, O'Hare, Goll, & Tuck, 2008) and often demonstrate challenges in areas not included in the diagnostic criteria, such as executive functioning deficits and sensory sensitivities (Epstein et al., 2008). Consequently, it is critical that professionals recognize the challenges that parents face and not assume that children with HFA have fewer problem behaviors than children with more classic autism.

D. E. Gray (2003) reported that HFA is an exceptionally stressful condition, and the experience of coping with it has not been adequately addressed in the research literature. Tobing and Glenwick (2007) found that mothers of children with AS indicated greater parenting stress than mothers of children with autism or pervasive development disorder not otherwise specified. Lee et al. (2009) found that income and stress consistently predicted the physical and mental health of parents of children with HFA. They hypothesized that raising a child with HFA leads to significant parental stress, which then has a negative impact on their physical and mental health. Although access to support through increased income may buffer the stressors, Lee et al. recommended that professionals investigate the way parents view income as a barrier to their physical and mental health so that they can assist in offering services that directly address parental needs (e.g., respite care). Furthermore, to address issues associated with ASD, Lee et al. recommended forums for parents, such as psychoeducational training about HFA, social skills training for the children outside of the clinical settings, advocacy training for the parents, and training in working with professionals including physicians, psychologists, and school personnel.

Sofronoff and Farbotko (2002) found that when parents of children with AS ages 6 to 12 years were given training in managing behavior problems, either in a 1-day workshop format or in six individual sessions, they indicated fewer behavior problems and increased self-efficacy following training at both 4 weeks and at 3 months compared with a control group who demonstrated decreased self-efficacy. The two training formats included education on AS and instruction in the following: (a) Comic Strip Conversations; (b) Social Stories; (c) strategies to reduce anxiety; and (d) management of behavior problems, rigid behaviors, routines, and special interests. Mothers in the intervention groups demonstrated a significant increase in self-efficacy after intervention, whereas fathers showed no change. Sofronoff and Farbotko indicated that several of the fathers displayed characteristics of AS and hypothesized that because most of the training was presented orally, incorporating visual presentations, role play, and reading components in future training may be more helpful for the fathers.

Marcus, Kunce, and Schopler (2005) indicated that the fundamental goals of parent training and family-based interventions should include (a) decreasing the child's inappropriate behaviors and increasing positive behaviors, (b) improving the quality of relationships within the family and increasing their adaptive functioning, and (c) including family members in the change process. Tonge et al. (2006) found that when parents of young children recently diagnosed with autism participated in a parent education and counseling intervention or parent education and behavior management skills training, they experienced significant improvement in mental health and adjustment. Their findings suggest that including parent training in early intervention programs is critical, especially for parents who are experiencing mental health problems. Interestingly, Tonge and colleagues found that both intervention programs led to significant and progressive improvement in mental health at follow-up. Moreover, at the 6-month follow-up, parents in the education and behavior management group reported greater relief from anxiety, insomnia, somatic symptoms, and family dysfunction than did those from the education and counseling group. On the basis of these research findings (Sofronoff & Farbotko, 2002; Tonge et al., 2006), it would appear that equipping parents with behavior management skills is a critical component in parent education training.

Understanding parents' perspectives and their level of involvement and participation is critical in developing comprehensive plans. Parents have expressed concerns regarding the following issues related to their children with ASD: (a) poor long-term outcomes, (b) protection and safety, (c) self-injurious behaviors and aggression, (d) food refusals, (e) poor sleeping habits and personal care skills, (f) poor language skills, (g) disruption and destruction in the home, (h) inappropriate sexual expressions, (i) social rejection and stigma for the parents and the child, (j) child's future when the parents are no longer living, and (k) depletion of time available to care for siblings and themselves (Barnhill, 2002; D. E. Gray, 2002; Ivey, 2004, Rogers & Dawson, 2010). Some parents have reported experiencing an ambiguous loss because their child is physically present but may not be entirely psychologically present (O'Brien, 2007). In addition, significant discouragement with the diagnostic process, including the length of time to reach diagnosis and the poor interpersonal skills of some professionals, has been voiced (Sansosti et al., 2012).

On the basis of their research, Webber, Simpson, and Bentley (2000) presented five levels of parental involvement:

1. The *awareness level* is considered a baseline situation in which parents and families receive information about autism. When parent involvement is low, however, professionals must actively provide information to families regarding basic facts pertaining to the characteristics of autism, appropriate interventions, and available services and programs.

2. The *open communication level* refers to effective sharing and communication between parents, family members, and professionals, and should be the desired level. Regardless of other levels of involvement, Webber et al. (2000) recommended engagement in open communication among all stakeholders.

3. The *advocacy and participation level* involves parents and family members who desire to be actively engaged in promoting services and programs for their children. They may be members on an autism board, volunteer their services to organizations serving individuals with autism, or they may be active participants in their child's education.

4. The *problem-solving and procedural application level* is an option for parents and families who are able and inspired to implement programs and procedures for individuals with ASD in natural environments. These activities may include home-based tutoring, toileting, and eating programs.

5. The *partnership level* means that parents and families are on an equal footing with professionals in recognizing, implementing, and assessing programs for children and youth with ASD. Parents

may independently ascertain goals for their child, develop train-ing procedures for achieving each goal, and assess the general-ization of the skills in other situations.

Parents and families may be at more than one level at a given time, and these levels may change over time. Professionals should recognize the level(s) at which families are operating and be willing to assist them if they want to move to a different level. It is also important to note that individualizing parent and family participation is the first step to satisfying parent and family needs. Furthermore, increased parent and family involvement does not nec-essarily mean "better involvement" (Webber et al., 2000, p. 310).

Understanding Parental Stress and Parent–Child Relationships

Only in the last decade has research focused on examining the effects having a child with autism or AS has on the parents. The impact of autism on the family is seen in the area of finances and in the parents' mental and physical health and coping skills (D. E. Gray, 2006; Tehee, Honan, & Hevey, 2009). Common themes in the research literature indicate that compared with families without a child with autism, these families experience the fol-lowing: (a) increased risk of divorce; (b) decrease in the father's involvement; (c) greater parenting and psychological stress; (d) higher levels of depression in the parents; (e) higher levels of anxiety, especially in mothers; (f) more strain on the family system; (g) worse physical and health-related issues; (h) fewer adaptive coping skills; and (i) greater stress on mothers than fathers (Epstein et al., 2008; D. E. Gray, 2002, 2003; Hoffman, Sweeney, Hodge, Lopez-Wagner, & Looney, 2009; Lee, 2009; Little, 2002; Pottie & Ingram, 2008; Sivberg, 2002; Tobing & Glenwick, 2007). More research should be conducted with families of various socioeconomic levels and ethnicity because most of the research to date has focused on Caucasian families.

D. E. Gray (2003) found that fathers typically were committed to their work, which led to a lower degree of child rearing. Furthermore, they per-ceived the impact of autism indirectly, with the most serious impact on them a result of the stress experienced by their wives. Generally, fathers reported seeing themselves "as being a reserve support" for their wives during times of extreme stress (p. 635). Mothers typically were primarily responsible for their child's medical and educational appointments, interventions, and child rearing, and they reported that their child's autism significantly affected their careers through missing work or needing to reduce their employment to part-time work. In addition, mothers, more than fathers, reported that they talked to friends and families as a way to handle their emotions. Little (2002) sug-gested that mothers may perceive their child's challenges to be a reflection on themselves and, therefore, are more susceptible to stress and seek assistance for depression.

Resiliency and adaptive coping also were observed in parents of children with ASD. Montes and Halterman (2007) found that families of children with autism used compensatory strategies to maintain family stability in the face of increased stress and poor mental health. In a large national sample, they did not find an increased risk of divorce. Moreover, when parents used *reframing* as a coping strategy (changing their view of a stressful situation to see it in a more positive manner), they reported benefits associated with autism (Altiere & von Kluge, 2009). Almost every parent in the Altiere and von Kluge (2009) study reported significant, positive experiences as a result of raising their child with autism, and most reported an increase in their coping skills. For example, several couples reported that they viewed life with their child as "a priceless experience" and that they now "appreciate life more in general" (p. 148). Furthermore, research has suggested that psychological acceptance may be a vital factor in coping for parents who are dealing with chronic behavior challenges (Weiss, Cappadocia, MacMullin, Viecili, & Lunsky, 2012).

In a longitudinal study, D. E. Gray (2006) demonstrated that the outcomes for approximately two thirds of the parents studied were reasonably favorable in that parents reported their situation was better than it had been 10 years previous. The author noted that little was known about how parents of children with ASD coped over time, because previous research was cross-sectional in nature and hypothesized that positive outcomes may have been attributed to the access to appropriate services and increased coping abilities. The study also found that parents used fewer coping strategies than they had 10 years previous and relied more on their religious faith and emotion-focused coping strategies. Furthermore, social withdrawal as a coping strategy declined over time. D. E. Gray (2006) hypothesized that parents also may have been able to accept the permanence of their child's autism by putting it into a more meaningful perspective through their faith.

Research conducted by Pottie and Ingram (2008) demonstrated that, after controlling for personality and contextual factors, the use of the following coping strategies was predictive of higher levels of daily positive mood for parents of children with ASD: "Problem Focused, Social Support, Positive Reframing, Emotional Regulation, and Compromise coping" (p. 861). Furthermore, decreases in daily positive mood correlated with "Escape, Blaming, Withdrawal and Helplessness coping" (p. 861). Higher levels of negative mood were predicted by "increased use of Problem-Focused, Blaming, Worrying, and Withdrawal coping" (p. 861). Pottie and Ingram were surprised to find that *problem-focused coping* (dealing with the problem in a concrete, organized way) was correlated with both higher negative mood and higher positive mood. They concluded that this coping strategy may not always be adaptive because many of the difficulties parents face are not amenable to change and, therefore, a flexible repertoire of coping may be most beneficial. Also, using *emotional regulation coping* (controlling emotions or communicating them in a constructive way) and less worrying coping were found to be especially adaptive on highly stressful days. Interestingly, Pottie and Ingram found that none of the coping strategies they investigated were more or less effective for mothers or fathers, and the level of ASD symptoms did not predict parents' positive or negative moods. In contrast, D. E. Gray (2006) found that parents of aggressive and violent children experienced more stress and had fewer resources.

Being Sensitive to Relationships Among Siblings

Research on the effects of autism on siblings has produced mixed results (Beyer, 2009; Meadan, Halle, & Ebata, 2010; Petalas, Hastings, Nash, Dowey, & Reilly, 2009; Tomeny, Barry, & Bader, 2012). Beyer (2009) indicated that this may be due to factors such as the family environment, which includes the number, gender, and age of children, as well as finances, coping skills, support available, and the severity of the ASD. Beyer also indicated that the research tended to group together siblings of persons with ASD from early childhood through adolescence and that this may have obscured differences between these different developmental periods. Although overall the research has suggested more negative than positive impacts on siblings, these results should be interpreted cautiously because more research is needed in this area (Beyer, 2009).

In contrast to the findings of the Beyer (2009) study, Tomeny et al. (2012) found that having a sibling with autism was neither a protective factor nor a risk factor for maladjustment of the typically developing sibling beyond that found among brothers and sisters in general. Petalas et al. (2009) found that having a brother with ASD was an experience unique to each sibling (ages 8–17), given the complex nature of ASD. Unlike findings in other studies, Petalas et al. indicated that most siblings expressed acceptance toward their brother with ASD and provided several positive facets of their sibling relationship. Also, siblings frequently reported that they experienced prejudice and misunderstanding from others, which caused them to answer questions and provide explanations to others to dispel the lack of knowledge. Most siblings reported using different sources of support to cope, such as obtaining help from parents, peers, and professionals in the form of respite and sibling support groups. Furthermore, some siblings stated that they became socially isolated, changed their behavior to cope with their brother's unusual behaviors and aggression, and had less time for family leisure and recreation. Other researchers (Oppenheim-Leaf, Leaf, Dozier, Sheldon, & Sherman, 2012) taught typically developing siblings between the ages of 4 and 6 years to encourage social play with their sibling with ASD by using clear instructions, prompts, and reinforcement. Clearly, more research is needed specifically to explore children's coping strategies in the context of the sibling relationship and ASD (Petalas et al., 2009).

Interpreting and Communicating Assessment Findings for Parents

Research supports parents as key team members in the success of their children's education programs (National Research Council, 2001), and parent participation is mandated as one of the six key principles of the Individuals With Disabilities Education Act (IDEA; 2004). However, if parents are immobilized with grief, anger, or fear, how can they be effective team members? School psychologists and professionals who have knowledge about the unique stressors these parents face and the current research on effective strategies are in a strategic position to assist them during the diagnostic process and throughout the education of the child. Moreover, "the identification of parenting stress and parent–child relationship problems can also alert the assessment team the need for additional support or counseling" (Wilkinson, 2010, p. 71).

Best practices in supporting school–family partnerships include beginning with the building blocks of Esler et al.'s (2008) eight P philosophy for school–family collaboration. These are: "1. Partnership as a priority, 2. Planned effort, 3. Proactive and persistent communication, 4. Positive, 5. Personalized, 6. Practical suggestions, 7. Program monitoring, and 8. Attend to the Process for building relationships with families" (p. 925). Schools have to extend the invitation to partner with families, and they should be informed by the families about the students' learning and needs (Esler et al., 2008). One way to collaborate is to integrate the nine elements of Handleman and Harris's (1986) CONSULTED strategy: (a) Confer, (b) Observe, (c) Name problems, (d) Set priorities, (e) Utilize resources, (f) Label obstacles, (g) Try intervention, (h) Evaluate outcome, and (i) Determine the next step to guide the family problem-solving process (as cited in Webber et al., 2000).

It is critical that professionals know themselves (their values, prejudices, and beliefs) first before engaging in collaboration with families, so that their issues do not present barriers to collaboration. It also is critical that school personnel and consultants be familiar with Fiedler, Simpson, and Clark's (2007) 12 trust enhancement suggestions for working with families. These include (a) sustaining a positive attitude, (b) striving to be receptive to families' emotional and psychological needs, (c) exhibiting respect and professionalism toward the information shared, (d) willingness to acknowledge one's limitations and the limitations of the organization, (e) taking time to consider information so that hasty judgments are not made about families, (f) making only promises that can be kept, (g) including families in decision making, (h) engaging in actions that permit an understanding of students' home and personal life, (i) following through with commitments, (j) showing warmth and honoring families, (k) encouraging families to consider novel coping approaches, and (l) keeping in mind that trust is a process that takes time to build. School professionals can apply these best practices and suggestions within the framework of one of the parent–educator consultation models.

PARENT–EDUCATOR CONSULTATION MODELS

Conjoint behavioral consultation (CBC) is an indirect model of consultation that involves parents and educators each taking responsibility in working to address a student's academic, behavioral, or social needs (Sheridan et al., 2001). The CBC model uses the traditional behavioral consultation model and problem-solving model, which includes (a) identifying the concern, (b) analyzing the problem, (c) developing and implementing a plan, and (d) assessing the plan (Peacock & Collett, 2010). Wilkinson (2005) used CBC as a framework in a school setting to teach a 9-year-old boy with AS self-management strategies. Findings revealed an improvement in behavioral control, which was exhibited by increased on-task behavior and compliance. Data collected 4 weeks after the completion of the study indicated maintenance of positive intervention effects following consultation. Implications suggest that CBC may be used by school psychologists to successfully support students with AS in the general education setting.

The *family-centered care model* (FCC) has been considered a best practice method for working with children with health care needs; however, there is limited research regarding the use of this model with children with ASD and their families (Gabovitch & Curtin, 2009). The National Center for Family-Centered Care (1989) identified the following 10 components of FCC: (a) It acknowledges the family as the constant in a child's life; (b) it builds on family strengths; (c) it supports the child in learning about and participating in his or her care and decision making; (d) it honors cultural diversity and family traditions; (e) it recognizes the importance of community-based services; (f) it promotes an individual and developmental approach; (g) it encourages family-to-family and peer support; (h) it supports youth as they transition to adulthood; (i) it develops policies, practices, and systems that are family friendly and family centered in all settings; and (j) it celebrates successes (Family Voices, 2008, p. ii).

To date, the *collaborative model for promoting competence and success for students with ASD* (COMPASS) "is the first consultation model that has been validated by randomized controlled experiments and by objective, trained evaluators" (Ruble, Dalyrymple, & McGrew, 2012, p. x) to specifically increase the individualized educational plan (IEP) outcomes of students with ASD. COMPASS is unique in that it focuses on competency development and awareness of individuals in context, and the key impact with parents, who are considered experts on their child, is empowerment. The goal of consultation is not to have the student attain normality but rather to measure success by looking at core competencies of individuals with ASD. COMPASS is a proactive, dynamic, and collaborative model that involves setting goals and planning interventions (consultation) and putting these into practice during the coaching phase to enhance the quality of life of the individual with ASD so that he or she can participate to the fullest extent possible and "achieve his or her maximum potential and competence" (Ruble et al., 2012, p. 12). Consultation begins with the consultant gathering information from student observations and from the documents given to the parents and teachers requesting information on student challenges and supports. Three hours of direct interactions begin first with a review of the student's strengths and preferences and then the student's fears and frustrations, which is followed by a review of their adaptive skills, problem behaviors, play and social skills, communication skills, sensory skills and challenges, and learning skills. A consensus of the top three concerns is determined, and measurable IEP goals are written to address these concerns. In addition, personal and environmental challenges and personal and environmental supports are identified. Follow-up coaching sessions consist of 1- to 1.5-hour sessions throughout the year, yielding a total consultation time of 9 hours for the year. Research has indicated that COMPASS does not negatively affect teacher time or stress. Furthermore, coaching was related to changes in teacher behavior, and teachers needed several months after the initial consultation to apply interventions with fidelity. Ruble et al. (2012) provided step-by-step instructions for the implementation of COMPASS and numerous examples of completed consultation forms, as well as research results attained from the implementation of this model for students with ASD.

RECOMMENDATIONS FOR INTERVENTION IN SCHOOL AND HOME

Parents of children with ASD have indicated that they want to work with professionals who provide them opportunities to ask questions, take into account their earlier worries, give them useful information, and approach them in an open-minded, honest, supportive, empathetic, and understanding manner (Moh & Magiati, 2012). O'Brien and Daggett (2006) reported that families that had good diagnostic experiences were more likely to assume more effective roles in partnerships with professionals. I recommend beginning interactions by sharing positive statements with the parents regarding their child and establishing a relationship of trust and respect proactively before problems arise.

The first contact with the family may be on the phone or in person. Professionals should be aware of their body language and demonstrate an openness and willingness to communicate effectively by removing physical barriers in face-to-face face meetings. Greet the family warmly as they arrive for the scheduled meeting, and lean in and nod as the parents speak to demonstrate interest and genuine concern for them and their child. It is critical to allow enough time for the meeting so that parents do not feel rushed and are able to express their concerns. Extra time spent during the first collaborative meeting will demonstrate a true interest in getting to know the family and their child. Professionals should ensure that all collaborative partners are included in the discussions. Furthermore, they should demonstrate eye contact, empathy, a nonjudgmental attitude, tactful statements, and frequent statements of encouragement. These building blocks for effective communication can be summarized as *BETTER LISTENING*: Begin, Eye contact, Trusted, Tactful, Empathy, Respectful, Lean in, Interest, Share, Time, Encouragement, Nod, Include, Nonjudgmental, and Greet warmly.

In addition to proactively contacting parents at the beginning of the school year to set up a time to meet to gain an understanding of their child and their future hopes and dreams for their child, I suggest the following:

- Send home positive notes about the child each day.
- Use journals to communicate between the home and the school.
- Carefully consider who should be at meetings. Sometimes it may be appropriate to have fewer people in attendance so that the parents are not overwhelmed..
- Be mindful that there is a broader phenotype of autism and, although parents may not have a diagnosis of ASD, one or both of the parents may share some of the characteristics of ASD.
- Avoid the use of jargon and technical terms and frequently check for understanding.
- Remember that parents have a life-long role in their child's life.
- Learn about the various community agencies that can help support the family.
- Realize that the family's needs will change over time and that they often have other children to care for and other family responsibilities in addition to their child with autism.

Sivberg (2002) suggested that parents (a) balance their attention between the child with autism and their other children as much as possible,

(b) be cautious about expecting a great deal of help from the siblings in caring for the child with ASD, (c) use consistent and coordinated methods with the child with autism, and (d) be careful not to see the child with autism as the only source of strain in the family. Sivberg found that parents developed distancing and escape as a coping mechanism to handle the stress related to the child with autism. Although these coping strategies are rational and may be helpful in the short term, caution should be exercised so that they are not used in nonfunctional ways. Sivberg noted that this finding was in contrast to the earlier assumption that the mother's distancing personality (e.g., the old refrigerator mother theory) hindered the child's development when he found that distancing was developed later as a reaction to stress.

Compensatory Tools to Teach Parents

Parents can be taught evidence-based strategies that successfully support their children with ASD (National Research Council, 2001). The National Professional Development Center (NPDC) on Autism Spectrum Disorders (2010) included parent-implemented intervention as an evidence-based practice. *Parent-implemented intervention* involves parents directly using individualized intervention practices with their child to increase positive learning opportunities and acquisition of important skills. Parents learn to implement these practices in their home and/or community through a structured parent-training program.

The NPDC (2010) reported that parent-implemented interventions improved the child's communication skills and reduced aggression and disruptive behaviors, as well as increased the functioning of the entire family. Parents are taught by professionals how to implement strategies and goals, and practices are adjusted over time to meet the changing needs of the child and family through collaboration and a problem-solving approach that includes (a) determination of the family's needs; (b) goal selection for the child, parents, and family; (c) creation of the implementation plan; (d) parent training; (e) executing the intervention; and (f) monitoring progress. Although the National Autism Center (NAC; 2009) did not specifically list parent-implemented intervention as an evidence-based practice in their free online publication *Evidence-based Practice and Autism in the Schools: A Guide to Providing Appropriate Interventions to Students with Autism Spectrum Disorder*, 24 of the studies they reviewed under other strategies involved parent implementation. The NAC (2011) also published a free online manual specifically for parents titled *A Parent's Guide to Evidence-Based Practice and Autism*. Parents can implement compensatory strategies such as social narratives or story-based interventions and visual supports, which are considered evidence-based practices, as reported by the NAC (2009) and the NPDC (2010). Chapter 7 of this volume provides a matrix illustrating the evidence-based strategies and interventions identified by the NAC and the NPDC.

Social Narratives

Social Stories, originally created by Carol Gray in 1991, describe a situation, skill, or idea in the first or third person by providing relevant social cues, perspectives of others, and conventional responses in a prescribed format that is tailored to the individual's preferences and interests (C. Gray, 2004). Social Stories can be used to record an achievement, address a specific skill, describe when a child does something well, or help a child navigate through a challenging situation. They put real-life situations into a visual format and allow children to practice the skill and gain a perspective on emotions, thoughts, and behaviors of others. They also give children the opportunity to make predictions. C. Gray (2010) recommended that Social Stories contain at least twice as many sentences that describe as sentences that coach so that each story describes more than directs. In addition, she made the following suggestions:

- Consider the child's age and ability level. Stories for younger children should be brief. Although shorter stories are more challenging to write, three to 12 short sentences are recommended for younger children.
- Write everything first and then edit the story. You may find that you actually need to create two or more stories.
- Include repetition, rhythm, and rhyme because they capture attention and are predictable.
- Consider using illustrations based on the person's ability level and interests.

I also recommend that the writer of the Social Story carefully consider when to have the child read the story. Always insisting that the child read the story immediately after misbehavior occurs could lead to escape and avoidance behavior related to the story. Having the child read the Social Story prior to a potential behavioral problem would be a preventive approach. Also, remember to have the child read stories about their successes. For more information on C. Gray's Social Stories, see http://www.thegraycenter.org.

Visual Supports

Research has revealed that persons with ASD frequently exhibit strength in visual learning. Visual supports supplement and clarify verbal instructions and organize a sequence of actions, thus improving a person's ability to understand, anticipate, and take part in these actions or circumstances (Smith, 2012). The term *visual support* refers to any tool that is presented visually to assist the person as he or she moves through the day. Examples include schedules, maps, labels, organizational systems, timelines, scripts, visual boundaries, calendars, notes, recipes, checklists, menus, rules, and the Picture Exchange Communication System (Frost & Bondy, 2002). They can be as simple as a note stating, "Do spelling; then computer."

The NPDC (2010) indicated that visual supports are an evidenced-based intervention for early childhood, elementary, and middle-school-age students. The NAC (2009) found that schedules have been effective in improving self-regulation skills for children ages 3 to 14 years. Schedules can use photos, Boardmaker icons (symbols software from Dynavox Mayer-Johnson), 3-D objects, or written or typed words. They can even be placed on touch-screen tablet computers. "Visual supports are a simple, yet very powerful intervention for individuals with ASD" (Smith, 2012, para. 4). More information on visual supports can be found on the Autism Internet Modules created by the Ohio Center for Autism and Low Incidence at http://www.autisminternetmodules.org/mod_list.php

Community Resources

Parents need support in three basic areas—information, knowledge, and skills to deal with their child—and support from outside the family to develop coping and problem-solving skills (Webber et al., 2000). The Autism Society of America has local chapters that can provide families with information on resources in their local area. There are also many universities with autism centers and clinics that provide assessment, intervention, and support services to the community. Other organizations include Autism Speaks, which provides parents of newly diagnosed children with a free 100-day kit. They also provide several other free resources, such as kits for AS and HFA, for dental professionals, for medical procedures such as blood draws, for toilet training, for applied behavior analysis, and so forth. In addition, the Organization for Autism Research, founded by parents and grandparents of children and adults on the autism spectrum, focuses on "applying" research to address issues of daily concern for those living with autism.

In addition to providing parents with information on autism-related organizations, outside support may take the form of accessing community agencies such as social services, Social Security, Medicaid, counselors and psychologists, and other medical professionals for the frequent comorbid conditions such as sensory motor impairments, seizure disorders, gastrointestinal difficulties, immune dysfunction, and mental health problems (Ellis et al., 2007). The Internet has facilitated advocacy and support groups; however, the National Research Council (2001) cautioned that this information has often "conveyed perspectives that were not balanced or well supported scientifically" (p. 215). Parents also should be given resources for information regarding creating a special needs trust that will protect their child's assets in adulthood when he or she may be accessing government supports. Issues of guardianship, conservatorship, and power of attorney may need to be addressed before the child reaches the age of majority at 18 years.

Advocacy for Expanding Services

"Many of the scientists and fund-raisers who have helped advance knowledge around the world about autism are themselves parents of children with autism" (Grinker, 2007, p. 197). To advocate for the needs of individuals with ASD and their families, it is critical that parents and professionals become aware of the current information on effective interventions based on scientific research, the current status of service delivery for ASD, and current litigation issues. Autism has been the target of fads and unproven therapies that have victimized parents who have been desperate for treatment for their children (Marcus et al., 2005). It is imperative that parents and professionals become better consumers of strategies for ASD. According to Simpson (2005), the following questions should be asked when selecting an intervention or treatment (p. 143):

- What are the efficacy and anticipated outcomes that align with a particular practice, and are the anticipated outcomes in harmony with the needs of the student?
- What are the potential risks associated with the practice?
- What are the most effective means of evaluating a particular method or approach?

In the area of education, students with ASD accounted for almost one third of the published court decisions regarding free and appropriate public education and least restrictive environment under IDEA, and the overall proportionality ratio of autism litigation to autism enrollments was 10:1 based on Zirkel's (2011) compilation of IDEA court decisions. Research conducted by Hill, Martin, and Nelson-Head (2011) indicated that the lack of well-trained teachers combined with increased accountability requirements and mandated participation by parents has led to the increase in special education litigation for students with ASD. Furthermore, the trend in who prevails in litigation has changed from parents prevailing in the 1990s, to split decisions in 2002–2004, to school districts prevailing more in 2007–2008.

Although the specific choice of teaching method cannot be litigated, the most frequently related methodology requested was applied behavior analysis. Moreover, Yell and Drasgow (2000) found that parents previously prevailed in 76% of the cases regarding applied behavior analysis and discrete trial instruction. However, when school districts have established that their method of instruction afforded a "basic floor of opportunity" and demonstrated progress, then the courts have ruled in their favor, according to Hill et al. (2011, p. 220). When challenging student behavior was involved, school districts prevailed almost 3 to 1, and when a functional behavioral assessment or behavior intervention plan was included in the litigation, school districts won more than twice as often.

Recently, school districts have tended to prevail when complaints were focused on procedural violations, whereas parents have won when substantive issues were involved. Hill et al. (2011) contended that this points to the importance of IEP development, which is critical to IDEA and a free and appropriate public education. Nevertheless, the focus should be on building a positive alliance between families and schools that results in the development of IEPs that meet the needs of the individual student and avoids "the emotional, monetary and temporal toll taken when full-blown litigation is pursued" (Hill et al., 2011, p. 220). The IEP process and legal issues under IDEA are discussed in Chapters 8 and 11 of this volume, respectively.

CHALLENGES FOR PARENTS AND TEACHERS

Barriers to successful communication include structural and psychological barriers for families, educators, and the school–family relationship. Structural barriers for families may include a lack of economic resources and a supportive environment; psychological barriers for families may include feelings of inadequacy and cultural and linguistic differences. Educators' structural barriers may include a lack funding for family programs and for training on how to create and maintain family partnerships, and their psychological barriers may include stereotypes and concerns regarding family roles and abilities. Barriers specific to the school–family relationship may include absence of communication procedures, time constraints for important discussions, or communication mainly at times of crisis. Psychological barriers in the school–family partnership may include cultural differences and an inability to see each other's differences as strengths (Esler et al., 2008).

Often, parents cannot attend meetings because of work constraints, child care issues, or transportation challenges. Schools should brainstorm solutions to these issues by securing funding and/or volunteers to provide transportation and child care and by being flexible in scheduling meetings at a mutually agreeable time. Professionals should be aware that some parents have unpleasant memories of their own school experiences and may be reluctant to come to school for meetings. Parents may be hesitant to ask a question when they do not understand what is being shared about their child, so it is critical for professionals to check often for understanding. Peacock and Collett (2010) suggested asking the parent, "How does this fit with what you know about your child?" or "Were there other questions or concerns that you had that we haven't addressed yet?" (p. 13).

Individuals with ASD frequently have a typical physical appearance; however, this combined with significant social and communication issues, uneven pattern of development, and problems ascertaining whether they "can't versus won't" comply with demands confounds professionals and families alike and often leads to stress and the erroneous conclusion that their misbehavior is willful and volitional when it often is not (Marcus et al., 2005, p. 1057). Professionals and families need training that addresses how to determine when misbehavior is a result of a lack of understanding or ability or due to a willful refusal.

Finally, professionals can be instrumental in educating families on the differences between the terminology used by medical and educational professionals in the diagnosis and treatment of ASD. Medical professionals use the *Diagnostic and Statistical Manual of Mental Disorders* (5th ed.; American Psychiatric Association, 2013) to diagnosis ASD, whereas schools follow IDEA criteria to determine eligibility for special education services under the diagnostic category of autism. Clinical and educational classification systems are reviewed in Chapter 3 of this volume.

CONCLUSION

In summary, collaboration between families and schools is critical for the success of students with ASD. Professionals and families can work collaboratively to advocate for expanded services and overcome barriers to effective collaboration. The research literature offers several models for effective collaboration. COMPASS is the first consultation model to be experimentally validated to increase the IEP outcomes of students with ASD. CBC, an indirect service delivery model, has demonstrated effectiveness in supporting inclusion for individuals with various disabilities.

Educators should be aware that parents worldwide experience a range of emotions when their child receives a diagnosis of ASD, and many go through stages of grief. One conceptual model that may be used to assess parent participation with professionals was suggested by Webber et al. (2000) and includes five levels of involvement: awareness, open communication, advocacy and participation, problem solving and procedural application, and partnership. Open communication is recommended for all stakeholders. It is also critical for professionals to understand that due to the severe and pervasive features of ASD, parents face significant emotional demands raising their children.

Professionals can assist families by using effective communication and by offering parent training in behavior management, which has been shown to increase parents' self-efficacy and decrease their children's problematic behaviors. The building blocks for effective communication can be summarized as BETTER LISTENING: Begin, Eye contact, Trust, Tactful, Empathy, Respect, Lean in, Interest, Share, Time, Encouragement, Nod, Include, Nonjudgmental, and Greet warmly. Best practices also include Esler et al.'s (2008) eight P philosophy for school–family collaboration and Fiedler et al.'s (2007) 12 trust enhancements. In closing, it is of paramount importance to remember that parents are an integral part of their child's treatment plan and are capable of implementing compensatory strategies (e.g., social narratives, visual supports) to assist their children with ASD.

REFERENCES

Altiere, M. J., & von Kluge, S. (2009). Searching for acceptance: Challenges encountered when raising a child with autism. *Journal of Intellectual & Developmental Disability, 34,* 142–152.

American Psychiatric Association. (2013). *Diagnostic and statistical manual of mental disorders* (5th ed.). Washington, DC: Author.

Barnhill, G. P. (2002). *Right address . . . wrong planet: Children with Asperger syndrome becoming adults.* Shawnee Mission, KS: Autism Asperger Publishing Company.

Beyer, J. (2009). Autism spectrum disorders and siblings relationships: Research and strategies. *Education and Training in Developmental Disabilities, 44,* 444–452.

Boardmaker Software [Computer software]. Pittsburgh, PA: Dynavox Mayer-Johnson.

Christenson, S. L. (2004). The family–school partnership: An opportunity to promote the learning competence of all students. *School Psychology Review, 33,* 83–104.

Christenson, S. L., & Sheridan, S. M. (2001). *Schools and families: Creating essential connections for children's learning.* New York, NY: Guilford Press.

Ellis, C. R., Lutz, R. E., Schaefer, G. B., & Woods, K. N. (2007). Physician collaboration involving students with autism spectrum disorders. *Psychology in the Schools, 44,* 737–747. doi:10.1002/pits.20262

Epstein, T., Saltzman-Benaiah, J., O'Hare, A., Goll, J. C., & Tuck, S. (2008). Associated features of Asperger syndrome and their relationship to parenting stress. *Child: Care, Health and Development, 34,* 503–511. doi:10.1111/j.1365-2214.2008.00834.x

Esler, A. N., Godber, Y., & Christenson, S. L. (2008). Best practices in supporting school–family partnerships. In A. Thomas & J. Grimes (Eds.), *Best practices in school psychology* (pp. 917–936). Bethesda, MD: National Association of School Psychologists.

Family Voices. (2008). *Family-centered care self-assessment tool*. Retrieved from https://org2.democracyinaction.org/o/6739/images/fcca_FamilyTool.pdf

Fiedler, C. R., Simpson, R. L., & Clark, D. M. (2007). *Parents of children with disabilities: Effective school-based support services*. Upper Saddle River, NJ: Pearson.

Frost, L., & Bondy, A. (2002). *The Picture Exchange Communication System training manual*. Newark, DE: Pyramid.

Gabovitch, E. M., & Curtin, C. L. (2009). Family-centered care for children with autism spectrum disorders: A review. *Marriage & Family Review, 45*, 469–498. doi:10.1080/01494920903050755

Gray, C. (2004). Social Stories 10.0: The new defining criteria and guidelines. *Jenison Autism Journal, 15*(4), 2–20.

Gray, C. (2010). *The new Social Story™ book*. Arlington, TX: Future Horizons.

Gray, D. E. (2002). Ten years on: A longitudinal study of families of children with autism. *Journal of Intellectual & Developmental Disability, 27*, 215-–222. doi:10.1080/136682502100000863 9

Gray, D. E. (2003). Gender and coping: The parents of children with high functioning autism. *Social Science & Medicine, 56*, 631–642. doi:10.1016/S0277-9536(02)00059-X

Gray, D. E. (2006). Coping over time: The parents of children with autism. *Journal of Intellectual Disability Research, 50*, 970–976. doi:10.1111/j.1365-2788.2006.00933.x

Grinker, R. R. (2007). *Unstrange minds: Remapping the world of autism*. New York, NY: Basic Books.

Handleman, J. S., & Harris, S. L. (1986). *Educating the developmentally disabled: Meeting the needs of children and families*. San Diego, CA: College-Hill Press.

Hill, D. A., Martin, E. D., & Nelson-Head, C. (2011). Examination of case law (2007–2008) regarding autism spectrum disorder and violations of the Individuals With Disabilities Education Act. *Preventing School Failure, 55*, 214–225. doi:10.1080/1045988X.2010.542784

Hoffman, C. D., Sweeney, D. P., Hodge, D., Lopez-Wagner, M. C., & Looney, L. (2009). Parenting stress and closeness: Mothers of typically developing children and mothers of children with autism. *Focus on Autism and Other Developmental Disabilities, 24*, 178–187. doi:10.1177/1088357609338715

Individuals With Disabilities Education Act of 2004, 20 U.S.C. § 1400 (2004).

Ivey, J. K. (2004). What do parents expect? A study of the likelihood and importance issues for children with autism spectrum disorders. *Focus on Autism and Other Developmental Disabilities, 19*, 27–33. doi:10.1177/10883576040190010401

Koegel, L. K., & LaZebnik, C. (2004). *Overcoming autism*. New York, NY: Penguin Books.

Lee, G. K. (2009). Parents of children with high functioning autism: How well do they cope and adjust? *Journal of Developmental and Physical Disabilities, 21*, 93–114. doi:10.1007/s10882-008-9128-2

Lee, G. K., Lopata, C., Volker, M. A., Thomeer, M. L., Nida, R. E., Toomey, J. A., . . . Smerbeck, A. M. (2009). Health-related quality of life of parents of children with high-functioning autism spectrum disorders. *Focus on Autism and Other Developmental Disabilities, 24,* 227–239. doi:10.1177/108835760 9347371

Little, L. (2002). Differences in stress and coping for mothers and fathers of children with Asperger's syndrome and nonverbal learning disorders. *Pediatric Nursing, 28,* 565–570.

Marcus, L. M., Kunce, L. J., & Schopler, E. (2005). Working with families. In F. R. Volkmar, P., Rhea, A. Klin, & D. Cohen (Eds.), *Handbook of autism and pervasive developmental disorders: Vol. II. Assessment, interventions and policy* (3rd ed., pp. 1055–1086). Hoboken, NJ: Wiley.

McCabe, H. (2008). Autism and family in the People's Republic of China: Learning from parents' perspectives. *Research and Practice for Persons with Severe Disabilities, 33,* 37–47. doi:10.2511/rpsd.33.1-2.37

Meadan, H., Halle, J. W., & Ebata, A. T. (2010). Families with children who have autism spectrum disorders: Stress and support. *Exceptional Children, 77,* 7–36.

Moh, T. A., & Magiati, I. (2012). *Factors associated with parental satisfaction during the process of diagnosis of children with autism spectrum disorders. Research in Autism Spectrum Disorders, 6,* 293–303. doi: 10.1016/j.rasd.2011.05.011

Montes, G., & Halterman, J. S. (2007). Psychological functioning and coping among mothers of children with autism: A population-based study. *Pediatrics, 119,* e1040–e1046. doi:10.1542/peds.2006-2819

National Autism Center. (2009). *Evidence-based practice and autism in the schools: A guide to providing appropriate interventions to students with autism spectrum disorders.* Randolph, MA: Author. Retrieved from http://www.nationalautismcenter.org/pdf/NAC%20Ed%20Manual_FINAL.pdf

National Autism Center. (2011). *A parent's guide to evidence-based practice and autism: Providing information and resources for families of children with autism spectrum disorders.* Randolph, MA: Author. Retrieved from http://www.nationalautism center.org/pdf/nac_parent_manual.pdf

National Center for Family-Centered Care. (1989). *Family-centered care for children with special needs.* Bethesda, MD: Association for the Care of Children's Health.

National Professional Development Center on Autism Spectrum Disorders. (2010). *Evidence-based practices.* Retrieved from http://autismpdc.fpg.unc.edu/content/briefs

National Research Council. (2001). *Educating children with autism.* Washington, DC: National Academy Press.

O'Brien, M. (2007). Ambiguous loss in families of children with autism spectrum disorders. *Family Relations, 56,* 135–146. doi:10.1111/j.1741-3729.2007.00447.x

O'Brien, M., & Daggett, J. A. (2006). *Beyond the autism diagnosis—A professional's guide to helping families.* Baltimore, MD: Paul H. Brookes.

Oppenheim-Leaf, M. L., Leaf, J. B., Dozier, C., Sheldon, J. B., & Sherman, J. A. (2012). Teaching typically developing children to promote social play with their siblings with autism. *Research in Autism Spectrum Disorders, 6,* 777–791. doi: 10.1016/j.rasd.2011.10.010

Peacock, G. G., & Collett, B. R. (2010). *Collaborative home/school interventions: Evidence-based solutions for emotional, behavioral, academic problems.* New York, NY: Guilford Press.

Petalas, M. A., Hastings, R. P., Nash, S., Dowey, A., & Reilly, D. (2009). "I like that he always shows who he is": The perceptions and experiences of siblings with a brother with autism spectrum disorder. *International Journal of Disability, Development and Education, 56,* 381–399. doi:10.1080/10349120903306715

Pottie, C. G., & Ingram, K. M. (2008). Daily stress, coping, and well-being in parents of children with autism: A multilevel modeling approach. *Journal of Family Psychology, 22,* 855–864. doi:10.1037/a0013604

Rogers, S. J., & Dawson, G. (2010). *Early start Denver model for young children: Promoting language, learning, and engagement.* New York, NY: Guilford Press.

Ruble, L. A., Dalyrymple, N. J., & McGrew, J. H. (2012). *Collaborative model for promoting competence and success for students with ASD.* New York, NY: Springer. doi:10.1007/978-1-4614-2332-4

Sansosti, F. J., Lavik, K. B., & Sansosti, J. M. (2012). Family experiences through the autism diagnostic process. *Focus on Autism and Other Developmental Disabilities, 27,* 81–92. doi:10.1177/1088357612446860

Sheridan, S. M., Eagle, J. W., Cowan, R. J., & Mickelson, W. (2001). The effects of conjoint behavioral consultation: Results of a 4-year investigation. *Journal of School Psychology, 39,* 361–385. doi:10.1016/S0022-4405(01)00079-6

Simpson, R. L. (2005). Evidence-based practices and students with autism spectrum disorders. *Focus on Autism and Other Developmental Disabilities, 20,* 140–149. doi: 10.1177/10883576050200030201

Sivberg, B. (2002). Family system and coping behaviors: A comparison between parents of children with autistic spectrum disorders and parents with non-autistic children. *Autism, 6,* 397–409. doi:10.1177/1362361302006004006

Smith, S. (2012). *Visual supports.* Retrieved from http://www.autisminternetmodules. org/mod_intro.php?mod_id=2

Sofronoff, K., & Farbotko, M. (2002). The effectiveness of parent management training to increase self-efficacy in parents of children with Asperger syndrome. *Autism, 6,* 271–286. doi:10.1177/1362361302006003005

Tehee, E., Honan, R., & Hevey, D. (2009). Factors contributing to stress in parents of individuals with autism spectrum disorders. *Journal of Applied Research in Intellectual Disabilities, 22,* 34–42. doi:10.1111/j.1468-3148.2008.00437.x

Tobing, L. E., & Glenwick, D. S. (2007). Predictors and moderators of psychological distress in mothers of children with pervasive developmental disorders. *Journal of Family Social Work, 10*(4), 1–22. doi:10.1300/J039v10n04_01

Tomeny, T. S., Barry, T. D., & Bader, S. H. (2012). Are typically developing siblings of children with autism spectrum disorder at risk for behavioral, emotional, and social maladjustment? *Research in Autism Spectrum Disorders, 6,* 508–518. doi:10.1016/j.rasd.2011.07.012

Tonge, B., Brereton, A., Kiomall, M., MacKinnon, A., King, N., & Rinehart, N. (2006). Effects of parental health of an education and skills training program for parents of young children with autism: A randomized controlled trial. *Journal of the American Academy of Child and Adolescent Psychiatry, 45,* 561–569. doi:10.1097/01.chi.0000205701.48324.26

Turnbull, A. P., & Turnbull, H. R. (2001). *Families, professionals, and exceptionality: Collaborating for empowerment* (4th ed.). Upper Saddle River, NJ: Merrill Prentice Hall.

Webber, J., & Scheuermann, B. (2008). *Educating students with autism: A quick start manual.* Austin, TX: PRO-ED.

Webber, J., Simpson, R. L., & Bentley, J. K. C. (2000). Parents and families of children with autism. In M. J. Fine & R. L. Simpson (Eds.), *Collaboration with parents and families of children and youth with exceptionalities* (2nd ed., pp. 303–324). Austin, TX: PRO-ED.

Weiss, J. A., Cappadocia, M. C., MacMullin, J. A., Viecili, M., & Lunsky, Y. (2012). The impact of child problem behaviors of children with ASD on parent mental health: The mediating role of acceptance and empowerment. *Autism, 16,* 261–274. doi:10.1177/1362361311422708

Wilkinson, L. A. (2005). Supporting the inclusion of a student with Asperger syndrome: A case study using conjoint behavioural consultation and self-management. *Educational Psychology in Practice, 21,* 307–326. doi:10.1080/02667360500344914

Wilkinson, L. A. (2010). *A best practice guide to assessment and intervention for autism and Asperger syndrome in schools.* London, England: Jessica Kingsley.

Yell, M. L., & Drasgow, E. (2000). Litigating a free and appropriate education: The Lovaas hearings and cases. *The Journal of Special Education, 30,* 205–214. doi:10.1177/002246690003300403

Zirkel, P. A. (2011). Autism litigation under IDEA: A new meaning of "disproportionality"? *Journal of Special Education Leadership, 24,* 92–103.

11

LEGAL ISSUES UNDER IDEA

PERRY A. ZIRKEL

The legal issues for children with autism spectrum disorder (ASD) arise primarily under Part B of the Individuals With Disabilities Education Act (IDEA; 2011), which—unlike the early intervention services of Part C—covers ages 3 through 21. Although the cases cover the full range of issues under the IDEA, the two categories specific to ASD are eligibility, or identification, and free appropriate public education (FAPE), construed broadly to include related services and least restrictive environment (LRE). Other IDEA categories, such as discipline, attorneys' fees, and compensatory education services, are not different for children with ASD than for other eligible students under the IDEA. These categories where ASD is incidental account for approximately half of the case law (Zirkel, 2001). As a final but secondary matter, Section 504 of the Rehabilitation Act of 1973 and its regulations (Nondiscrimination on the Basis of Handicap in Programs or Activities Receiving Federal Financial Assistance, 2011) provide additional or alternate coverage.

http://dx.doi.org/10.1037/14338-012
Autism Spectrum Disorder in Children and Adolescents: Evidence-Based Assessment and Intervention in Schools, L. A. Wilkinson (Editor)

This chapter provides an overview of these legal issues. First, it provides a brief primer of key concepts under the IDEA and, to a secondary extent, Section 504. It then analyzes the ASD-distinctive issues of eligibility and FAPE under the IDEA in terms of the legislation and regulations, U.S. Office of Special Education Programs (OSEP) policy interpretations, and case law. Next, it highlights the corresponding relevant features of Section 504. The chapter concludes with observations and recommendations.

KEY LEGAL CONCEPTS

The primary federal framework for the legal issues specific to students from preschool to Grade 12 in public schools is the IDEA, which started as funding legislation in 1975 and which has been the subject of successive amendments—with the most recent being in 2004—and regulations—with the most recent being in 2006. For example, one of the additions in the latest amendments is the requirement that the special education component of the individualized education program (IEP) be based on "peer-reviewed research to the extent practicable" (20 U.S.C. § 1414(d)(1)(A)(i)(IV), 2011).

The key concepts under the IDEA include evaluation to determine eligibility, FAPE and LRE, and two avenues for formal dispute resolution. Although one avenue is the state education agency's complaint resolution process, the one that is primary in terms of providing precedents and other evolving guidance is the adjudicative route (Zirkel & McGuire, 2010). More specifically, this route under the IDEA starts with an impartial hearing—often called a *due process hearing*. Per the latitude provided in the IDEA, the states vary considerably in terms of the nature of the hearing officers (e.g., from part-timers who may not be attorneys to full-time administrative law judges; approximately 10 states have a second administrative tier, in the form of a review officer or reviewing panel; Zirkel & Scala, 2010).

As the next level in the adjudicative avenue, the IDEA provides concurrent jurisdiction between state and federal courts; the vast majority of the cases go to the federal courts. In either event, the judiciary has three levels: the trial court, the intermediate appellate court, and the highest court. For the federal judiciary, these three levels are the district court, the circuit courts of appeal, and the U.S. Supreme Court. The Supreme Court has issued only a dozen or so decisions under the IDEA, with the landmark FAPE decision being *Board of Education v. Rowley* (1982; hereafter *Rowley*) and with none of them specific to students with ASD (e.g., Zirkel, 2001).

Via the doctrine of *stare decisis,* or precedent, the officially published decisions of the higher courts are binding on the lower courts in the same jurisdiction. Thus, for example, a decision by the Third Circuit Court of Appeals is binding on the three states in its jurisdiction—Delaware, New Jersey, and Pennsylvania—regardless of which of these three was the state of origin for the case. Cases from other jurisdictions may be persuasive but are not binding on the court deciding the case; generally, more weight is attached to published than unpublished decisions and to those of higher as compared with lower courts.

The IDEA's administering agency, the OSEP, provides additional legal guidance via its policy interpretations, which it issues as commentary to the regulations, general memoranda, and policy letters. Courts often defer to these policy interpretations as persuasive, although they are not binding (Zirkel, 2003).

The other federal legislation and regulations specific to students with disabilities are Section 504, along with its sister statute, the Americans With Disabilities Act of 1990. The key differences from the IDEA are that Section 504 is a civil rights rather than a funding act and that it has a broader definition of disability. Like the IDEA, it obligates districts to provide evaluations for eligibility, FAPE for eligible children, and impartial hearings as one of the procedural safeguards. However, its administering agency within the U.S. Department of Education is the Office for Civil Rights (OCR), which provides both policy interpretations and a complaint resolution process (e.g., Zirkel, 2011d).

Finally, state laws complement the coverage of the IDEA and Section 504, with the general rule being that they may add to, but not subtract from, the foundational requirements in these federal laws. Only a few states have added requirements for students with ASD. For example, Connecticut passed legislation that requires school districts, as of July 1, 2012, to provide applied behavioral analysis (ABA) services to any child with ASD if the student's IEP or 504 plan requires these services (Conn. Gen. Stat. § 10-76ii, 2013). This law also provides necessary qualifications for the ABA service provider in terms of state or professional certification.

IDEA ISSUES: ELIGIBILITY AND FAPE

Legal analysis of the central and successive issues of eligibility and FAPE consists of legislation and regulations, OSEP policy interpretations, and case law. This section synthesizes these three sources of law first in terms of eligibility and then in terms of FAPE.

Legislation/Regulations on Eligibility

The IDEA regulations for Part B (Assistance to States for the Education of Children With Disabilities, 2012) define *child with a disability* and, thus, set forth the criteria for eligibility in terms of two essential elements: (a) an IDEA-listed classification and (b) a resulting need for special education (34 C.F.R. § 300.8, 2012). The connecting adverse effect on educational performance is the final part of the first of these two essential elements.

The IDEA did not recognize autism as one of its listed classifications until the 1990 amendments to the legislation. The definition of the *autism* classification, which is in the resulting regulations, includes a significant effect on (a) verbal communication, (b) nonverbal communication, and (c) social interaction (34 C.F.R. § 300.8(c)(1), 2012). This definition does not entirely square with the *Diagnostic and Statistical Manual of Mental Disorders* (5th ed. [DSM–5]; American Psychiatric Association, 2013). The *DSM–5* includes a new single diagnostic category of ASD and shifts from a three-domain symptom model to a two-domain symptom model. But another classification under the IDEA—other health impairment (OHI)—serves as a broader backup. The differences between educational and psychiatric classification for ASD are discussed in Chapter 3 of this volume.

OSEP Policy Interpretations of Eligibility

The policy interpretations of the OSEP, which is the arm of the U.S. Department of Education that administers the IDEA, help clarify the meaning and application of these definitions. For example, in response to a query from the field, OSEP clarified that (a) children with pervasive developmental disorder (PDD) and its subcategory autism in the *Diagnostic and Statistical Manual of Mental Disorders* (4th ed. [DSM–IV]; American Psychiatric Association, 1994) are eligible under the IDEA only if they meet the IDEA definition of autism or other specified classification, such as OHI; (b) states may have eligibility criteria so long as those criteria do not conflict with those in the IDEA; and (c) children with PDD ages 3 through 9 may qualify as *developmentally delayed* if the state and district utilize this optional classification (Letter to Coe, 1999). In a subsequent policy letter, OSEP provided a similar answer for children with Asperger's disorder (Letter to Williams, 2000).

Case Law Regarding Eligibility

Although a review of IDEA cases reveals that courts follow the IDEA definition to the extent of any difference from *DSM–IV* (Zirkel, 2011c), the number of court cases concerning eligibility of students with ASD is relatively small, with the majority being at the hearing officer, rather than the court, level. The paucity of litigation is likely due to the severity of the effect for many of these children and the broader alternate coverage of OHI for others (Fogt, Miller, & Zirkel, 2003). Although not controlling as compared with the minimum requirements in the IDEA for evaluation, best practices may serve as another contributor to the relatively low level of litigation. In other words, doing more than the law requires in terms of effective identification practices and having this implementation and expertise available for cogent testimony tend to avoid litigation.

A pair of court decisions concerning students with Asperger's disorder serves as a relatively recent example of the case law. In both of these decisions, the issue was whether the child's condition, regardless of whether classified as autism or OHI, adversely affected educational performance; each student did well academically but not socially and emotionally. In the first of these two decisions, which arose in Maine, the First Circuit Court of Appeals' decision ruled that the child was eligible based on a broad definition of educational performance in that state's law, which included nonacademic areas (*Mr. I. v. Maine School Administrative District No. 55*, 2007). In contrast, in the subsequent decision, a federal district court in New York followed precedent in the Second Circuit interpreting educational performance to be specific to academic progress, thus ruling that the child was not eligible under autism or, in effect, any other IDEA classification (*A.J. v. Board of Education*, 2010). These cases show that rather than an overemphasis on autism, whether as defined under *DSM–IV* or the IDEA, eligibility of children with ASD warrants due attention to the other elements of the definition of disability under the IDEA and related state laws. They also show that such determinations are not devoid of ambiguity and jurisdictional variance.

FAPE Legislation and *Rowley*

The IDEA and the pertinent case law more generally establish two standards for FAPE—one procedural and the other substantive. On the procedural side, for denial of FAPE, the parent must prove not only that the district violated one or more of the various procedural requirements of the IDEA but also that the violation(s) resulted in educational harm to the child. The present provisions of the IDEA, as a result of the 2004 amendments, provide one arguable exception; the pertinent language may be interpreted as establishing a per se, or automatically harmful, violation is if the district "significantly impeded the parent's opportunity to participate in the decision-making process regarding the provision of a FAPE to the parent's child" (20 U.S.C. § 1415(f)(3)(E), 2011). In any event, the corresponding substantive standard is, according to the Supreme Court's landmark ruling in *Rowley* (1982), whether the child's IEP is "reasonably calculated to enable the child to receive educational benefits" (pp. 206–207). Although varying to a limited extent from one jurisdiction to another, this relatively low substantive standard remains the law of the land (Zirkel, 2013).

OSEP Policy Interpretations of FAPE

In its policy letters, OSEP has addressed the broader FAPE issues of related services and LRE for students with ASD. First, OSEP clarified that the answer to whether the child with ASD, once determined eligible under the IDEA, is entitled to related services, such as speech pathology, occupational therapy, or social skills training, depends on whether the child needs these services to benefit from special education (Letter to Williams, 2000). The obligation is on the IEP team, not the parent, although the ultimate determination is left to adjudication—initially under the IDEA at the impartial hearing officer level and ultimately in the courts. More recently, in response to the question as to whether the IDEA permits separate schools for students with autism, OSEP emphasized that placement must be on an individual basis in accordance with the applicable procedures and criteria for LRE (Letter to Autin, 2011). In the interim between these two policy letters, OSEP accompanied the final IDEA regulations with commentary (Assistance to States for the Education of Children With Disabilities and Preschool Grants for Children With Disabilities, 2006) on a question pertinent, although not specific, to students with ASD. Specifically, OSEP repeated its longstanding position, in the absence of such a requirement in the IDEA, that "if an IEP Team determines that specific instructional methods are necessary for the child to receive FAPE, the instructional methods may be addressed in the IEP" (Assistance to States for the Education of Children With Disabilities and Preschool Grants for Children With Disabilities, 2006, p. 46,665).

Case Law Concerning FAPE

For students with ASD, the litigation concerning FAPE is much more extensive than that concerning eligibility. Indeed, the proportion of FAPE cases for children with autism outpaces by far that of any other classification in relation to their proportion in the school population, thus revealing that the dramatically rising percentage of children with autism since 1990 is only one contributing factor (Zirkel, 2011a).

Various other analyses have examined successive segments of this FAPE case law for students with ASD. For example, Etscheidt (2003) reviewed 68 cases decided between 1997 and 2002, finding that the majority was at the hearing officer level and that the prevailing party was districts 57% of the time and parents 43% of the time. Among the key factors that Etscheidt identified were goals aligned to the evaluation and methods tailored to the goals. In an analysis of the cases during the same period but limited to the segment specific to court decisions where Lovaas and discrete trial training (DTT) was at issue ($n = 19$), Nelson and Huefner (2003) found a much higher ratio of decisions in favor of districts. In a subsequent analysis of ASD methodology cases more generally for the period 1980–2001, Choutka, Doloughty, and Zirkel (2004) found that the clear majority was at the hearing or review officer level, that approximately one third of the cases concerned implementation rather than selection, and that the overall outcomes were relatively evenly split between parents and districts. The outcome-related factors that they identified included effectiveness of witnesses and documentation of progress. More recent analyses found markedly district-favorable outcomes for court decisions specific to ABA methodology from 1975 to 2009 (Decker, 2012) and for those more general to FAPE/LRE in 2007–2008 (Hill, Martin, & Nelson-Head, 2011). Although these studies varied in scope (e.g., issue categories, time period, and adjudicative level) and outcome scales (e.g., ranging from two to seven categories), the overall trend appears on balance to favor districts in cases limited to methodology, more recent years, and the court level.

Although a relatively recent comprehensive listing of pertinent court decisions is available (Zirkel, 2011b), it will suffice here to discuss in detail (a) one particular case as an effective example for FAPE in general and (b) a pair of other cases specific to the most recent relevant FAPE issue, peer-reviewed research (PRR).

The Deal Case

For the first case-study example, the IEPs at issue were for the preschool year 1998–1999 and for the kindergarten year 1999–2000 for a child who had been identified as eligible under the autism classification and had been receiving district services since age 3. The 95-page proposed IEP for 1998–1999 provided for 35 hours per week in a specialized class that included multiple methodologies, including DTT, and various related services, including physical therapy (PT) and occupational therapy (OT). The parents' minority report proposed that the district instead fund their home-based Lovaas-style ABA program designed by the Center for Autism and Related Disorders. Their child only attended the district program for 16% of the year while continuing with the parents' home-based program. For 1999–2000, the district's proposed, detailed IEP included (a) continued placement in a specialized class; (b) mainstreaming in the regular kindergarten for lunch and brief additional periods each week; (c) an eclectic TEACCH methodology that had a one-on-one DTT component; (d) use of the picture exchange communication system and hand-over-hand physical prompts; and (e) speech/language therapy for 30 minutes per day, PT for 30 minutes per week, and OT for 30 minutes every 2 weeks. Dissatisfied with this proposal, the parents—without notice to the district—unilaterally placed the child in a private regular preschool class for 6 hours per week. In addition, they continued their one-on-one Lovaas-style ABA program and requested an impartial hearing.

After 27 days of testimony from various witnesses, including outside experts, the hearing officer concluded that the district had denied the child FAPE via significant procedural violations, including making a predetermination of what the IEP should be and not having the regular kindergarten teacher and an ABA-knowledgeable person on the IEP team, and via substantively lacking intensive Lovaas-style ABA. Conversely concluding that the parents had provided this methodology, the hearing officer ordered the district to reimburse them for up to 30 hours for their home-based ABA program. However, the hearing officer refused their requested reimbursement for the private school tuition because they had failed to provide the district with the IDEA-required notice.

Both sides appealed, and the federal trial court reversed the hearing officer's FAPE ruling, finding that (a) the parents had not proven predetermination; (b) the absence of the regular kindergarten teacher did not result in substantive harm in this case; (c) the IDEA does not require an IEP team member who is an expert in the parents' preferred methodology; and (d) the district's proposed eclectic approach met the substantive standard of *Rowley*, with due deference to districts for methodology questions. However, after the parents appealed, in a widely cited decision, the Sixth Circuit reversed the trial court's decision (*Deal v. Hamilton County Board of Education*, 2004).

The Sixth Circuit's decision merits careful attention, particularly in light of subsequent proceedings in the case. First, on the procedural side, the appellate court concluded:

> The evidence reveals that the School System, and its representatives, had pre-decided not to offer Zachary intensive ABA services regardless of any evidence concerning Zachary's individual needs and the effectiveness of his private program. Because it effectively deprived Zachary's parents of meaningful participation in the IEP process, the pre-determination caused substantive harm and therefore deprived Zachary of a FAPE. (*Deal v. Hamilton County Board of Education*, 2004, p. 857)

Similarly, the Sixth Circuit found fatal the absence of the regular education teacher on the IEP team because her unique perspective was critical for the LRE issue that was one of the primary points of disagreement with the proposed IEP. On the substantive side, the appeals court warned that the due deference to school districts for methodology must have limits due to the individual orientation of the IDEA and that "even greater weight is due to [a hearing officer's] determinations on matters for which educational expertise is relevant" (*Deal v. Hamilton County Board of Education*, 2004, p. 865). As a result, the Sixth Circuit remanded the case to the trial court, concluding that the parents were entitled to reimbursement based on the prejudicial procedural violation but that the extent of the reimbursement would depend on the lower court's reconsideration of the substantive FAPE issue.

After the Supreme Court declined the district's request to the review the Sixth Circuit's decision (*Hamilton County Department of Education v. Deal*, 2005), the trial court, on remand, cited various other ASD court decisions in concluding that the district's proposed eclectic IEPs were reasonably calculated to provide this individual child with educational benefit (*Deal v. Hamilton County Department of Education*, 2006a). In contrast, the court concluded, the hearing officer had erred by focusing on whether the district's proposed program was better than the parents' preferred method. In a separate decision, the court awarded the parents reimbursement for $25,205 of their requested expenses of $54,610 and payment for $410,770 of their requested attorneys' fees of $801,466 (*Deal v. Hamilton County Department of Education*, 2006b). The parents again appealed.

In a brief unpublished decision, the Sixth Circuit affirmed the trial court's most recent rulings (*Deal v. Hamilton County Department of Education*, 2008). First, observing that "different methodologies may be appropriate for treating autism and provide a FAPE as long as the student's individual needs are considered and the program is reasonably calculated to provide educational benefit" (*Deal v. Hamilton County Department of Education*, 2008, p. 865), the appellate court upheld the substantive appropriateness of the district's proposed IEPs. Second, the Sixth Circuit concluded that the lower court had not abused its discretion in determining the appropriate amounts for reimbursement and attorneys' fees.

No one was the winner in this case. Nevertheless, the lessons learned include (a) the two-part, harmless-error analysis for procedural FAPE claims, with the potential exception of significantly impeding the parental opportunity for participation; (b) the multipart and equitable analysis for tuition reimbursement claims, starting with the requirement of prompt parental notice; (c) the variance in interpreting the relatively low substantive standard for FAPE, including due deference for methodology issues; (d) the motivation for and implementation of a 95-page IEP; and (e) the major transaction costs, including time, money, and adversariness, of the multilevel adjudicative process under the IDEA.

The PRR Cases

The other two cases illustrate the polar interpretations of the PRR provision as applied to students with ASD in terms of its effect on *Rowley*'s substantive standard for FAPE. In the first case, in Iowa, a hearing officer who was also a professor of special education addressed two issues, one concerning LRE and the other—relevant here—concerning PRR. In the pertinent relevant part of her decision, she concluded that the district's behavioral interventions with the child, an 8-year-old with autism, violated the IDEA IEP requirement with regard to PRR (*Waukee Community School District*,

2007). This part of her decision is remarkable because she primarily relied on a whole host of studies published in peer-reviewed journals while also citing, as a responsible academician, various articles in the professional literature questioning the assumptions underlying PRR. However, subsequent legal developments mitigated the thrust of her reasoning.

First, in rejecting the district's appeal in an unpublished decision, the federal trial court upheld her FAPE ruling but largely sidestepped the PRR issue by folding it into the *Rowley* standard (*Waukee Community School District v. Douglas L.*, 2008). More specifically, the court concluded that the hearing officer's delineation of criteria for behavioral interventions as substantive rights constituted legal error but that she could permissibly consider these factors in applying *Rowley*. Subordinate to this conclusion, the court responded to the parents' citation of the IDEA's PRR provision with the following brief footnote: "An IEP which relies on behavioral interventions which are not supported by, or are contrary to, the relevant research may be such that it is not 'reasonably calculated' to provide an educational benefit" (*Waukee Community School District v. Douglas L.*, 2008, ¶ 20). Applying this merged use of PRR, the court concluded that the preponderance of the evidence, with notable reliance on expert testimony and no citation of peer-reviewed studies, supported the hearing officer's decision that the formulation and implementation of the behavioral interventions fell short of the *Rowley* standard.

Second, the contrasting case in this pair started with a hearing officer decision in the same year. Specifically, in a California case concerning whether a particular district had provided FAPE to a 6-year-old with autism, the pertinent issue was whether the district's eclectic approach, which included ABA, was appropriate as compared with the parents' proposed ABA-only method (*Rocklin Unified School District*, 2007). The California hearing officer, a full-time administrative law judge, upheld the district's IEP with this much more deferential reasoning:

> If the component parts of a plan are peer-reviewed, then it follows that the sum of those parts should be considered as peer-reviewed as well, particularly in light of the moral, legal and ethical constraints that prevent the truest form of scientific study from being conducted. The ultimate test is not the degree to which a methodology has been peer-reviewed, but rather, whether the methodology chosen was believed by the IEP team to be appropriate to meet the individual needs of the child. (p. 1036)

On appeal, the federal district court upheld the hearing officer, reasoning much more concisely as follows:

> It does not appear that Congress intended that the service with the greatest body of research be used in order to provide FAPE. Likewise there is nothing in the Act to suggest that the failure of a public agency to

provide services based on [PRR] would automatically result in a denial of FAPE. As other Ninth Circuit courts have noted, if Congress intended to modify the *Rowley* standard, it would have said so. (*Joshua A. v. Rocklin Unified School District*, 2008, p. 1142)

Next, the Ninth Circuit affirmed, with this reasoning:

This eclectic approach, while not itself peer-reviewed, was based on "peer-reviewed research to the extent practicable." We need not decide whether District made the best decision or a correct decision, only whether its decision satisfied the requirements of the IDEA. In doing so, we "must be careful to avoid imposing [the court's] view of preferable education methods upon the State" [citing *Rowley*]. (*Joshua A. v. Rocklin Unified School District*, 2009, p. 695)

Third, two other developments left the academic, best practice orientation of the Iowa hearing officer as the outlier in this case law. More specifically, a whole host of subsequent court decisions followed the district-deferential view of PRR such that it did not significantly affect the *Rowley* substantive standard (e.g., *Doe v. Hampden-Wilbraham Regional School District*, 2010; *S.M. v. State of Hawaii Department of Education*, 2011), and Iowa changed its hearing officer system to full-time, administrative law judges, akin to the California model.

SECTION 504

Section 504 has a broader definition of disability than does the IDEA, which is any mental or physical impairment that substantially limits one or more major life activities. Thus, Section 504 provides alternate protection for not only students covered by the IDEA but also those covered only by Section 504 (e.g., Zirkel, 2011d). For students with ASD, Section 504 may be relevant in two different ways. First, for students with ASD who qualify for IEPs under the IDEA, Section 504 offers alternate avenues for dispute resolution, such as filing a complaint with its federal administering agency—OCR (Zirkel & McGuire, 2010). Second, for students who do not qualify for an IEP under the IDEA, the broader coverage of Section 504 presents the possibility of eligibility under Section 504. For example, the Third Circuit recently recognized that social interaction qualifies as a major life activity under Section 504 (*Weidow v. Scranton School District*, 2012), thus providing the potential for additional or alternate coverage of high-functioning students with Asperger's disorder.

In either case, depending on the jurisdiction, Section 504 may provide further legal leverage. First, it may offer the possibility of obtaining money damages, a remedy not available under the IDEA. For example, in the aforementioned

Iowa case, the parents separately filed in federal court for this additional form of relief based on various federal and state claims, and the court denied the defendants' motion to dismiss the Section 504 claim (*D.L. v. Waukee Community School District*, 2008). Although the published ruling merely preserved the issue for further proceedings, the eventual outcome was not reported, thus probably being the subject of settlement. Second, Section 504 may offer a different substantive standard for FAPE than does the IDEA. A case in Hawaii concerning two siblings with autism illustrates this possibility, which the Ninth Circuit recognized on appeal and which is still subject to further proceedings upon being sent back to the trial court (*Mark H. v. Hamamoto*, 2010).

All of these issues under Section 504 are newly developing and, thus, relatively unsettled and speculative at this point. Nevertheless, they merit at least secondary attention in terms of the legal protections for students with ASD.

CONCLUSION

In sum, for students with ASD, the IDEA presents the primary governing legal framework, with eligibility and FAPE being the distinctive issues. For eligibility, the litigation is relatively infrequent, and the primary recommendation is to avoid confusion with *DSM–5*. For FAPE, the litigation is relatively voluminous in terms of both the harmless-error approach to alleged procedural violations and the relatively relaxed *Rowley* substantive standard. The primary recommendations are to be aware of judicial deference to school districts, especially in methodology cases, and to hearing officer decisions, especially for factual findings. Finally, Section 504 provides alternative standards of eligibility and FAPE and alternative avenues for dispute resolution, including the complaint resolution process of OCR.

Thus, legal issues specific to students with ASD are constantly evolving based on knowledge about ASD, political decisions primarily in the form of legislation and regulations at the federal and state levels, and the cumulative development of the case law. This process is a costly and complicated one, and it is not synonymous with best practice, professional ethics, or scholarly research. As a result, parents, district personnel, and other interested individuals need to maintain their legal literacy while at the same time doing their best in terms of communication, coordination, and creativity to (a) inform and improve the law and (b) engage in preventive practice that avoids the necessity of overlegalized dispute resolution.

For the special and central role of school psychologists, the legal lessons include (a) keeping in its proper place the expertise of the medical community—as do the courts (e.g., *Marshall Joint School District No. 2 v. C.D.*, 2010)—as compared with the specialized knowledge and experience of educators, including school psychologists; (b) being careful but not fearful about legal proceedings (Zirkel, 2012); (c) balancing but not confusing ethical and legal duties (e.g., Zirkel, 2008, 2009); and (d) effectively facilitating communications among parents, teachers, administrators, and support personnel for the common interest of the individual child and the school system.

REFERENCES

A.J. v. Board of Education, 679 F. Supp. 2d 299 (E.D.N.Y. 2010).

American Psychiatric Association. (1994). *Diagnostic and statistical manual of mental disorders* (4th ed.). Washington, DC: Author.

American Psychiatric Association. (2013). *Diagnostic and statistical manual of mental disorders* (5th ed.). Washington, DC: Author.

Americans With Disabilities Act of 1990, 42 U.S.C. § 12101 *et seq.* (2011).

Assistance to States for the Education of Children With Disabilities, 34 C.F.R. § 300.1 *et seq.* (2012).

Assistance to States for the Education of Children With Disabilities and Preschool Grants for Children With Disabilities, 71 Fed. Reg. 46,540 (Aug. 14, 2006).

Board of Education v. Rowley, 458 U.S. 176 (1982).

Choutka, C. M., Doloughty, P. T., & Zirkel, P. A. (2004). The "discrete trials" of applied behavior analysis for children with autism. *Journal of Special Education, 38*, 95–103.

Conn. Gen. Stat. § 10-76ii (2013).

D.L. v. Waukee Community School District, 578 F. Supp. 2d 1178 (S.D. Iowa 2008).

Deal v. Hamilton County Board of Education, 392 F.3d 840 (6th Cir. 2004).

Deal v. Hamilton County Department of Education, 259 F. Supp. 2d 687 (E.D. Tenn. 2006a).

Deal v. Hamilton County Department of Education, No. 1:01-cv-295, 2006 WL 2854463 (E.D. Tenn. August 1, 2006b).

Deal v. Hamilton County Department of Education, 258 F. App'x 863 (6th Cir. 2008).

Decker, J. (2012). A comprehensive analysis of Applied Behavior Analysis (ABA) litigation trends for students with autism. *Education Law Reporter, 274*, 1–26.

Doe v. Hampden-Wilbraham Regional School District, 715 F. Supp. 2d 185 (D. Mass. 2010).

Etscheidt, S. (2003). An analysis of legal hearings and cases related to IEPs for children with autism. *Research & Practice for Persons With Severe Disabilities, 28*, 51–69.

Fogt, J. B., Miller, D. N., & Zirkel, P. A. (2003). Defining autism: Professional best practices and published case law. *Journal of School Psychology, 41*, 201–216.

Hamilton County Department of Education v. Deal, 546 U.S. 936 (2005).

Hill, D. A., Martin, E. D., & Nelson-Head, C. (2011). Examination of case law (2007-2008) regarding autism spectrum disorder and violations of the Individuals With Disabilities Education Act. *Preventing School Failure, 55*, 214–225.

Individuals With Disabilities Education Act, 20 U.S.C. § 1401 *et seq.* (2011).

Joshua A. v. Rocklin Unified School District, 49 IDELR ¶ 249 (E.D. Cal. 2008)

Joshua A. v. Rocklin Unified School District, 52 IDELR ¶ 64 (9th Cir. 2009)

Letter to Autin, 58 IDELR ¶ 51 (Office of Special Education Programs 2011).

Letter to Coe, 32 IDELR ¶ 204 (Office of Special Education Programs 1999).

Letter to Williams, 33 IDELR ¶ 249 (Office of Special Education Programs 2000).

Mark H. v. Hamamoto, 620 F.3d 1090 (9th Cir. 2010), *on remand*, 849 F. Supp. 2d 990 (D. Hawaii 2012), *reconsideration denied*, 58 IDELR ¶ 212 (D. Hawaii 2012).

Marshall Joint School District No. 2 v. C.D., 616 F.3d 632 (7th Cir. 2010).

Mr. I. v. Maine School Administrative District No. 55, 480 F.3d 1 (1st Cir. 2007).

Nelson, C., & Huefner, D. S. (2003). Young children with autism: Judicial responses to the Lovaas and discrete trial training debates, *Journal of Early Intervention, 26*, 1–19.

Nondiscrimination on the Basis of Handicap in Programs or Activities Receiving Federal Financial Assistance, 34 C.F.R. § 104.1 *et seq.* (2011).

Rehabilitation Act of 1973, 29 U.S.C. §§ 705(20) & 794. (2011).

Rocklin Unified School District, 48 IDELR ¶ 234 (Cal. SEA 2007).

S.M. v. State of Hawaii Department of Education, 56 IDELR ¶ 193 (D. Hawaii 2011).

Waukee Community School District, 48 IDELR ¶ 26 (Iowa SEA 2007).

Waukee Community School District v. Douglas L., 51 IDELR ¶ 15 (S.D. Iowa 2008).

Weidow v. Scranton School District, 460 F. App'x 18 (3d Cir. 2012).

Zirkel, P. (2003). Do OSEP policy letters have legal weight? *Education Law Reporter, 171*, 391–396.

Zirkel, P. A. (2001). *Autism and the law: Rulings and expert analysis.* Horsham, PA: LRP.

Zirkel, P. A. (2005, January/February). What does the law say? *Teaching Exceptional Children, 38*(3), 62–63.

Zirkel, P. A. (2008, February). Child advocacy and "freedom" of expression: Ethical obligation and the First Amendment. *Communiqué, 36*(5), 1, 8–9.

Zirkel, P. A. (2009, January/February). Ethical duties are not necessarily legal duties. *Communiqué, 37*(5), 8.

Zirkel, P. A. (2011a). Autism litigation under the IDEA: A new meaning of "disproportionality"? *Journal of Special Education Leadership, 24*, 92–103.

Zirkel, P. A. (2011b). The case law on eligibility and methodology for students with autism: An update. *West's Education Law Reporter, 262*, 23–41.

Zirkel, P. A. (2011c, January/February). The role of the DSM in IDEA case law. *Communiqué, 39*(5), 30–31.

Zirkel, P. A. (2011d). *Section 504, the ADA, and the schools.* Horsham, PA: LRP.

Zirkel, P. A. (2012, September). Mistaken evaluation: The school psychologist or the case law? *Communiqué, 41*(1), 1, 16–18.

Zirkel, P. A. (2013). Is it time for elevating the substantive standard for FAPE under the IDEA? *Exceptional Children, 79*, 503–508.

Zirkel, P. A., & McGuire, B. L. (2010). A roadmap to legal dispute resolution for students with disabilities. *Journal of Special Education Leadership, 23*, 100–112.

Zirkel, P. A., & Scala, G. (2010). Due process hearing systems under the IDEA: A state-by-state survey. *Journal of Disability Policy Studies, 21*, 3–8.

INDEX

CAPS. *See* Comprehensive Autism Planning System
Caregivers, 59
Caron, C., 127
Carpentieri, S., 78
Carr, K., 110
CARS2. *See* Childhood Autism Rating Scale, Second Edition
CARS2–HF. *See* Childhood Autism Rating Scale, Second Edition—High Functioning Version
CARS2–QPC. *See* Childhood Autism Rating Scale, Second Edition—Parent Questionnaire
CARS2–ST. *See* Childhood Autism Rating Scale, Second Edition—Standard Version
CAS. *See* Cognitive Assessment System
Case conferences, 197–199
Case finding, 45–46
Case law, regarding eligibility, 246–247
Categorical diagnoses, 39
Cattell-Horn-Carroll model of intelligence, 78, 79
CBAs (curriculum-based assessments), 68, 208
CBC (conjoint behavioral consultation), 228
CBT (cognitive behavioral therapy), 142
CCC–2 (Children's Communication Checklist—Second Edition), 43
CDA model. *See* Comprehensive development approach to assessment model
CDC. *See* Centers for Disease Control and Prevention
CDD. *See* childhood disintegrative disorder
Center for Autism and Related Disorders, 249
Centers for Disease Control and Prevention (CDC), 3, 19, 55
Central coherence, 23
Chakrabarti, S., 55
Chambless, D. L., 156
Child Behavior Checklist, 136, 138, 141
Childhood Autism Rating Scale, Second Edition (CARS2), 62

Childhood Autism Rating Scale, Second Edition—High Functioning Version (CARS2–HF), 62, 63
Childhood Autism Rating Scale, Second Edition—Questionnaire for Parents or Caregivers (CARS2–QPC), 62
Childhood Autism Rating Scale, Second Edition—Standard Version (CARS2–ST), 62–63
Childhood disintegrative disorder (CDD), 18, 21
Children's Communication Checklist—Second Edition (CCC–2), 43
Children's Depression Inventory–2, 141
Children's Impairment Rating Scale, 136
Child Symptom Inventory—Fourth Edition, 138
Chinese parents, 220–221
Choral responding, 212
Choutka, C. M., 249
Clark, D. M., 227
Classification systems, 52–53
Classroom aides, 204, 206
Classroom pivotal response teaching (CPRT)
    development of, 161
    in evidence-based interventions, 161
    implementation of, 161–166
Classrooms
    general education, 184, 202, 203
    self-contained, 184, 202, 204
Cleary, J., 106
Clinical Evaluation of Language Fundamentals—Fourth Edition, 67
Clinical formulation, 7
Cloze procedure, 212
Cognitive Assessment System (CAS), 79
Cognitive behavioral therapy (CBT), 142
Cognitive flexibility, 84–85
Cognitive functioning, 76–81
    measures of, 64–66, 76–81
    nonlanguage tests for assessing, 79–81
    as predictor of outcomes, 28
    severity of impairment in, 22

General education classrooms, 184, 202, 203
General intelligence, 22, 28
Generalization (social-language intervention), 121
Generalized anxiety disorder, 24
Genetics, 54
Georgia, 180, 183
Georgia Parent Mentor Partnership, 188
Geurts, H. M., 85
Gilchrist, A., 28
Gilliam Autism Rating Scale—Second Edition (GARS–2), 64
Gilotty, L., 87
Glenwick, D. S., 221
Goldstein, G., 82, 83, 85, 110
Goldstein, S., 40, 63
Gordon's Diagnostic System (GDS), 82–83
Gray, C., 232
Gray, D. E., 221, 224, 225
Green, J., 28
Gresham, F. M., 175
Grieving, with autism diagnosis, 220
Griffith, E. M., 157
Grillon, C., 83
Grinker, R. R., 234
Group homes, 185

Hallucinations, 24
Halterman, J. S., 225
Handleman, J. S., 227
Hanzel, E., 77
Hardware, assistive technology, 211
Harris, S. L., 227
Hauck, M., 83–84
Hawaii, 254
Health services, 183
Heller, M., 214
Hermalin, B., 83
Higher level behaviors, 20
High-functioning autism (HFA)
    later diagnosis of, 221
    parents of children with, 221–222
    and scores on WISC–IV, 65
Hill, D. A., 234, 235
Hill, E., 85
Hollon, S. D., 156
Holman, K., 106
Home Situations Questionnaire, 136

Hooper, S. R., 86
Howlin, P., 28, 29
Huefner, D. S., 181, 248–249
Hunsley, J., 7, 58
Hyperactivity, 130

I
IDEA. *See* Individuals With Disabilities Education Act
IEPs. *See* Individualized education plans
Imitation, 20
Implementation science, 157
Inattention, 126, 130
Income barriers, 221
Indirect fidelity assessment, 213
Individualized education plans (IEPs), 173–189
    accommodations and modifications in, 184
    and continuum of services, 176–177, 196
    evaluation of, 186–187
    goals in, 180–182, 229
    importance of, 177, 235
    interpreting assessments for, 182–183
    legal issues with, 247, 249–253
    measuring progress of, 181–182
    and parents, 178–179, 187–189
    participants in creation of, 179–180
    and performance evaluation, 180–181
    placement options in, 184–185, 196
    postsecondary transitions in, 185–186
    related services in, 183, 248
    and special education classifications, 174–176
    and student-centered planning, 197
    understanding of procedures for developing, 173–174
Individuals With Disabilities Education Act (IDEA)
    autism as separate education category in, 151
    court decisions surrounding, 234, 243–245
    disability classification system outlined in, 53
    effects of, 5, 6, 24–25
    eligibility criteria in, 236, 245–247

Nelson-Head, C., 234
NEPSY–II. *See* Developmental Neuro-
psychological Assessment—
Second Edition
Neuroimaging research on autism,
54–55
Neuropsychological assessment, 81–87
of attention, 82–83
of cognitive flexibility, 84–85
executive functioning, 23, 81–82
of memory, 83–84
of planning skills, 85–87
New York State, 247
NIRN. *See* National Implementation
Research Network
NNAT. *See* Naglieri Test of Nonverbal
Abilities
No Child Left Behind Act (NCLB), 6,
152, 181, 208
Noncompliance, 137
Nonverbal cognitive measures, 66
Nonverbal communication, 109–110,
246
Nonverbal individuals, 21, 26
NPDC. *See* National Professional
Development Center
NPV. *See* negative predictive value
NSP. *See* National Standards Project

O'Brien, M., 220, 229–230
Observations. *See* Direct observations
Obsessive-compulsive disorder (OCD)
as common comorbid diagnosis, 24,
55, 125
routine behaviors in, 140
Occupational therapy, 183, 249
OCD. *See* Obsessive-compulsive disorder
O'Conner, N., 83
ODD. *See* Oppositional defiant disorder
Odom, S. L., 156
Office of Special Education Programs, 4,
174, 244, 245, 246, 248
Ohio Center for Autism and Low Inci-
dence, 233
Ohio Department of Education, 188
Oppositional defiant disorder (ODD),
24, 127, 137
Organization for Autism Research, 233
Orientation services, 183

OSEP. *See* U.S. Office of Special Educa-
tion Programs
Osterling, J., 29
Other health impairment (IDEA clas-
sification), 174, 246
Outcomes, with autism, 7, 28–29
Ozonoff, S., 68, 77, 85

Pandolfi, V., 64
Parental stress, 224–226
Parent-educator consultation models,
228–229
Parent-implemented interventions,
231
Parents. *See also* Families
coping strategies of, 225–226
counseling and training for, 183
and individualized education plans,
178–179, 187–189
involvement of, 59, 179
stress of, 224–226
*A Parent's Guide to Evidence-Based Prac-
tice and Autism* (National Autism
Center), 231
Payton, J., 85
PDDNOS. *See* Pervasive developmental
disorder not otherwise specified
PDDs. *See* Pervasive developmental
disorders
Peabody Picture Vocabulary Test—IV, 67
Peacock, G. G., 236
Pearson, D. A., 89
Peer mediated interventions, 153
Peer programs, 184
Peer-reviewed research (PRR), 249,
251–253
PEP–3. *See* Psychoeducational Profile—
Third Edition
Performance evaluation, 180–181
Perra, O., 107
Perrett, D. I., 107
Perry, A., 90
Pervasive developmental disorder not
otherwise specified (PDDNOS),
8, 19, 22
Pervasive developmental disorders
(PDDs)
autism spectrum disorder classifica-
tion under, 8, 18–19

School psychologists, *continued*
  interdisciplinary approach of, 59
  and knowledge of autism, 54–55
  and language functioning
    assessment, 68
  resources required for, 8
  role of, 29, 30, 69
School Situations Questionnaire, 136
Schopler, E., 222
Schwartz, J. M., 120
SCQ. *See* Social Communication
  Questionnaire
Screening. *See* Multitier screening and
  identification
Section 504 (Rehabilitation Act of
  1973), 253–254
Selective attention, 82
Selective mutism, 140
Self-contained classrooms, 184, 202, 204
Self-injury, 137, 140
Self-management strategies, 153
Self-monitoring, 23
Seltzer, M. M., 185
Semistructured interviews, 133
Senator, Susan, 3
Sensitivity (diagnostic validity), 39
Sensorimotor repetitive behaviors, 22
Separation anxiety disorder, 24, 140
Severity, of symptoms
  measures for determining, 40–45,
    60–64
  overview of, 20–22
  as risk factor for comorbid conditions,
    131–132
Shattuck, P. T., 185
Shaw, J. B., 89
Siblings, 226–227
SIDI. *See* Social Interaction Difference
  Index
Sigman, M., 106
Siller, M., 106
Simpson, R. L., 223, 227, 234
Sirian, L., 87
Sivberg, B., 230–231
Skill performance, 210
Skills, parental, 233
Skinner, B. F., 103
SLDT. *See* Social Language Development
  Test
SLPs. See speech-language pathologists

*S.M. v. State of Hawaii Department of
  Education*, 253
Smith, L., 85
Smith, S., 233
Social cognition, 132
Social communication
  challenges with, 4–5, 37–38,
    112–115
  and disruptive behaviors, 138
  in legal definitions of autism, 53, 246
  and theory of mind, 22–23, 106–109
Social Communication Questionnaire
  (SCQ), 43–44, 62
Social information processing, 54
Social Interaction Difference Index
  (SIDI), 43
Social Language Development Test
  (SLDT), 118
Social-language learning, 104–105
Social narratives, 232
Social phobia, 140
Social-pragmatic view of language
  development, 103–105
Social Responsiveness Scale (SRS–2),
  44–45, 63
Social services, 233
Social skills
  and cognitive skills, 22
  as core difficulty, 20
  training groups for, 26
Social Skills Improvement System, 175
Social Stories (C. Gray), 232
Social work services, 183
Sofronoff, K., 222
Software, 211
Sparrow, S. S., 67
Special education. *See also* "Free appro-
  priate public education"
  classifications in, 53, 174–176
  eligibility for, 53, 245–247
  research-to-practice gap in, 158–160
Special education teachers, 161, 179
Specificity (diagnostic validity), 39
Specific phobia, 24
Speech-generating devices, 211
Speech-language pathologists (SLPs),
  67–68, 197, 211
Speech-language therapy, 183
SRS–2. *See* Social Responsiveness
  Scale—Second Edition

ABOUT THE EDITOR

Lee A. Wilkinson, PhD, NCSP, is an applied researcher, educator, and practitioner. He is a nationally certified school psychologist, licensed school psychologist, chartered educational psychologist, and certified cognitive–behavioral therapist. Dr. Wilkinson currently practices in South Florida, where he provides diagnostic and consultation services for children with autism spectrum disorder and their families. He is also a university educator and serves on the school psychology faculty at Capella University and Nova Southeastern University, where he mentors doctoral researchers and teaches courses in assessment and intervention, child and adolescent psychopathology, legal and ethical issues in the school, research methods, and consultation. Dr. Wilkinson's research and professional writing have focused primarily on behavioral consultation and therapy, and children and adults with autism spectrum disorders. He has published numerous journal articles on these topics both in the United States and internationally and has been an ad hoc reviewer for peer-reviewed journals such as the *Journal of Remedial and Special Education*, the *Journal of Child Psychology and Psychiatry*, *Learning and Individual Differences*, and *Autism: The International Journal of Research and Practice*. Dr. Wilkinson is the author of the award-winning book A *Best Practice Guide to Assessment and Intervention for Autism and Asperger Syndrome in Schools* (2010).

Date Due

JAN 0 6 2015		
SEP 3 0 2016		

BRODART, CO.   Cat. No. 23-233   Printed in U.S.A.